# A2-Level
# Chemistry

JOHNNY
QIN

$9^{\circ}/_{0} + 98^{\circ}/_{0} + 87^{\circ}/_{0} + 98^{\circ}/_{0} + 95^{\circ}/_{0} + 95^{\circ}/_{0}$

# The Revision Guide
## Exam Board: Edexcel

*Editors*:

Amy Boutal, Mary Falkner, David Hickinson, Sarah Hilton, Paul Jordin, Sharon Keeley, Simon Little, Tim Major, Sam Norman, Ami Snelling, Michael Southorn, Hayley Thompson.

*Contributors*:

Mike Bossart, Robert Clarke, Ian H. Davis, John Duffy, Max Fishel, Lucy Muncaster, Jane Simoni, Paul Warren, Chris Workman.

*Proofreaders*:

Barrie Crowther, Julie Wakeling, Paul Jordin.

Published by Coordination Group Publications Ltd.

ISBN: 978 1 84762 266 2

With thanks to Laura Stoney for the copyright research
and thanks to Science Photo Library for the image on p67

Groovy website: www.cgpbooks.co.uk
Jolly bits of clipart from CorelDRAW®
Printed by Elanders Hindson Ltd, Newcastle upon Tyne.

Every effort has been made to locate copyright holders and obtain permission to reproduce sources. For those sources where it has been difficult to trace the originator of the work, we would be grateful for information. If any copyright holder would like us to make an amendment to the acknowledgements, please notify us and we will gladly update the book at the next reprint. Thank you.

# Contents

## How Science Works

The Scientific Process ................................................ 2

## Unit 4

### Section 1 — Rates of Reaction

Reaction Rates ....................................................... 4
Orders of Reaction .................................................. 6
Rate Equations ...................................................... 8
Deducing Orders and Rate Equations ....................... 10
Rates and Reaction Mechanisms ............................. 12
Halogenoalkanes and Reaction Mechanisms ............. 14
Activation Energy and Catalysts .............................. 16

### Section 2 — Entropy

Entropy ............................................................... 19
Entropy Change ..................................................... 21
Dissolving ............................................................ 24

### Section 3 — Equilibria

Dynamic Equilibria .................................................. 26
Equilibrium Constants ............................................. 28
Gas Equilibria ....................................................... 30
Equilibrium Constants and Entropy ........................... 32
Le Chatelier's Principle ........................................... 34
Equilibria in Industrial Processes ............................. 36

### Section 4 — Acid-Base Equilibria

Acids and Bases ..................................................... 38
pH Calculations ..................................................... 40
Titration Curves and Indicators ................................ 43
Buffers ................................................................. 45

### Section 5 — Further Organic Chemistry

Isomerism ............................................................. 47
Aldehydes and Ketones ............................................ 50
More on Aldehydes and Ketones ............................... 52
Carboxylic Acids .................................................... 54
Esters .................................................................. 57
Acyl Chlorides ....................................................... 59

### Section 6 — Spectroscopy and Chromatography

UV and Microwave Radiation .................................... 60
Mass Spectrometry ................................................. 62
NMR Spectroscopy ................................................. 64
More About NMR ................................................... 66
Infrared Spectroscopy ............................................. 68
Chromatography .................................................... 70

## Unit 5

### Section 7 — Electrochemistry

Redox Reactions .................................................... 72
Electrode Potentials ................................................ 74
The Electrochemical Series ...................................... 76
Redox Titrations .................................................... 78
More Redox Titrations ............................................ 80
Uses of Fuel Cells .................................................. 82

### Section 8 — Transition Metals

Transition Metals — The Basics ................................ 84
Complex Ions and Colour ........................................ 86
Complex Ions — Ligand Reactions ............................ 89
Copper and Chromium ............................................ 91
Uses of Transition Metals & Their Compounds ........... 94

### Section 9 — Organic Compounds

Aromatic Compounds .............................................. 96
Reactions of Aromatic Compounds ........................... 98
More Reactions of Aromatic Compounds ................... 100
Amines ................................................................ 102
Amides and Aromatic Amines ................................. 104
Amino Acids ........................................................ 106
Polymers ............................................................. 108
More Condensation Polymers .................................. 110

### Section 10 — Organic Synthesis

Empirical and Molecular Formulas ........................... 112
Practical Techniques .............................................. 114
Organic Functional Groups ..................................... 116
Organic Synthesis ................................................. 118

Practical and Investigative Skills .............................. 121

Answers .............................................................. 124

Index .................................................................. 133

# *How Science Works*

# The Scientific Process

*'How Science Works' is all about the scientific process — how we develop and test scientific ideas.*
*It's what scientists do all day, every day (well except at coffee time — never come between scientists and their coffee).*

## Scientists Come Up with **Theories** — Then **Test Them**...

Science tries to explain **how** and **why** things happen. It's all about seeking and gaining **knowledge** about the world around us. Scientists do this by **asking** questions and **suggesting** answers and then **testing** them, to see if they're correct — this is the **scientific process**.

1) **Ask** a question — make an **observation** and ask **why or how** whatever you've observed happens.
   *E.g. Why does sodium chloride dissolve in water?*

2) **Suggest** an answer, or part of an answer, by forming a **theory** or a **model** (a possible **explanation** of the observations or a description of what you think is actually happening).
   *E.g. Sodium chloride is made up of charged particles, which are pulled apart by the polar water molecules.*

3) Make a **prediction** or **hypothesis** — a **specific testable statement**, based on the theory, about what will happen in a test situation.
   *E.g. A solution of sodium chloride will conduct electricity much better than water does.*

4) Carry out **tests** — to provide **evidence** that will support the prediction or refute it.
   *E.g. Measure the conductivity of water and of sodium chloride solution.*

The evidence supported Quentin's Theory of Flammable Burps.

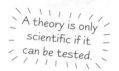

A theory is only scientific if it can be tested.

## ...Then They **Tell** Everyone About Their **Results**...

The results are **published** — scientists need to let others know about their work. Scientists publish their results in **scientific journals**. These are just like normal magazines, only they contain **scientific reports** (called papers) instead of the latest celebrity gossip.

1) Scientific reports are similar to the **lab write-ups** you do in school. And just as a lab write-up is **reviewed** (marked) by your teacher, reports in scientific journals undergo **peer review** before they're published.

   Scientists use standard terminology when writing their reports. This way they know that other scientists will understand them. For instance, there are internationally agreed rules for naming organic compounds, so that scientists across the world will know exactly what substance is being referred to.

2) The report is sent out to **peers** — other scientists who are experts in the **same area**. They go through it bit by bit, examining the methods and data, and checking it's all clear and logical. When the report is approved, it's **published**. This makes sure that work published in scientific journals is of a **good standard**.

3) But peer review **can't guarantee** the science is **correct** — other scientists still need to **reproduce** it.

4) Sometimes **mistakes** are made and bad work is published. Peer review **isn't perfect** but it's probably the best way for scientists to self-regulate their work and to publish **quality reports**.

## ...Then **Other Scientists** Will **Test** the Theory Too

1) Other scientists read the published theories and results, and try to **test the theory** themselves. This involves:
   - Repeating the **exact same experiments**.
   - Using the theory to make **new predictions** and then testing them with **new experiments**.

2) If all the experiments in the world provide evidence to back it up, the theory is thought of as **scientific 'fact'** (for now).

3) If **new evidence** comes to light that **conflicts** with the current evidence the theory is questioned all over again. More rounds of **testing** will be carried out to try to find out where the theory **falls down**.

This is how the scientific process works — evidence supports a theory, loads of other scientists read it and test it for themselves, eventually all the scientists in the world agree with it and then bingo, you get to learn it.

This is exactly how scientists arrived at the structure of the atom — and how they came to the conclusion that electrons are arranged in shells and orbitals. It took years and years for these models to be developed and accepted — this is often the case with the scientific process.

# The Scientific Process

## If the **Evidence** Supports a Theory, It's **Accepted** — for Now

Our currently accepted theories have survived this '**trial by evidence**'. They've been tested **over and over again** and each time the results have backed them up. **BUT**, and this is a big but (teehee), they never become totally indisputable fact. Scientific **breakthroughs or advances** could provide new ways to question and test the theory, which could lead to **changes and challenges** to it. Then the testing starts all over again...

And this, my friend, is the **tentative nature of scientific knowledge** — it's always **changing** and **evolving**.

In 1865, when Kekulé suggested the structure of benzene was a ring of carbon atoms, joined by alternating single and double bonds, it was widely accepted — it was the best fit for the evidence at the time. It was only once electrons had been discovered and orbital theory was developed that scientists came up with the modern 'delocalised model', which explains the behaviour of benzene better than Kekulé's model. See page 96.

## **Evidence** Comes From **Lab Experiments**...

1)  Results from **controlled experiments** in **laboratories** are great.
2)  A lab is the easiest place to **control variables** so that they're all **kept constant** (except for the one you're investigating).
3)  This means you can draw meaningful **conclusions**.

For example, if you're investigating how temperature affects the rate of a reaction you need to keep everything but the temperature constant, e.g. the pH of the solution, the concentration of the solution, etc.

## ...But You **Can't** Always do a Lab Experiment

There are things you **can't** study in a lab. And outside the lab controlling the variables is tricky, if not impossible.

- *Are increasing $CO_2$ emissions causing climate change?*
  There are other variables which may have an effect, such as changes in solar activity. You can't easily rule out every possibility. Also, climate change is a very **gradual process**. Scientists won't be able to tell if their predictions are correct for donkey's years.

- *Does eating food containing trans fatty acids increase the risk of heart disease and strokes?*
  There are always differences between groups of people. The best you can do is to have a **well-designed study** using **matched groups** — **choose two groups** of people (those who eat a lot of trans fats and those who don't) which are **as similar as possible** (same mix of ages, same mix of diets etc.). But you still can't rule out every possibility. Taking newborn identical twins and treating them identically, except for making one consume a lot of trans fats and the other none at all, might be a fairer test, but it would present huge **ethical problems**.

*Samantha thought her study was very well designed — especially the fitted bookshelf.*

See page 58 for more about trans fatty acids.

## Science Helps to Inform **Decision-Making**

Lots of scientific work eventually leads to **important discoveries** that **could** benefit humankind — but there are often **risks** attached (and almost always **financial costs**).

**Society** (that's you, me and everyone else) must weigh up the information in order to **make decisions** — about the way we live, what we eat, what we drive, and so on. Information is also used by **politicians** to devise policies and laws.

- Scientific advances mean that **hydrogen-oxygen fuel cells** can now be made (see page 82). They're better for the **environment** than batteries, because their only waste product is **water**. But you do need to **use energy** to produce the **hydrogen** and **oxygen** in the first place. And hydrogen is **highly flammable**, so it's tricky to store safely.
- Pharmaceutical drugs are really expensive to develop, and drug companies want to make money. So they put most of their efforts into developing drugs that they can sell for a good price. Society has to consider the **cost** of buying new drugs — the **NHS** can't afford the most expensive drugs without **sacrificing** something else.
- **Synthetic polymers** are very useful — they're **cheap** to produce and very **durable**. But they're **hard to dispose of** (they don't break down easily). So we need to make choices about how we can best dispose of plastics and whether we should try to **reduce** the amount that we use, or work to develop more **biodegradable plastics**.

## So there you have it — how science works...

*Hopefully these pages have given you a nice intro to how science works, e.g. what scientists do to provide you with 'facts'. You need to understand this, as you're expected to know how science works yourself — for the exam and for life.*

# Reaction Rates

*Welcome, one and all to the start of A2 Chemistry. Please keep all limbs inside the vehicle at all times. Thank you.*

## The **Reaction Rate** tells you How Fast **Reactants** are Converted to **Products**

The **reaction rate** is the **change in the amount** of reactants or products **per unit time** (normally per second).

If the reactants are in **solution**, the rate'll be **change in concentration per second** and the units will be **mol dm$^{-3}$ s$^{-1}$**.

## There are **Loads** of Ways to **Follow the Rate of a Reaction**

Although there are a lot of ways to follow reactions, not every method works for every reaction.
You've got to **pick a property** that **changes** as the reaction goes on.

### Gas volume

If a **gas** is given off, you could **collect it** in a gas syringe and record how much you've got at **regular time intervals**. For example, this'd work for the reaction between an **acid** and a **carbonate** in which **carbon dioxide gas** is given off.

$CO_2$
acid
carbonate

### Loss of mass

If a **gas** is given off, the system will **lose mass**.
You can measure this at regular intervals with a **balance**.

$CO_2 \rightarrow$

Balance

### Colour change

You can sometimes track the colour change of a reaction using a gadget called a **colorimeter**.
For example, in the reaction between propanone and iodine, the **brown** colour fades.

$CH_3COCH_{3(aq)} + I_{2(aq)} \rightarrow CH_3COCH_2I_{(aq)} + H^+_{(aq)} + I^-_{(aq)}$
colourless    brown
                colourless

### Clock reaction

For some reactions there is a **sudden** colour change when a product reaches a certain concentration. The **rate of reaction** can be worked out from measuring **the time** it takes for the colour change to happen — the **shorter** the time, the **faster** the rate.

### Electrical conductivity

If the **number of ions** changes, so will the **electrical conductivity**.
This also happens in the reaction between propanone and iodine.

## Work Out **Reaction Rate** from a **Concentration-Time Graph**

1) If you draw a graph of the **concentration of a reactant against time**, you can use it to work out the reaction rate.

2) The rate at any point in the reaction is given by the **gradient** at that point on the graph.

3) If the graph is a curve, you'll have to draw a **tangent** to the curve and find the gradient of that.

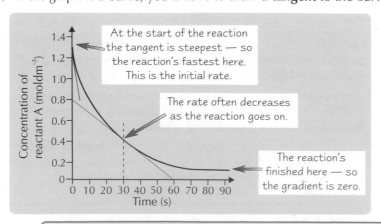

At the start of the reaction the tangent is steepest — so the reaction's fastest here. This is the initial rate.

The rate often decreases as the reaction goes on.

The reaction's finished here — so the gradient is zero.

A tangent is a line that just touches a curve and has the same gradient as the curve does at that point.

The gradient of the blue tangent is the rate of the reaction after **30 seconds**.

Gradient $= \dfrac{-0.8}{60} = $ **−0.013 mol dm$^{-3}$ s$^{-1}$**

So, the rate after 30 seconds is **0.013 mol dm$^{-3}$ s$^{-1}$**

The sign of the gradient doesn't really matter — it's a negative gradient when you're measuring reactant concentration because the reactant decreases. If you measured the product concentration, it'd be a positive gradient.

# Reaction Rates

## Reaction Rates can be **Calculated** from **Other Types** of Graph

**Measuring** the **concentration** of a reactant or product can be a bit **tricky**. It's sometimes easier to measure a **property** of a reactant or product instead — like those found on the previous page. You can still use these measurements to **draw a graph** and work out the **reaction rate** in the same way as before but the units might be different. Here are a couple of examples.

*Dave didn't know how he was going to monitor alcohol absorption but figured after the second drink he wouldn't care.*

### Absorbance vs Time

The reaction between aqueous bromine (orange-yellow) and methanoic acid can be followed by using a colorimeter. The percentage absorbance falls as the bromine is used up.

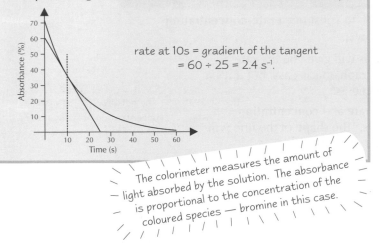

rate at 10s = gradient of the tangent
= 60 ÷ 25 = 2.4 s⁻¹.

*The colorimeter measures the amount of light absorbed by the solution. The absorbance is proportional to the concentration of the coloured species — bromine in this case.*

### Gas Volume vs Time

The decomposition of hydrogen peroxide can be followed by recording the volume of oxygen produced at regular time intervals.

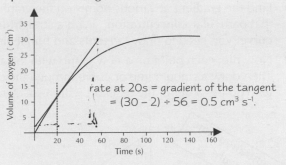

rate at 20s = gradient of the tangent
= (30 − 2) ÷ 56 = 0.5 cm³ s⁻¹.

## Practice Questions

Q1 Define the term 'reaction rate'.
Q2 You can follow some reactions by measuring electrical conductivity. What causes this change in conductivity?
Q3 In a clock reaction, how does time relate to the rate of the reaction?
Q4 When plotting a graph to work out reaction rate, what variable is on the x-axis?

## Exam Questions

1 The reaction between iodine and propanone in acidic conditions was investigated.

$$I_{2(aq)} + CH_3COCH_{3(aq)} \xrightarrow{H^+_{(aq)}} CH_3COCH_2I_{(aq)} + H^+_{(aq)} + I^-_{(aq)}$$

a) Apart from colorimetry, suggest, with a reason, one method that could be used to follow the reaction rate. [2 marks]
b) Outline how the rate of reaction with respect to propanone, at any particular time, could be determined. [3 marks]

2 Benzene diazonium chloride (BDC) decomposes in acidic aqueous solution.

$$C_6H_5N_2Cl_{(aq)} + H_2O_{(l)} \xrightarrow{H^+_{(aq)}} C_6H_5OH_{(aq)} + HCl_{(aq)} + N_{2(g)}$$

The following data was collected at 25 °C.

| Time (s) | 0 | 10 | 20 | 30 | 40 |
|---|---|---|---|---|---|
| Concentration of BDC (mol dm⁻³) | 0.20 | 0.070 | 0.025 | 0.0098 | 0.0031 |

a) Using the data provided, plot a graph and use it to determine the rate of reaction after 15 seconds. [6 marks]
b) Suggest an alternative method that could have been used to follow this reaction. [2 marks]

## This reaction has been rated A2 by the Board of Chemistry classification...

*I get the feeling that A2 is going to be a bit of a roller coaster. And it begins at a pretty fast rate. Oh dear... not a good start to the jokes and I can't promise they're going to get any better. Anyhow, this whole section is gonna cover a lot of different stuff to do with reaction rates, so it's worth making sure you understand the gradient = rate thing.*

# Orders of Reaction

*You might think the rate of a reaction will change if you change the concentration of the reactants. But this isn't always the case...*

## Orders Tell You How a Reactant's Concentration Affects the Rate

1) The **order of reaction** with respect to a particular reactant tells you how the **reactant's concentration** affects the **rate**.

If you increase a reactant's concentration by x and the rate **stays the same**, the order with respect to that reactant is **0**.

If you increase a reactant's concentration by x and the rate **increases by x**, the order with respect to that reactant is **1**.

If you increase a reactant's concentration by x and the rate **increases by $x^2$**, the order with respect to that reactant is **2**.

2) You can only find **orders of reaction** from **experiments**. You **can't** work them out from chemical equations.

## The Shape of a Rate-Concentration Graph Tells You the Order

You can use the **concentration–time graphs** from page 4, to construct a **rate-concentration graph**, which can tell you the **reaction order**. Here's how...

1) Find the **gradient** at various points on the graph. This will give you the **rate** at that particular concentration. With a **straight-line graph**, this is easy, but if it's a **curve**, you need to draw **tangents** and find their gradients.

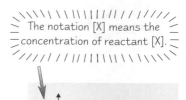
The notation [X] means the concentration of reactant [X].

2) Now plot each point on a new graph with the axes **rate** and **concentration**. Then draw a smooth line or curve through the points. The shape of the line will tell you the order of the reaction with respect to that reactant.

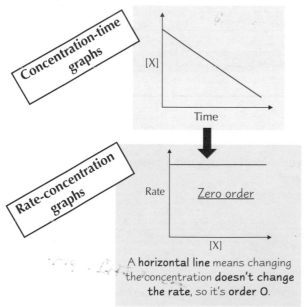

*Concentration-time graphs*

*Rate-concentration graphs*

Rate — Zero order — [X]
A **horizontal line** means changing the concentration **doesn't change the rate**, so it's **order 0**.

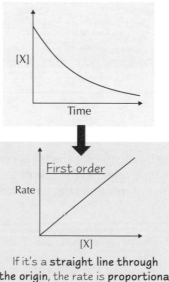

Rate — First order — [X]
If it's a **straight line through the origin**, the rate is **proportional to [X]**, and it's order 1.

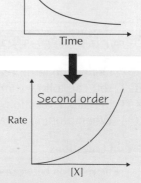

Rate — Second order — [X]
A curve means it's order 2. The rate will be proportional to $[X]^2$
(In theory, a curve could mean a higher order than 2 but you won't be asked about them.)

## Half-Life is the Time Taken for Half the Reactant to React

The **half-life** ($t_{1/2}$) of a reaction is the time it takes for **half of the reactant** to be used up.

To work out the half-life, plot a **concentration–time graph**. Then **draw lines** across from the y-axis at points where the **concentration has halved** and read off the time taken.

### Example

The graph shows the decomposition of hydrogen peroxide, $H_2O_2$ to $O_2$ and $H_2$.

$[H_2O_2]$ from 4 to 2 mol dm$^{-3}$ = 200 sec,
$[H_2O_2]$ from 2 to 1 mol dm$^{-3}$ = 200 sec,
$[H_2O_2]$ from 1 to 0.5 mol dm$^{-3}$ = 200 sec.

You can see how half-lives are useful for working out orders of reaction on the next page.

# Orders of Reaction

## Orders can also be Worked Out from looking at the Half-Life...

You can use the half-life to work out the order of a reaction without having to draw a rate-concentration graph.

**Zero order** reactions are easy to spot from a concentration-time graph because **the rate doesn't change** so they produce a straight line. But the half-life can help distinguish **first order** and **second order** reactions.

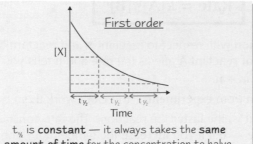

The rate **doesn't change** as concentration falls — the graph is a **straight line**.

$t_{1/2}$ is **constant** — it always takes the **same amount of time** for the concentration to halve. The half-life is independent of the concentration

The half-life **isn't** constant — it **increases** as the reaction goes on. You can get higher orders than second but you don't need to worry about them.

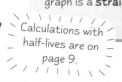

Calculations with half-lives are on page 9.

## Practice Questions

Q1 If a reaction is first order with respect to a reagent, what happens to the rate if the concentration of that reagent is doubled?

Q2 Sketch rate-concentration graphs for zero, first and second order reactions.

Q3 How does the half-life change with time in a first order reaction?

Q4 Describe two ways to determine the order of a reaction using a concentration-time graph.

**Exam Questions**

1 The decomposition of hydrogen peroxide is a first order reaction.
   a) Under certain conditions, the decomposition has a half-life of 250 s. If the original concentration of hydrogen peroxide was 2.0 mol dm⁻³, complete the table of results for this decomposition.

| Time (s) | 0 | 250 | 500 | 750 | 1000 |
|---|---|---|---|---|---|
| $[H_2O_2]$ (mol dm⁻³) | 2.0 | 1 | 0.5 | 0.25 | 0.125 |

[2 marks]

   b) Sketch a rate-concentration graph for this decomposition. [3 marks]

2 The table shows the results of an experiment on the decomposition of nitrogen(V) oxide at constant temperature.
$$2N_2O_5 \rightarrow 4NO_2 + O_2$$

| Time (s) | 0 | 50 | 100 | 150 | 200 | 250 | 300 |
|---|---|---|---|---|---|---|---|
| $[N_2O_5]$ (mol dm⁻³) | 2.50 | 1.66 | 1.14 | 0.76 | 0.50 | 0.32 | 0.22 |

   a) Plot a graph of these results. [3 marks]
   b) From the graph, find the times for the concentration of $N_2O_5$ to decrease:
      i) to half its original concentration, [2 marks]
      ii) from 2.0 mol dm⁻³ to 1.0 mol dm⁻³. [2 marks]
   c) Giving a reason, deduce the order of this reaction. [2 marks]

## Describe the link between concentration and rate, soldier — that's an order...

*There's quite a lot on this page, graphically speaking. And graphs are always great, easy marks. Just remember — labelled axes, accurately plotted points and a smooooooooth curve or a smooooooooth line of best fit. If you do these things then all the other calculations will become a lot easier. And remember smooooooooth — like a freshly licked lollipop.*

# Rate Equations

*This is when it all gets a bit mathsy. You've just got to take a deep breath, dive in, and don't bash your head on the bottom.*

## The Rate Equation links Reaction Rate to Reactant Concentrations

Rate equations look ghastly, but all they really do is tell you how the **rate** is affected by the **concentrations of reactants**. For a general reaction: **A + B → C + D**, the **rate equation** is:

The units of rate are mol dm$^{-3}$ s$^{-1}$.

$$\text{Rate} = k[A]^m[B]^n$$

Remember — square brackets mean the concentration of whatever's inside them.

1) **m** and **n** are the **orders of the reaction** with respect to reactant A and reactant B. **m** tells you how the **concentration of reactant A** affects the **rate** and **n** tells you the same for **reactant B**.

2) The **overall order of the reaction** is **m + n**.

3) You can only find **orders of reaction** from **experiments**. You **can't** work them out from chemical equations.

4) **k** is the **rate constant** — the bigger it is, the **faster** the reaction. The rate constant is **always the same** for a certain reaction at a **particular temperature** — but if you **increase** the temperature, the rate constant's going to rise too. The **units** vary, so you have to **work them out**. The example further down the page shows you how.

**Example:**

The chemical equation below shows the acid-catalysed reaction between propanone and iodine.

$$CH_3COCH_{3(aq)} + I_{2(aq)} \xrightarrow{H^+_{(aq)}} CH_3COCH_2I_{(aq)} + H^+_{(aq)} + I^-_{(aq)}$$

This reaction is first order with respect to propanone and $H^+_{(aq)}$ and zero order with respect to iodine. Write down: a) the rate equation, b) the overall order of the reaction.

Even though $H^+_{(aq)}$ is a catalyst, rather than a reactant, it can still be in the rate equation.

a) The **rate equation** is: rate = $k[CH_3COCH_3]^1[H^+]^1[I_2]^0$

But $[X]^1$ is usually written as **[X]**, and $[X]^0 = 1$, so it can be **left out** of the rate equation.

So you can **simplify** the rate equation to: **rate = $k[CH_3COCH_3][H^+]$**

Think about the indices laws from maths.

b) The overall order of the reaction is $1 + 1 + 0 = \textbf{2}$

## You can Calculate the Rate Constant from the Orders and Rate of Reaction

Once the rate and the orders of the reaction have been found by experiment, you can work out the **rate constant, k**.

**Example:**

The reaction below was found to be second order with respect to NO and zero order with respect to CO and $O_2$. At a certain temperature the rate is $1.76 \times 10^{-3}$ mol dm$^{-3}$ s$^{-1}$, when [NO] = [CO] = [$O_2$] = $2.00 \times 10^{-3}$ mol dm$^{-3}$.

$$NO_{(g)} + CO_{(g)} + O_{2(g)} \rightarrow NO_{2(g)} + CO_{2(g)}$$

Calculate the rate constant for the reaction at this temperature.

First write out the **rate equation**:

$$\text{Rate} = k[NO]^2[CO]^0[O_2]^0 = k[NO]^2$$

Next insert the **concentration** and the **rate**. **Rearrange** the equation and calculate the value of **k**:

$$\text{Rate} = k[NO]^2, \text{ so, } 1.76 \times 10^{-3} = k \times (2.00 \times 10^{-3})^2 \Rightarrow k = \frac{1.76 \times 10^{-3}}{(2.00 \times 10^{-3})^2} = 440$$

Find the **units for k** by putting the other units in the rate equation:

$$\text{Rate} = k[NO]^2, \text{ so mol dm}^{-3}\text{s}^{-1} = k \times (\text{mol dm}^{-3})^2 \Rightarrow k = \frac{\text{mol dm}^{-3}\text{s}^{-1}}{(\text{mol dm}^{-3})^2} = \frac{\text{s}^{-1}}{\text{mol dm}^{-3}} = \text{dm}^3 \text{ mol}^{-1} \text{ s}^{-1}$$

So the answer is: **k = 440 dm$^3$ mol$^{-1}$ s$^{-1}$**

# Rate Equations

## Reaction Rates Can Be Used to Calculate the Half-Life of a Reaction...

If you're given the **rate constant**, $k$, the **order** of the reaction and the reactant **concentrations** then you can work out the **half-life**. Each order has an equation — you **don't** need to remember them, but you might be asked to **use** them. So here they are...

| | | |
|---|---|---|
| 1) **Zero Order** $t_{1/2} = [X] \div 2k$ | The decomposition of X to Y and Z is zero order. Under certain conditions, the rate constant = 0.2 mol dm$^{-3}$ s$^{-1}$. So if the original concentration of X is 1.0 mol dm$^{-3}$, then $t_{1/2} = 1.0 \div (2 \times 0.2) = 2.5$ s | |
| 2) **First Order** $t_{1/2} = 0.69 \div k$ | The decomposition of $N_2O_5$ to $NO_2$ and $O_2$ is first order. At a certain temperature, the rate constant is $1.10 \times 10^{-2}$ s$^{-1}$. At this temperature, $t_{1/2} = 0.69 \div 1.10 \times 10^{-2} = 62.7$ s | |
| 3) **Second Order** $t_{1/2} = 1 \div k[X]$ | The decomposition of hydrogen iodide is a second order reaction. At a certain temperature, the rate constant is $2.50 \times 10^{-3}$ dm$^3$ mol$^{-1}$ s$^{-1}$. If the initial concentration of hydrogen iodide is 1.0 mol dm$^{-3}$, $t_{1/2} = 1 \div (2.50 \times 10^{-3} \times 1.0) = 400$ s | |

## ...And Half-Lives can be used to Figure Out the Rate Equation from a Graph

On page 7, **half-lives** were used to find the **reaction order** — you can take this one step further and use the half life to work out the **rate equation**.

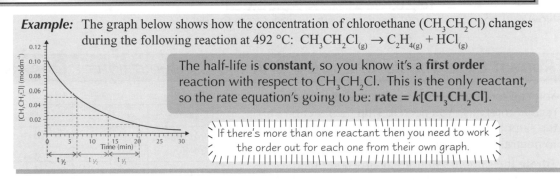

**Example:** The graph below shows how the concentration of chloroethane ($CH_3CH_2Cl$) changes during the following reaction at 492 °C: $CH_3CH_2Cl_{(g)} \rightarrow C_2H_{4(g)} + HCl_{(g)}$

The half-life is **constant**, so you know it's a **first order** reaction with respect to $CH_3CH_2Cl$. This is the only reactant, so the rate equation's going to be: **rate = $k[CH_3CH_2Cl]$**.

If there's more than one reactant then you need to work the order out for each one from their own graph.

## Practice Questions

Q1 What are the units for rate in a rate equation?

Q2 What happens to the value of the rate constant when the temperature is increased?

Q3 What is the order of a reaction if the half-life is independent of the reactant concentration?

**Exam Questions**

1 The following reaction is second order with respect to NO and first order with respect to $H_2$.
$$2NO_{(g)} + 2H_{2(g)} \rightarrow 2H_2O_{(g)} + N_{2(g)}$$
   a) Write a rate equation for the reaction and state the overall order of the reaction. [2 marks]
   b) The rate of the reaction at 800 °C was determined to be 0.00267 mol dm$^{-3}$ s$^{-1}$ when $[H_2] = 0.0020$ mol dm$^{-3}$ and $[NO] = 0.0040$ mol dm$^{-3}$.
   i) Calculate a value for the rate constant at 800 °C, including units. [3 marks]
   ii) Predict the effect on the rate constant of decreasing the temperature of the reaction to 600 °C. [1 mark]
   *decrease.*

2 In a reaction between A and B, the rate equation has been determined to be
$$Rate = k[A][B]^2$$
   *B. au*
   What happens to the reaction rate, at constant temperature, when:
   a) the initial concentrations of both A and B are doubled. [3 marks]
   b) the initial concentration of A is halved and B is doubled. [3 marks]

## If you thought this was fun, just wait till you get a load of...

...page 10. That's even better. It's got an entire example on this stuff. Like, wow! And speaking of things that are fun, can I also recommend to you... flying kites, peeling bananas, making models of your friends out of apples, the literary works of Jan Pieńkowski, counting spots on the carpet, the 1980s, goats, eating all the pies and cuddling boys.

# Deducing Orders and Rate Equations

*OK, now it's time to try and bring the previous few pages together and actually work some stuff out.*

## You can **Work Out** Orders Of Reaction and Rate Equations by **Experimentation**

The way to solve these kinds of problem is generally the same.

1) Do a series of experiments **monitoring** the **rate of the reaction**.
2) In each separate experiment, **vary** the concentration of **only one reactant**. Keep everything else the same.
3) **Plot** each experiment on a **concentration-time graph** and **calculate** the **initial rate of reaction** (gradient at t = 0).
4) Analyse the results to see how changing the concentration affects the rate, and work out the **rate equation**.

## Worked Example — Reaction of **Propanone** and **Iodine**

The **equation** for this reaction is:

$$CH_3COCH_{3(aq)} + I_{2(aq)} \xrightarrow{H^+_{(aq)}} CH_3COCH_2I_{(aq)} + H^+_{(aq)} + I^-_{(aq)}$$

And from this you can write the **rate equation**.

$$Rate = k\,[CH_3COCH_3]^x\,[H^+]^y\,[I_2]^z$$

Now you need to work out the values of x, y and z from the data.

## **Repeat** Experiments **Changing** Only the Concentration of **One** Reactant

You can monitor the reaction by **taking samples** at regular intervals. You need to **stop** the reaction in the sample by adding sodium hydrogen carbonate to neutralise the acid.

**Titrate** the sample solutions against sodium thiosulfate and starch to work out the **concentration of the iodine** (see p43 for more about titration).

Carry out the experiment several times. In each experiment, you should **only** change the concentration of **one reactant**.

| Experiment | 1 | 2 | 3 | 4 | 5 | 6 | 7 |
|---|---|---|---|---|---|---|---|
| [Propanone] (mol dm$^{-3}$) | 0.4 | 0.8 | 1.2 | 0.4 | 0.4 | 0.4 | 0.4 |
| [Iodine] (mol dm$^{-3}$) | 0.002 | 0.002 | 0.002 | 0.004 | 0.006 | 0.002 | 0.002 |
| [H$^+$] (mol dm$^{-3}$) | 0.4 | 0.4 | 0.4 | 0.4 | 0.4 | 0.8 | 1.2 |

## Plot **Concentration-Time** Graphs to Work Out the **Rate Of Reaction**

Here is the **table of data** from each of the seven experiments. The volume of sodium thiosulfate is proportional to the concentration of iodine, so the results can be used to draw a series of **concentration-time graphs**. From each graph you can work out the **initial rate of reaction** by **measuring the gradient** at t = 0.

| | Volume of sodium thiosulfate (cm$^3$) | | | | | | |
|---|---|---|---|---|---|---|---|
| Experiment | 1 | 2 | 3 | 4 | 5 | 6 | 7 |
| 0 seconds | 19.0 | 19.0 | 19.0 | 38.0 | 57.0 | 19.0 | 19.0 |
| 60 seconds | 17.0 | 15.3 | 13.5 | 36.0 | 55.0 | 15.5 | 13.4 |
| 120 seconds | 15.0 | 12.1 | 8.7 | 33.9 | 53.3 | 12.0 | 8.6 |
| 180 seconds | 13.0 | 9.2 | 5.1 | 31.9 | 51.6 | 9.0 | 4.9 |
| 240 seconds | 11.0 | 6.7 | 3.0 | 29.8 | 49.9 | 6.5 | 3.1 |

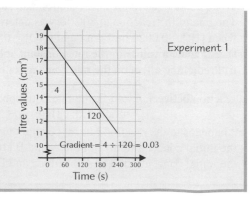

In this experiment the graph is a **straight line**, so it's easy to measure the gradient.
If the graph was a **curve**, you'd need to measure the **initial gradient** (gradient at t = 0) to work out the **initial rate**.

# Deducing Orders and Rate Equations

## Compare the Results to Determine the Effect of Concentration on the Rate

Once you've worked out the rate for each experiment it's time to make another table.
This time it shows how **changing** the concentration of the **reactants** affects the **rates of reaction**.

| Expt | Change compared to Expt 1 | Rate Of Reaction | Change |
|------|---------------------------|------------------|--------|
| 1 | — | 0.033 | — |
| 2 | [propanone] doubled | 0.062 | Rate doubled |
| 3 | [propanone] trebled | 0.092 | Rate trebled |
| 4 | [iodine] doubled | 0.034 | No change in rate |
| 5 | [iodine] trebled | 0.032 | No change in rate |
| 6 | [$H^+$] doubled | 0.058 | Rate doubled |
| 7 | [$H^+$] trebled | 0.094 | Rate trebled |

*The rates of reaction aren't exactly double or triple because of experimental error.*

## Work Out the Rate Equation

From the table above, you can say...

1) The **rate is proportional** to [propanone], so the **order is 1** with respect to propanone.
2) The **rate is independent** of [iodine], so the **order is 0** with respect to iodine.
3) The **rate is proportional** to [$H^+$], so the **order is 1** with respect to [$H^+$].

*See p6 for how changing the concentration of reactants relates to the rate order.*

You can now write the full rate equation...
Rate = $k[CH_3COCH_3]^1[H^+]^1[I_2]^0$ = $k[CH_3COCH_3][H^+]$

*You can now see that the rate is independent of [iodine], which is why the graphs of [iodine] vs time are a straight line.*

## Practice Questions

Q1 Why are samples from the reaction between propanone and iodine added to sodium hydrogencarbonate?

Q2 What is the indicator used when titrating samples of the reaction mixture with sodium thiosulfate?

Q3 In this investigation, why is the concentration-time graph a straight line?

Q4 If the graph was a curve, where would you measure the gradient?

### Exam Questions

1 The table shows the results of a series of initial rate
experiments for the reaction between substances D and E.
   a) Find the order of the reaction with respect
      to reactants D and E. Explain your reasoning. [4 marks]
   b) Write the rate equation for the reaction. [1 mark]

| Experiment | [D] (mol dm$^{-3}$) | [E] (mol dm$^{-3}$) | Initial rate × 10$^{-3}$ (mol dm$^{-3}$ s$^{-1}$) |
|-----------|------|------|------|
| 1 | 0.2 | 0.2 | 1.30 |
| 2 | 0.4 | 0.2 | 5.19 |
| 3 | 0.2 | 0.4 | 2.61 |

2 X and Y react together according to the equation
$$X + 3Y \rightarrow XY_3$$
In a series of experiments carried out at 288 K,
the following results were obtained
   a) What is the order of reaction with respect to X? [2 marks]
   b) What is the order of reaction with respect to Y? [2 marks]
   c) Write the rate equation for the reaction between X and Y. [1 mark]

| Experiment | initial [X] (mol dm$^{-3}$) | initial [Y] (mol dm$^{-3}$) | initial rate (mol dm$^{-3}$ s$^{-1}$) |
|-----------|------|------|------|
| 1 | 0.100 | 0.100 | 0.00198 |
| 2 | 0.100 | 0.300 | 0.01801 |
| 3 | 0.200 | 0.100 | 0.00401 |

## The fun just never stops...

*I know experiments like these might not seem the most exciting in the world. But you have got to learn them. Besides once upon a time they were exciting. At some point in history people would have been positively enthusiastic about a titration. They'd love the opportunity to swirl a flask of liquid until the colour changed. Honest...*

# Rates and Reaction Mechanisms

*It's a cold, miserable grey day outside, but on the plus side I just had a really nice slice of carrot and ginger cake. Anyway, this page is about the connection between rate equations and reaction mechanisms.*

## The **Rate-Determining Step** is the **Slowest Step** in a Multi-Step Reaction

Mechanisms can have **one step** or a **series of steps**. If there's a series of steps, then each step can have its own **rate**. The **overall rate** is decided by the step with the slowest rate — the **rate-determining step**.

It's a bit like a busy supermarket with only one checkout open. It **doesn't matter** how many customers come into the store or how quickly they choose their items, the number of customers that can complete their shopping will **mainly** be decided by the number that can get through the checkout — this is the **rate-determining step**.

## Reactants in the **Rate Equation** Affect the **Rate**

The rate equation is handy for working out the **mechanism** of a chemical reaction.

You need to be able to pick out which reactants from the chemical equation are involved in the **rate-determining step**. Here are the **rules** for doing this:

> If a reactant appears in the **rate equation**, it must be affecting the **rate**.
> So this reactant must be in the **rate-determining step**.
>
> If a reactant **doesn't** appear in the **rate equation**,
> then it **won't** be involved in the **rate-determining step**.

*Catalysts can appear in rate equations, so they can be in rate-determining steps too.*

Some **important points** to remember about rate-determining steps and mechanisms are:
1) The rate-determining step **doesn't** have to be the first step in a mechanism.
2) The reaction mechanism **can't** usually be predicted from **just** the chemical equation.

## You Can Predict the **Rate Equation** from the **Rate-Determining Step**...

> The **order of a reaction** with respect to a reactant shows the **number of molecules** of that reactant which are involved in the **rate-determining step**.

So, if a reaction's second order with respect to X, there'll be two molecules of X in the rate-determining step.

For example, the mechanism for the reaction between **chlorine free radicals** and **ozone**, $O_3$, consists of **two steps**:

$$Cl\bullet_{(g)} + O_{3(g)} \rightarrow ClO\bullet_{(g)} + O_{2(g)} \text{ — slow (rate-determining step)}$$

$$ClO\bullet_{(g)} + O\bullet_{(g)} \rightarrow Cl\bullet_{(g)} + O_{2(g)} \text{ — fast}$$

$Cl\bullet$ and $O_3$ must both be in the rate equation, so the rate equation will be of the form: **rate = $k[Cl\bullet]^m[O_3]^n$**.

There's only **one** $Cl\bullet$ radical and **one** $O_3$ molecule in the rate-determining step, so the **orders**, m and n, are both **1**.

So the predicted rate equation is **rate = $k[Cl\bullet][O_3]$**.

## ...And You Can Predict the **Mechanism** from the **Rate Equation**

Knowing exactly which reactants are in the **rate-determining step** gives you an idea of the reaction **mechanism**.

For example, the nucleophile **OH⁻** can substitute for **Br** in 2-bromo-2-methylpropane. Here are two possible mechanisms:

The actual **rate equation** was worked out by rate experiments: **rate = $k[(CH_3)_3CBr]$**

**OH⁻** isn't in the **rate equation**, so it **can't** be involved in the rate-determining step.

The **second mechanism** is most likely to be correct because OH⁻ **isn't** in the rate-determining step.

# Rates and Reaction Mechanisms

## Example — *Propanone* and *Iodine... again*

You've seen it before and it's back again. The reaction between **propanone** and **iodine**, catalysed by hydrogen ions. On pages 10–11 you worked out the **rate equation** from some experimental data. Now you can use the rate equation to come up with a **reaction mechanism**.

As a quick reminder, the rate equation for the reaction is...

$$Rate = k[CH_3COCH_3][H^+]$$

So, using the rules from the previous page here's what you can say about the reaction —

1) Propanone and $H^+$ are **in the rate equation** — so they must be **in the rate-determining step.**

2) Iodine is **not in the rate equation** so it's **not in the rate-determining step.**

3) The **order** of reaction for both propanone and $H^+$ is **1** — so the rate-determining step must use **1 molecule** of each.

4) $H^+$ is a **catalyst** — so it must be **regenerated** in another step.

And when you put all that together you could come up with a reaction mechanism like this...

Step 1 **only** involves **one** molecule of propanone and **one** of $H^+$.

The first step is the slow **rate-determining step.**

Iodine is **not** in the rate equation, so **doesn't** appear in the rate-determining step — instead it appears in step three.

The **hydrogen** ion is **regenerated** in Step 2. So is acting as a **catalyst**.

The $H^+$ made here is the one in the full equation.

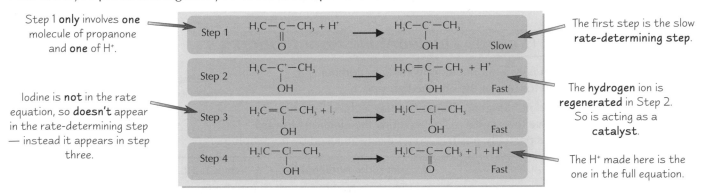

## Practice Questions

Q1 In a multi-step reaction, what's the name given to the step with the slowest rate?

Q2 Knowing the order of reaction is important for suggesting a rate-determining step. Why?

Q3 In the reaction of iodine with propanone, why doesn't iodine appear in the rate equation?

## Exam Questions

1 The following reaction is first order with respect to $\underline{H_2}$ and first order with respect to $\underline{ICl}$.

$$H_{2(g)} + 2ICl_{(g)} \rightarrow I_{2(g)} + 2HCl_{(g)}$$

a) Write the rate equation for this reaction. $Rate = k[H_2] \cdot [ICl]^2$. [1 mark]

b) The mechanism for this reaction consists of two steps.

   i) Identify the molecules that are in the rate-determining step. Justify your answer. $H_2$ and $ICl$. [3 marks]

   ii) A chemist suggested the following mechanism for the reaction.

$$2ICl_{(g)} \rightarrow I_{2(g)} + Cl_{2(g)} \qquad slow$$
$$H_{2(g)} + Cl_{2(g)} \rightarrow 2HCl_{(g)} \qquad fast$$

$k[ICl]^2$

Suggest, with reasons, whether this mechanism is likely to be correct. No, because the rds must be the slow mechanism and it must contain reactants $I_2$ and $ICl$. [2 marks]

2 The reaction between hydrogen bromide and oxygen was studied at 400 °C.

$$4HBr_{(g)} + O_{2(g)} \rightarrow 2H_2O_{(g)} + 2Br_{2(g)} \qquad Rate = k[HBr][O_2]$$

a) What is the order of reaction with respect to each reactant? $HBr = 1 \quad O_2 = 1$ [1 mark]

b) What species must be involved in the rate-determining step, and in what molar ratio? $[HBr][O_2] \quad 1 = 1$ [2 marks]

c) The following steps have been suggested for the mechanism. Re-write them in the correct order and label the rate-determining step.

$$2HBrO + 2HBr \rightarrow 2H_2O + 2Br_2$$
$$HBr + O_2 \rightarrow HBrO_2$$
$$HBrO_2 + HBr \rightarrow 2HBrO$$

$HBr + O_2 \rightarrow HBrO_2 \quad RDS$
$HBrO_2 + HBr \rightarrow 2HBrO$
$2HBrO + 2HBr \rightarrow 2H_2O + 2Br_2$

[2 marks]

## *I found rate-determining step aerobics a bit on the slow side...*

*Left, right, left, right. Yes it's true, I go to step aerobics. Nothing wrong with a bit of exercise bouncing to the latest beats. Then I call in at the chippy on the way home. Don't judge me. It gets late and I'm hungry. Anyway, have you noticed that the propanone, iodine reaction crops up again... Hmmm, definitely worth checking that bit out properly, methinks.*

# Halogenoalkanes and Reaction Mechanisms

*'Lean hog on a lake' is an anagram of halogenoalkane. A good thing to know...*

## Halogenoalkanes can be Hydrolysed by Hydroxide Ions

There are three different types of halogenoalkane. They can all be hydrolysed (split) by heating them with sodium hydroxide — but they react using different mechanisms.

In primary halogenoalkanes, the halogen is joined to a carbon with just <u>one alkyl group</u> attached.

In secondary halogenoalkanes the halogen is joined to a carbon with <u>two alkyl groups</u> attached.

In tertiary halogenoalkanes, the halogen is attached to a carbon with <u>three alkyl groups</u> attached.

## Halogenoalkanes Undergo Nucleophilic Substitution

**Nucleophilic substitution** is when a nucleophile attacks another molecule and is **swapped** for one of the attached groups.

*Nucleophiles are particles that are attracted to positive charge, such as OH⁻ and CN⁻.*

The carbon–halogen bond in halogenoalkanes is **polar** — halogens are much more **electronegative** than carbon, so they draw the electrons **towards** themselves. The carbon is **partially positive**, so it's easily attacked by nucleophiles.

$$C^{\delta+}-Br^{\delta-}$$

1) OH⁻ is the **nucleophile** — it provides a pair of electrons for the $C^{\delta+}$.

2) The C–Br bond breaks **heterolytically** — both electrons from the bond are taken by Br⁻.

3) Br⁻ comes away as OH⁻ bonds to the carbon.

There are two different types of mechanism for nucleophilic substitution — **$S_N1$** and **$S_N2$**.

> $S_N1$ reactions only involve **1** molecule or ion in the **rate-determining step**.
> $S_N2$ reactions involve **2** molecules, 1 molecule and 1 ion or 2 ions in the **rate-determining step**.

**Primary halogenoalkanes** only react by the **$S_N2$** mechanism.
**Secondary halogenoalkanes** can react by **both** the $S_N1$ and $S_N2$ mechanisms — it depends what mood they're in.
**Tertiary halogenoalkanes** only react by the **$S_N1$** mechanism.

## The Rate Equation shows Primary Halogenoalkanes Use an $S_N2$ Mechanism

The equation for the reaction of the primary halogenoalkane **bromoethane** with **hydroxide ions** is:

$$CH_3CH_2Br + OH^- \rightarrow CH_3CH_2OH + Br^-$$

And the rate equation is: $rate = k[CH_3CH_2Br][OH^-]$

So, the **rate is dependent** on the concentration of **both** the reactants and the **order** with respect to **each** is **1**. This means the **rate-determining** step must include **one** of **each** reactant molecule — which is **two** in total so it's $S_N2$.

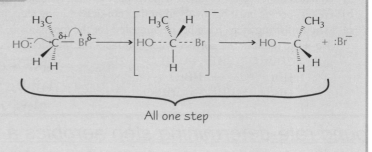

All one step

*Primary halogenoalkanes have lots of space around the carbon, which is surrounded mostly by H groups. This means there is space for the hydroxide ion to attack.*

# Halogenoalkanes and Reaction Mechanisms

## The Rate Equation shows Tertiary Halogenoalkanes Use $S_N1$

The equation for the reaction of the tertiary halogenoalkane **2-bromo-2-methylpropane** with **hydroxide ions** looks similar to the reaction with bromoethane on the previous page:

$$(CH_3)_3CBr + OH^- \rightarrow (CH_3)_3COH + Br^-$$

But the rate equation for this reaction is different:  $rate = k[(CH_3)_3CBr]$

The **rate is only dependent** on the concentration of the **halogenoalkane**. The **order of the reaction** with respect to the halogenoalkane is **1**. So the **rate-determining** step must only include **one** molecule of the halogenoalkane. The reaction happens in two steps. In the first step, the halogen leaves the halogenoalkane. The nucleophile is then able to attack in the second step.

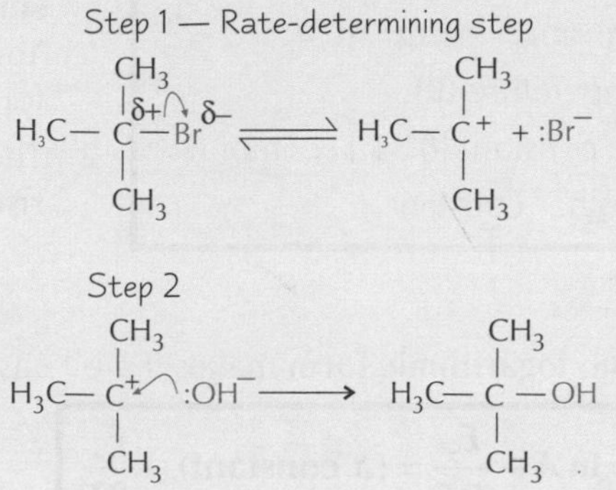

Step 1 — Rate-determining step

The reaction happens this way because there's very little space around the carbon (it's surrounded by alkyl groups).

Step 2

## Practice Questions

*[handwritten: Br / c–c–c–c]*

Q1 Which sort of bromoalkane is 2-bromobutane — primary, ~~secondary~~ or tertiary?

Q2 What is the role of the hydroxide ion in the hydrolysis of a halogenoalkane?  *[handwritten: nucleophile, substitude with Br]*

Q3 What do the terms $S_N1$ and $S_N2$ mean?  *[handwritten: $S_N1$ means the rate determine step includes 1 reactant molecule]*

Q4 What is the order of reaction with respect to hydroxide ions in the hydrolysis of a tertiary halogenoalkane?  *[handwritten: 0]*

## Exam Questions

*[handwritten: c–c–c–]*

1   For the reaction between sodium hydroxide and 1-chloropropane  *[handwritten: D]*

$$CH_3CH_2CH_2Cl + NaOH \rightarrow CH_3CH_2CH_2OH + NaCl$$

Which one of the following is the correct rate equation?

A  Rate = $k[NaOH]$                               B  Rate = $k[CH_3CH_2CH_2Cl]$

C  Rate = $k[CH_3CH_2CH_2Cl]^2$              D  Rate = $k[CH_3CH_2CH_2Cl][NaOH]$          [1 mark]

2   The hydrolysis of 2-bromo-2-methylpropane by hydroxide ions follows an $S_N1$ mechanism.  *[handwritten: A]*
Which one of the following is the rate-determining step?

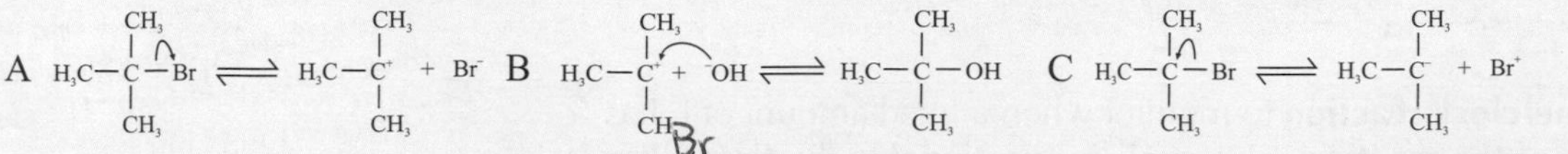

*[handwritten: Br / c–c–c / c]*                                                                                          [1 mark]

3   The following equation shows the hydrolysis of 1-iodobutane by hydroxide ions:

$$CH_3CH_2CH_2CH_2I + OH^- \rightarrow CH_3CH_2CH_2CH_2OH + I^-$$

a)  Is 1-iodobutane a primary, secondary or tertiary iodoalkane?  *[handwritten: a) primary]*          [1 mark]

b)  Write the rate equation for this reaction.  *[handwritten: b) Rate = k·[OH⁻][CH₃CH₂CH₂CH₂I]]*          [1 mark]

c)  What type of mechanism is involved in this reaction?          [2 marks]

d)  Write equation(s) to show the detailed mechanism of this reaction.  *[handwritten: (d) CH3CH2 CH2Cl, :OH⁻]*          [4 marks]

*[handwritten: c) $S_N2$]*

## Way-hay!!! — It's the curly arrows...  *[handwritten: c) a]*

Seriously, whenever I talk to someone who's done chemistry the one thing they've remembered is curly arrows. They have no idea how they work. But they know they exist. Now it's OK for them 'cos they don't have an exam, but you do — so make sure you understand where the arrows are coming from and going to. Check back to AS to be sure.

# Activation Energy and Catalysts

*It's more maths on this page. But keep going, the end is in sight — even though it's over the page.*

## Use the **Arrhenius Equation** to Calculate the **Activation Energy**

The **Arrhenius equation** (nasty-looking thing in the blue box) links the **rate constant** (*k*) with **activation energy** (*$E_a$*, the minimum amount of kinetic energy particles need to react) and **temperature** (T). This is probably the **worst** equation there is in A2 Chemistry. But the good news is, you **don't** have to learn it — you just have to understand what it's showing you. Here it is:

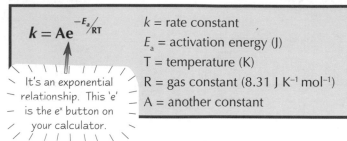

$$k = Ae^{-E_a/RT}$$

*k* = rate constant
*$E_a$* = activation energy (J)
T = temperature (K)
R = gas constant (8.31 J K⁻¹ mol⁻¹)
A = another constant

It's an exponential relationship. This 'e' is the $e^x$ button on your calculator.

1) As the activation energy, *$E_a$*, gets **bigger**, *k* gets **smaller**. So, a **large** *$E_a$* will mean a **slow rate**. You can **test** this out by trying **different numbers** for *$E_a$* in the equation... ahh go on, be a devil.

2) The equation also shows that as the temperature **rises**, *k* **increases**. Try this one out too.

Putting the **Arrhenius equation** into **logarithmic form** makes it a bit easier to use.

$$\ln k = \ln A - \frac{E_a}{RT} = \text{(a constant)} - \frac{E_a}{RT}$$

There's a handy 'ln' button on your calculator for this.

You can use this equation to create an **Arrhenius plot** by plotting **ln** *k* against $\frac{1}{T}$.

This will produce a graph with a **gradient** of $\frac{-E_a}{R}$. And once you know the gradient, you can find the **activation energy**.

*Example:*

The graph on the right shows an Arrhenius plot for the decomposition of hydrogen iodide. Calculate the activation energy for this reaction. R = 8.31 J K⁻¹ mol⁻¹.

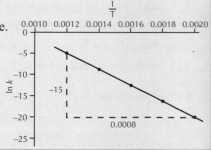

The gradient, $\frac{-E_a}{R} = \frac{-15}{0.0008} = -18\,750$

So, $E_a = -(-18\,750 \times 8.31) = 155\,812.5$ J mol⁻¹ ≈ **156 kJ mol⁻¹**

## To Calculate the Activation Energy, First **Collect** and **Process** the Data...

Here's another example of how to work out the activation energy.

$$S_2O_8^{2-}{}_{(aq)} + 2I^-{}_{(aq)} \rightarrow 2SO_4^{2-}{}_{(aq)} + I_{2(aq)}$$

You can only do this kind of mathematical trickery if all the concentrations are kept the same.

You can use the **iodine-clock reaction** to monitor when a fixed amount of $I_2$ has been made. The **rate of the reaction** is **inversely** proportional to the **time taken** (**t**) for the solution to change colour — a faster rate means a shorter time taken.

So, mathematically speaking, the rate is **proportional** to **1/time**. This means that 1/t can be used instead of *k* in the Arrhenius equation, which means you can calculate the activation energy. Hurrah!!

| Time, t (s) | Temp, T (K) | 1/t (s⁻¹) | ln 1/t | 1/T (K⁻¹) |
|---|---|---|---|---|
| 204 | 303 | 0.0049 | −5.32 | 0.00330 |
| 138 | 308 | 0.0072 | −4.93 | 0.00325 |
| 115 | 312 | 0.0087 | −4.74 | 0.00321 |
| 75 | 318 | 0.0133 | −4.32 | 0.00314 |
| 55 | 323 | 0.0182 | −4.01 | 0.00310 |

Here's some collected data for this reaction at different temperatures. The first two columns show the raw data and the other columns show the data that's needed to draw a graph of **ln (1/t)** against **1/T** (see the next page).

# Activation Energy and Catalysts

## Enthalpy Profiles and Boltzmann Distributions Show Why Catalysts Work

If you look at an **enthalpy profile** together with a **Maxwell-Boltzmann Distribution**, you can see **why** catalysts work.

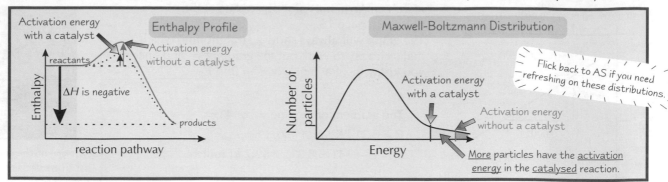

1) The catalyst provides an **alternative pathway** with **lower activation energy**, meaning there are **more particles** with **enough energy** to react when they collide. So, in a certain amount of time, **more particles will react**.

2) Catalysts are amazingly important in **industrial processes** — they save a fortune because they mean reactions can be carried out at lower temperatures.

## Practice Questions

Q1 The Arrhenius equation can be written as $\ln k$ = a constant – $E_a/RT$. What do the terms $k$, T and R represent?

Q2 The Arrhenius equation is $k = Ae^{-E_a/RT}$. Which one of the following answers is true as $E_a$ increases?
    A $k$ increases and rate of reaction increases
    B $k$ increases and rate of reaction decreases
    C $k$ decreases and rate of reaction increases
    D $k$ decreases and rate of reaction decreases

Q3 Give three examples of heterogeneous catalysts.

Q4 Explain how a catalyst works.

## Exam Questions

1 Finely divided iron catalyses the reaction of nitrogen and hydrogen in the Haber process.
  Which of the following statements is incorrect?

  A Iron is behaving as a heterogeneous catalyst in this reaction

  B The iron provides a surface for the reaction to take place

  C The iron provides an alternative route of higher activation energy

  D Finely dividing the iron increases its surface area [1 mark]

2 a) Explain what is meant by the term 'activation energy'. [2 marks]

  b) With the help of energy profiles, explain how catalysts work. [3 marks]

  c) The table gives values for the rate constant of the reaction between hydroxide ions and bromoethane at different temperatures.
     i) Complete the table and then plot a graph of $\ln k$ ($y$-axis) against 1/T ($x$-axis). [5 marks]
     ii) Measure the gradient of the straight line produced. [2 marks]
     iii) Using the Arrhenius equation, $\ln k$ = a constant $-E_a/RT$, calculate the activation energy of the reaction.
        (R = 8.31 J K$^{-1}$ mol$^{-1}$) [3 marks]

| T | $k$ | 1/T | $\ln k$ |
|---|-----|-----|---------|
| 305 | 0.181 | 0.00328 | −1.709 |
| 313 | 0.468 | | |
| 323 | 1.34 | | |
| 333 | 3.29 | 0.00300 | 1.191 |
| 344 | 10.1 | | |
| 353 | 22.7 | 0.00283 | 3.127 |

## Aaaaaaaaaaarrrrrrrrggggggggggghhhhhhhhhhhhhhhhh...

*This was my first thought when I saw the Arrhenius equation. A big chocolate covered marshmallow was my second but that's not really important. The thing to remember is that they will give you the formula in the exam. So concentrate on learning how to use it — which bits to plot on an Arrhenius graph and what things to calculate to work out the $E_a$.*

# Entropy

*Entropy. You're gonna love this. I really don't want to spoil the surprise, but seriously... just you wait...*

## Entropy Tells you How Much Disorder There Is

Entropy is a measure of the **number of ways** that **particles** can be **arranged** and the **number of ways** that the **energy** can be shared out between the particles.

Substances really **like** disorder — they're actually more **energetically stable** when there's **more disorder**. So the particles naturally move to try to **increase the entropy**.

> **Example:** A gas spontaneously diffusing across a room.
>
> If you open a bottle of something smelly, it will **diffuse** throughout the room **spontaneously** — you don't have to shake it or heat it to make it happen. This is because it has a **higher entropy** when filling the room (there are more ways to arrange the particles) than it has in the bottle.

Baby Jay's experiment into entropy and diffusion was about to begin.

There are a few things that affect entropy:

### Physical State affects Entropy

You have to go back to the good old **solid-liquid-gas** particle explanation thingy to understand this.

**Solid** particles just wobble about a fixed point — there's **hardly any** randomness, so they have the **lowest entropy**.

**Gas** particles whizz around wherever they like. They've got the most **random arrangements** of particles, so they have the **highest entropy**.

**Dissolving** a solid also increases its entropy — dissolved particles can **move freely** as they're no longer held in one place.

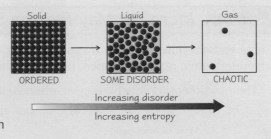

### The Amount of Energy a Substance has affects Entropy too

Energy can be measured in **quanta** — these are fixed '**packages**' of energy. The more energy quanta a substance has, the **more ways** they can be arranged and so the greater the **entropy**.

### More Particles means More Entropy

It makes sense — the more particles you've got, the **more ways** they and their energy can be **arranged** — so in a reaction like $N_2O_{4(g)} \rightarrow 2NO_{2(g)}$, entropy increases because the **number of moles** increases.

## The Entropy of A Substance Increases with Temperature

If you **raise the temperature** of a substance, you **increase the energy** of its particles. So the **higher** the temperature, the **more energy quanta** a substance has, and the **more ways** these quanta can be distributed — which means **higher entropy**.

The graph below shows how the entropy of a substance typically changes with temperature:

1) Within the solid, liquid and gas phases, entropy **increases slowly** with temperature.

2) When there's a change in **physical state**, there's also a **rapid change** in entropy. You can see this at points $T_m$ and $T_b$ on the graph.

3) There's a **larger** increase in entropy when a substance changes from **liquid to gas** than when it changes from **solid to liquid**.

4) The curve starts at the origin, (0, 0). In other words, at a temperature of **zero kelvin**, a substance will theoretically have **zero entropy**. This could only happen if you had a **perfectly ordered crystal**.

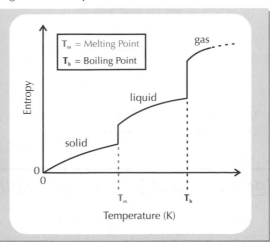

# Entropy

## Physical State and Complexity of a Substance Affect Standard Entropy

1) The **standard entropy** of a substance, $S^{\ominus}$, is the entropy of **1 mole** of that substance under **standard conditions** (**100 kPa** pressure and **298 K**). Its units are **J K$^{-1}$ mol$^{-1}$**.

2) The standard entropy of a substance depends **mainly** on its **physical state**. As a **general** rule solid substances tend to have **lower** standard entropies than liquids, which tend to have lower standard entropies than gases.

> **Example:** The standard entropy of liquid water is lower than the standard entropy for water vapour.
> $S^{\ominus}$ of $H_2O_{(l)}$ = 70 J K$^{-1}$ mol$^{-1}$     $S^{\ominus}$ of $H_2O_{(g)}$ = 189 J K$^{-1}$ mol$^{-1}$

3) The standard entropy of a substance also depends on its **complexity**.
**Simple** atoms or molecules tend to have **lower** standard entropies than more complicated molecules.

> **Example:** Carbon dioxide has more atoms than carbon monoxide and has a higher standard entropy.
> $S^{\ominus}$ of $CO_{2(g)}$ = 214 J K$^{-1}$ mol$^{-1}$     $S^{\ominus}$ of $CO_{(g)}$ = 198 J K$^{-1}$ mol$^{-1}$

## Entropy Increase May Explain Spontaneous Endothermic Reactions

Some **endothermic** reactions are **spontaneous** — which is a bit weird. You'd normally have to supply **energy** to make an endothermic reaction happen, but if the **entropy** increases enough, the reaction will happen by itself.

> The reaction of sodium hydrogencarbonate with hydrochloric acid is a **spontaneous endothermic reaction**.
>
> $$NaHCO_{3(s)} + H^+_{(aq)} \rightarrow Na^+_{(aq)} + CO_{2(g)} + H_2O_{(l)}$$
> 1 mole solid     1 mole aqueous ions     1 mole aqueous ions     1 mole gas     1 mole liquid
>
> It happens because of the large **increase in entropy** — the product has more particles and also the particles are in higher entropy states overall (gas and liquid, rather than solid).

*Both the enthalpy and the entropy have a say in whether a reaction is spontaneous — see the next page.*

## Practice Questions

Q1 How does the energy of a substance affect its entropy?

Q2 Why does entropy increase with increasing temperature?

Q3 Is the change in entropy greater at the melting point of a substance, or at its boiling point? Why?

Q4 In each of the following pairs choose the one with the greater entropy value:
    a) 1 mole of $NaCl_{(aq)}$ and 1 mole of $NaCl_{(s)}$        b) 1 mole of $Br_{2(l)}$ and 1 mole of $Br_{2(g)}$

### Exam Questions

1   a)  Define the term *entropy*.     **[2 marks]**

     b)  Explain whether each of the following reactions is likely to result in an increase or a decrease in entropy. Give a reason for your answer.

        i) $2NaNO_{3(s)} \rightarrow 2NaNO_{2(s)} + O_{2(g)}$     **[2 marks]**

        ii) $CO_{2(g)} + C_{(s)} \rightarrow 2CO_{(g)}$     **[2 marks]**

        iii) $N_{2(g)} + 3H_{2(g)} \rightarrow 2NH_{3(g)}$     **[2 marks]**

        iv) $H_{2(g)} + \frac{1}{2}O_{2(g)} \rightarrow H_2O_{(l)}$     **[2 marks]**

2   Based on just the equation, predict whether the reaction below is likely to be spontaneous. Give a reason for your answer.

$$Mg_{(s)} + \frac{1}{2}O_{2(g)} \rightarrow MgO_{(s)}$$

     **[2 marks]**

## Being neat and tidy is against the laws of nature...

*Well, there you go. Entropy in all its glory. We're not done yet though, oh no. There's plenty more where this came from. Which is why — if random disorder has left you in a spin — I'd suggest making sure you've really got your head around this lot before you turn over. You'll thank me for it, you will... Chocolates are always welcome... Flowers are nice too...*

# Entropy Change

*Here we go, as promised, more entropy. Never say I don't spoil you rotten...*

## The **Total Entropy Change** Includes the **System** and the **Surroundings**

During a reaction, there's an entropy change between the **reactants and products** — the entropy change of the **system**. The entropy of the **surroundings** changes too (because **energy** is transferred to or from the system). The **TOTAL** entropy change is the sum of the entropy changes of the **system** and the **surroundings**.

*The units of entropy are J K⁻¹ mol⁻¹*

$$\Delta S_{total} = \Delta S_{system} + \Delta S_{surroundings}$$

This equation isn't much use unless you know $\Delta S_{system}$ and $\Delta S_{surroundings}$. Luckily, there are formulas for them too:

This is just the difference between the entropies of the reactants and products.

$$\Delta S_{system} = S_{products} - S_{reactants}$$

and

$$\Delta S_{surroundings} = -\frac{\Delta H}{T}$$

$\Delta H$ = enthalpy change (in Jmol⁻¹)
$T$ = temperature (in K)

**Example:** Calculate the total entropy change for the reaction of ammonia and hydrogen chloride under standard conditions.

$$NH_{3(g)} + HCl_{(g)} \rightarrow NH_4Cl_{(s)} \qquad \Delta H = -315 \text{ kJ mol}^{-1} \text{ (at 298 K)}$$

$$S^{\ominus}[NH_{3(g)}] = 192.3 \text{ J K}^{-1}\text{mol}^{-1}, \ S^{\ominus}[HCl_{(g)}] = 186.8 \text{ J K}^{-1}\text{mol}^{-1}, \ S^{\ominus}[NH_4Cl_{(s)}] = 94.6 \text{ J K}^{-1}\text{mol}^{-1}$$

First find the entropy change of the **system**:

$$\Delta S_{system} = S_{products} - S_{reactants} = 94.6 - (192.3 + 186.8) = \mathbf{-284.5 \text{ J K}^{-1}\text{mol}^{-1}}$$

This shows a negative change in entropy. It's not surprising as 2 moles of gas have combined to form 1 mole of solid.

Now find the entropy change of the **surroundings**:

$$\Delta H = -315 \text{ kJmol}^{-1} = -315 \times 10^3 \text{ Jmol}^{-1}$$

Put $\Delta H$ in the right units.

$$\Delta S_{surroundings} = -\frac{\Delta H}{T} = \frac{-(-315 \times 10^3)}{298} = \mathbf{+1057 \text{ J K}^{-1}\text{mol}^{-1}}$$

Finally you can find the **total** entropy change:

$$\Delta S_{total} = \Delta S_{system} + \Delta S_{surroundings} = -284.5 + (+1057) = \mathbf{+772.5 \text{ J K}^{-1}\text{mol}^{-1}}$$

## For A **Spontaneous** Reaction, The **Total Entropy Change** Must Be **Positive**

1) The **total entropy** of a system and its surroundings **has to increase** for a spontaneous reaction to happen.

2) If $\Delta S_{total}$ is **positive** the reaction is **kinetically favourable** — it can happen spontaneously. If $\Delta S_{total}$ is **negative** the reactants are said to be **kinetically stable** — this means they won't react on their own.

3) As long as $\Delta S_{total}$ is **positive**, it doesn't matter if one of $\Delta S_{system}$ and $\Delta S_{surroundings}$ is negative. Whether or not the **total** entropy change is positive depends on the **balance** between the entropy changes of the system and the surroundings.

4) Remember, $\Delta S_{surroundings} = -\frac{\Delta H}{T}$.

This means:
- In an **exothermic** reaction $\Delta H$ is negative, so $\Delta S_{surroundings}$ is always **positive** — heat given out by the system **increases** the entropy of the surroundings.
- In an **endothermic** reaction $\Delta H$ is positive, so $\Delta S_{surroundings}$ is always **negative** — heat taken in by the system **lowers** the entropy of the surroundings.
- At **higher temperatures**, $\Delta S_{surroundings}$ gets **smaller**. As a result, it makes a **smaller contribution** to the total entropy change than it does at lower temperatures.

5) The **exothermic** reaction in the example above can happen because the **entropy increase** in the **surroundings** is big enough to make up for the **entropy decrease** in the **system** — the **total entropy** has still **increased**.

6) The same thing applies to endothermic reactions — there's a **drop** in $S_{surroundings}$, but if the **increase** in $S_{system}$ is big enough, the reaction **will happen**.

# Entropy Change

## You Can Relate **Reaction Results** to Changes in **Entropy** and **Enthalpy**

*Example:* The Instant Cold Pack.

A common type of instant cold pack consists of two bags, one inside the other. The inner bag contains **water** and the outer bag contains **ammonium nitrate crystals**. When you squeeze the pack, the inner bag bursts allowing the water and ammonium nitrate to mix. The **crystals dissolve** in the water in an **endothermic** reaction, **absorbing heat** from the surroundings. This causes the pack to **cool down** very quickly — ideal for first aid on sports injuries.

$$NH_4NO_{3(s)} \xrightarrow{H_2O_{(l)}} NH_4^+{}_{(aq)} + NO_3^-{}_{(aq)} \qquad \Delta H = +25.7 \text{ kJ mol}^{-1} \text{ (at 298 K)}$$

The entropy change of the system is **positive**: $\Delta S_{system} = +108.7 \text{ J K}^{-1}\text{mol}^{-1}$

This makes sense if you look at the equation — you'd expect an **increase** in the entropy of the system because a solid is dissolving to produce **freely moving** ions, **increasing disorder**.

The reaction is **endothermic**, so the entropy change of the **surroundings** must be **negative**: $\Delta S_{surroundings} = -\Delta H/T = -25\ 700 \div 298 = -86.2 \text{ J K}^{-1}\text{mol}^{-1}$

> The $\Delta H$ value given above is in **kJ**, $\Delta H$ in the equation $-\Delta H/T$ is in **J**. You need to multiply the figure above by **1000** to convert it into J.

The **total entropy change** is:

$$\Delta S_{total} = \Delta S_{system} + \Delta S_{surroundings} = 108.7 - 86.2 = +22.5 \text{ J K}^{-1}\text{mol}^{-1}$$

It's **positive**, which explains why the reaction takes place spontaneously.

---

*Example:* Reaction between barium hydroxide and ammonium chloride.

First, place a flask on top of a piece of damp cardboard. Add to the flask **solid barium hydroxide crystals**, $Ba(OH)_2.8H_2O$, and **solid ammonium chloride**, then stir. Within about 30 seconds, the smell of ammonia becomes noticeable and a short time later, the bottom of the flask will be **frozen** to the cardboard. The **temperature drops** to well below 0 °C.

$$Ba(OH)_2.8H_2O_{(s)} + 2NH_4Cl_{(s)} \rightarrow BaCl_{2(s)} + 10H_2O_{(l)} + 2NH_{3(g)} \qquad \Delta H = +164.0 \text{ kJ mol}^{-1} \text{ (at 298 K)}$$

Looking at the equation, you would expect an **increase** in the entropy of the system because two solids are combining to produce a solid, a liquid and a gas — that's an **increase** in disorder. Calculating $\Delta S_{system}$ using standard entropies confirms this:

$S^{\ominus}[Ba(OH)_2.8H_2O_{(s)}] = +427.0 \text{ J K}^{-1}\text{mol}^{-1}$, $S^{\ominus}[NH_4Cl_{(s)}] = +94.6 \text{ J K}^{-1}\text{mol}^{-1}$, $S^{\ominus}[BaCl_{2(s)}] = +123.7 \text{ J K}^{-1}\text{mol}^{-1}$,

$S^{\ominus}[H_2O_{(l)}] = +69.9 \text{ J K}^{-1}\text{mol}^{-1}$, $S^{\ominus}[NH_{3(g)}] = +192.3 \text{ J K}^{-1}\text{mol}^{-1}$

$S_{reactants} = 427.0 + (2 \times 94.6) = +616.2 \text{ J K}^{-1}\text{mol}^{-1}$
$S_{products} = 123.7 + (10 \times 69.9) + (2 \times 192.3) = +1207.3 \text{ J K}^{-1}\text{mol}^{-1}$

$$\Delta S_{system} = S_{products} - S_{reactants} = 1207.3 - 616.2 = +591.1 \text{ J K}^{-1}\text{mol}^{-1}$$

The reaction is **endothermic**, so the entropy change of the surroundings must be **negative**.

$$\Delta S_{surroundings} = -\Delta H/T = -164\ 000 \div 298 = -550.3 \text{ J K}^{-1}\text{mol}^{-1}$$

The reaction is spontaneous, so the **total entropy change** must be **positive**.

$$\Delta S_{total} = \Delta S_{system} + \Delta S_{surroundings} = 591.1 - 550.3 = +40.8 \text{ J K}^{-1}\text{mol}^{-1}$$

Yup.

Brian's mum didn't think his efforts to increase the total entropy of the bathroom were all that positive.

# Entropy Change

## Just Because A Reaction **Can** Happen, Doesn't Mean It Will Happen **Fast**

1) When you study the enthalpy and entropy changes of a reaction, you are looking at its **thermodynamics**. A **spontaneous** reaction or change happens without you having to input energy — it is thermodynamically **favourable**.

2) But just because a reaction can happen spontaneously, **doesn't** mean that it happens **quickly**. The thermodynamics of a reaction don't tell you anything about how **fast** it will go — that's the job of **reaction kinetics**.

*Example:* The conversion of diamond to graphite

$$C_{diamond} \rightarrow C_{graphite} \quad \text{At 298 K:} \quad \Delta H = -1.9 \text{ kJ mol}^{-1}, \Delta S = +3.3 \text{ J K}^{-1} \text{mol}^{-1}$$

So at 298 K $\Delta S_{total} = \Delta S_{system} + \Delta S_{surroundings} = 3.3 + (1900 \div 298) = 3.3 + 6.4 = +9.7 \text{ J K}^{-1} \text{mol}^{-1}$

The **total entropy change** is **positive**, so this reaction **can** happen spontaneously.
At room temperature and pressure though, the rate of reaction is **extremely slow** — in fact it takes millions of years. This is because the **activation energy** needed to start this reaction is so high. Diamond is said to be **kinetically inert**.

*Example:* The decomposition of limestone (calcium carbonate)

$$CaCO_{3(s)} \rightarrow CaO_{(s)} + CO_{2(g)} \quad \text{At 298 K:} \quad \Delta H = +178 \text{ kJ mol}^{-1}, \Delta S = +165 \text{ J K}^{-1} \text{mol}^{-1}$$

So at 298 K $\Delta S_{total} = \Delta S_{system} + \Delta S_{surroundings} = 165 - (178\ 000 \div 298) = 165 - 597 = -432 \text{ J K}^{-1} \text{mol}^{-1}$

The **total entropy change** is **negative** so, at 298 K, the decomposition **can't** happen.
At 298 K, limestone is said to be **thermodynamically stable**. The enthalpy and entropy changes involved **won't** let this reaction occur **spontaneously** at this temperature.

## Practice Questions

Q1 What is the formula for calculating the total entropy change of a system?

Q2 For a particular reaction, $\Delta H = -420 \text{ kJ mol}^{-1}$. What is the $\Delta S_{surroundings}$ at 298 K?

Q3 If a chemical reaction is exothermic, what must $\Delta S_{surroundings}$ be?

Q4 The decomposition of X has a positive $\Delta S_{total}$, but the rate of reaction is measured in thousands of years. What term is used to describe X?

### Exam Questions

1 When a small amount of ammonium carbonate solid is added to 10 cm³ of 1.0 mol dm⁻³ ethanoic acid, carbon dioxide gas is evolved. This is an endothermic reaction, so the temperature of the reaction mixture drops.

$$(NH_4)_2CO_{3(s)} + 2CH_3CO_2H_{(aq)} \rightarrow 2CH_3CO_2NH_{4(aq)} + H_2O_{(l)} + CO_{2(g)} \quad \Delta H^{\ominus} > 0$$

   a) Looking at the equation, what would you expect to happen to the entropy of the system during this reaction? Explain your answer. [3 marks]

   b) Explain how this reaction can be both endothermic and spontaneous. [3 marks]

2 Thin ribbons of magnesium burn brightly in oxygen to leave a solid, white residue of magnesium oxide. The equation for this reaction is:

$$2Mg_{(s)} + O_{2(g)} \rightarrow 2MgO_{(s)} \quad \Delta H = -1204 \text{ kJ mol}^{-1} \text{ (at 298 K)}$$

$$S^{\ominus}[Mg_{(s)}] = +32.7 \text{ J K}^{-1} \text{mol}^{-1}, \; S^{\ominus}[O_{2(g)}] = +205 \text{ J K}^{-1} \text{mol}^{-1}, \; S^{\ominus}[MgO_{(s)}] = +26.9 \text{ J K}^{-1} \text{mol}^{-1}$$

   a) From the equation, **predict** whether $\Delta S_{system}$ for the reaction will be positive or negative at 298 K. Give a reason for your answer. [2 marks]

   b) Using the data given, calculate $\Delta S_{system}$ at 298 K. [3 marks]

   c) Calculate $\Delta S_{total}$ for the reaction. [4 marks]

## The entropy of my surroundings is always increasing, take a look at my kitchen...

*Still awake? Great stuff. Let me be the first to congratulate you on making it to the end of this page — I nearly didn't. Bet you thought that instant cold pack stuff was pretty cool though right? I know, I'm clutching at straws. Never mind. As a reward I suggest ten minutes of looking at clips of reality TV auditionees on line. It'll cheer you up no end...*

# Dissolving

*Warning: this page may contain enthalpy cycles... Please remain calm... I repeat:  this page may contain enthalpy cycles...*

## Dissolving Involves **Enthalpy Changes**

The **enthalpy change of solution** is the overall effect on enthalpy when something dissolves.

> The **enthalpy change of solution**, $\Delta H_{solution}$, is the enthalpy change when **1 mole** of **solute** is dissolved in **sufficient solvent** that no further enthalpy change occurs on further dilution, e.g. $NaCl_{(s)} \rightarrow NaCl_{(aq)}$

You also need to know the **lattice enthalpy** of the compound and the **enthalpies** of hydration of the ions:

> The **standard lattice enthalpy**, $\Delta H_{latt}^{\ominus}$, is the enthalpy change when **1 mole** of a **solid ionic compound** is formed from **gaseous ions** under standard conditions, e.g. $Na^{+}_{(g)} + Cl^{-}_{(g)} \rightarrow NaCl_{(s)}$

> The **enthalpy change of hydration**, $\Delta H_{hyd}$, is the enthalpy change when **1 mole** of **aqueous ions** is formed from **gaseous ions**, e.g. $Na^{+}_{(g)} \rightarrow Na^{+}_{(aq)}$

## You can use **Enthalpy Cycles** to find the Enthalpy Change of Solution

1) OK, first up, you can't work out the enthalpy change of solution **directly**
   — to calculate it you'll need to use an **enthalpy cycle**.

2) Enthalpy cycles work on the principle of **Hess's Law**, which says that the
   **total enthalpy change** of a reaction is always **the same**, no matter what route is taken.

   This just means that **theoretically** there are **different ways** of turning a solid ionic compound (ionic lattice) into its aqueous ions, but whether you do it **directly** or **indirectly** the overall enthalpy change will be the same.  The enthalpy changes which take place on the different routes can be shown in an **enthalpy cycle**.

Here's how to draw the enthalpy cycle for working out the **enthalpy change of solution** for **sodium chloride**.

**1** Put the ionic lattice and the dissolved ions on the top — connect them by the enthalpy change of solution.  This is the **direct route**.

**2** Connect the ionic lattice to the gaseous ions by the reverse of the lattice enthalpy.
The breakdown of the lattice has the **opposite** enthalpy change to the formation of the lattice.

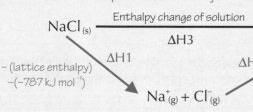

– (lattice enthalpy)
–(–787 kJ mol⁻¹)

Enthalpy change of solution

$NaCl_{(s)} \xrightarrow{\Delta H3} Na^{+}_{(aq)} + Cl^{-}_{(aq)}$

$\Delta H1$ $\Delta H2$

$Na^{+}_{(g)} + Cl^{-}_{(g)}$

Enthalpy of hydration of $Na^{+}_{(g)}$ (–406 kJ mol⁻¹)
Enthalpy of hydration of $Cl^{-}_{(g)}$ (–364 kJ mol⁻¹)

**3** Connect the gaseous ions to the dissolved ions by the hydration enthalpies of **each** ion.  This completes the **indirect route**.

From Hess's law:  $\Delta H3 = \Delta H1 + \Delta H2 = +780 + (-406 + -364) = +10 \text{ kJ mol}^{-1}$

The enthalpy change of solution is **slightly endothermic**, but this is compensated for by a small increase in **entropy**, so sodium chloride still dissolves in water.

And here's another.  This one's for working out the **enthalpy change of solution** for **silver chloride**.

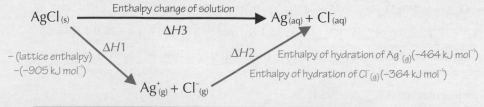

$AgCl_{(s)} \xrightarrow{\Delta H3} Ag^{+}_{(aq)} + Cl^{-}_{(aq)}$

Enthalpy change of solution

$\Delta H1$ $\Delta H2$ Enthalpy of hydration of $Ag^{+}_{(g)}$ (–464 kJ mol⁻¹)

– (lattice enthalpy)
–(–905 kJ mol⁻¹)

Enthalpy of hydration of $Cl^{-}_{(g)}$ (–364 kJ mol⁻¹)

$Ag^{+}_{(g)} + Cl^{-}_{(g)}$

From Hess's law:  $\Delta H3 = \Delta H1 + \Delta H2 = +905 + (-464 + -364) = +77 \text{ kJ mol}^{-1}$

This is much **more endothermic** than the enthalpy change of solution for sodium chloride.  There is an **increase in entropy** again, but it's pretty small and not enough to make a difference — so silver chloride is **insoluble** in water.

# Dissolving

## Ionic Charge and Size Affects Lattice Enthalpy

The **larger the charges** on the ions, the **more energy** is released when an ionic lattice forms. More energy released means that the lattice enthalpy will be **more negative**. So the lattice enthalpies for compounds with **2+ or 2– ions** (e.g. $Mg^{2+}$ or $S^{2-}$) are **more negative** than those with **1+ or 1– ions** (e.g. $Na^+$ or $Cl^-$).

For example, the lattice enthalpy of NaCl is only –780 kJ mol$^{-1}$, but the lattice enthalpy of $MgCl_2$ is –2526 kJ mol$^{-1}$. **MgS** has an even higher lattice enthalpy (–3406 kJ mol$^{-1}$) because both magnesium and sulfur ions have double charges.

The **smaller** the **ionic radii** of the ions involved, the **more exothermic** (more negative) the **lattice enthalpy**. Smaller ions attract **more strongly** because their **charge density** is higher.

The factors that affect lattice enthalpy also affect the **hydration enthalpy**. So the **smaller** and more **highly charged** the ion, the **more negative** the **hydration enthalpy**.

## Dissolving Also Involves Entropy Changes

You saw on page 21 how to predict whether a chemical reaction takes place by seeing if $\Delta S^{\ominus}_{total}$ is **positive**. Using the same method, you can predict whether an **ionic compound** will dissolve in water.

**Example 1 —** The dissolution of **sodium bromide**:

$$NaBr_{(s)} \rightarrow Na^+_{(aq)} + Br^-_{(aq)} \quad \text{At 298 K: } \Delta H = -0.6 \text{ kJ mol}^{-1}, \ \Delta S_{system} = +55.0 \text{ J K}^{-1} \text{mol}^{-1}$$

So at 298 K, $\Delta S_{surroundings} = -\Delta H/T = -(-600 \div 298) = +2.0 \text{ J K}^{-1} \text{mol}^{-1}$

$\Delta S_{total} = \Delta S_{system} + \Delta S_{surroundings} = +55.0 + 2.0 = \textbf{+57.0 J K}^{-1}\textbf{mol}^{-1}$. Sodium bromide **will** dissolve in water at 298 K.

**Example 2 —** The dissolution of **silver bromide**:

$$AgBr_{(s)} \rightarrow Ag^+_{(aq)} + Br^-_{(aq)} \quad \text{At 298 K: } \Delta H = +84.4 \text{ kJ mol}^{-1}, \ \Delta S_{system} = +47.7 \text{ J K}^{-1} \text{mol}^{-1}$$

So at 298 K, $\Delta S_{surroundings} = -\Delta H/T = -(+84\,400 \div 298) = -283.2 \text{ J K}^{-1} \text{mol}^{-1}$

$\Delta S_{total} = \Delta S_{system} + \Delta S_{surroundings} = +47.7 - 283.2 = \textbf{-235.5 J K}^{-1}\textbf{mol}^{-1}$. Silver bromide **won't** dissolve in water at 298 K.

## Practice Questions

Q1 Define the term 'enthalpy change of hydration'.
Q2 What other enthalpy changes do you need to know to work out the enthalpy change of solution?
Q3 Why do the hydration enthalpies become more negative along the series: $Na^+$, $Mg^{2+}$, $Al^{3+}$?
Q4 Why does the lattice enthalpy become more negative when the ions involved are smaller in size?

### Exam Questions

1    The dissolution of silver iodide is represented as follows:

$$AgI_{(s)} \rightarrow Ag^+_{(aq)} + I^-_{(aq)} \quad \text{At 298 K: } \Delta S_{system} = +69.1 \text{ JK}^{-1} \text{mol}^{-1}, \ \Delta H = +112.3 \text{ kJ mol}^{-1}$$

a) Define the term 'enthalpy change of solution'. [2 marks]

b) Write the equation that represents the lattice enthalpy of silver iodide. [2 marks]

c) Calculate $\Delta S_{total}$ for the dissolution of silver iodide and deduce its solubility in water at 298 K. [4 marks]

2    a) Draw an enthalpy cycle for the enthalpy change of solution of $SrF_{2(s)}$. Label each enthalpy change. [5 marks]

b) Calculate the enthalpy change of solution for $SrF_2$ from the following data:
$\Delta H^{\ominus}_{latt} [SrF_{2(s)}] = -2492 \text{ kJ mol}^{-1}, \quad \Delta H^{\ominus}_{hyd} [Sr^{2+}_{(g)}] = -1480 \text{ kJ mol}^{-1}, \quad \Delta H^{\ominus}_{hyd} [F^-_{(g)}] = -506 \text{ kJ mol}^{-1}$ [2 marks]

## Using enthalpy cycles — it's just like riding a bike...

*There is literally no end to the fun you can have calculating enthalpy changes. I'd liken it to observing your lovingly picked magnolia sunrise slowly dehydrate on the bedroom wall. It'd be a good idea to practise doing enthalpy cycles for the exam though — oh and make sure you know how to predict solubility using entropy changes. It's for your own good.*

# Dynamic Equilibria

*Dynamic equilibria. Sounds exciting right? I mean James Bond's dynamic isn't he? Well, sorry to disappoint...*

## At **Equilibrium** the Amounts of Reactants and Products **Stay the Same**

1) Lots of changes are **reversible** — they can go **both ways**. To show a change is reversible, you stick in a $\rightleftharpoons$.

2) As the **reactants** get used up, the **forward** reaction **slows down** — and as more **product** is formed, the **reverse** reaction **speeds up**. After a while, the forward reaction will be going at exactly the **same rate** as the backward reaction.

   The amounts of reactants and products **won't be changing** any more, so it'll seem like **nothing's happening**. It's a bit like you're **digging a hole** while someone else is **filling it in** at exactly the **same speed**. This is called a **dynamic equilibrium**.

3) Equilibria can be set up in **physical** systems...

   > *Example:* When **liquid bromine** is shaken in a closed flask, some of it changes to orange **bromine gas**. After a while, **equilibrium** is reached — bromine liquid is **still** changing to bromine gas and bromine gas is still changing to bromine liquid, but they are changing at the **same rate**.
   >
   > $$Br_{2(l)} \rightleftharpoons Br_{2(g)}$$

   ...and **chemical** systems...

   > *Example:* If **hydrogen gas** and **iodine gas** are mixed together in a closed flask, **hydrogen iodide** is formed.
   >
   > $$H_{2(g)} + I_{2(g)} \rightleftharpoons 2HI_{(g)}$$
   >
   > Imagine that **1.0 mole** of hydrogen gas is mixed with **1.0 mole** of iodine gas at a constant temperature of **640 K**. When this mixture reaches equilibrium, there will be **1.6 moles** of hydrogen iodide and **0.2 moles** of both hydrogen gas and iodine gas. No matter how long you leave them at this temperature, the **equilibrium** amounts **never change**. As with the physical system, it's all a matter of the forward and backward rates **being equal**.

4) A **dynamic equilibrium** can only happen in a **closed system** at a **constant temperature**.    *A closed system just means nothing can get in or out.*

## Many Important **Industrial Reactions** Are **Reversible**

1) The **Contact process** manufactures **sulfuric acid** for use in fertilisers, dyes, medicines and batteries. It is made up of several stages, one of which — the **conversion** of **sulfur dioxide** to **sulfur trioxide**, shown below — is reversible.

$$2SO_{2(g)} + O_{2(g)} \rightleftharpoons 2SO_{3(g)}$$

2) The **Haber process** manufactures **ammonia** for use in fertilisers and the production of other nitrogen-containing compounds. It is also reversible:

$$N_{2(g)} + 3H_{2(g)} \rightleftharpoons 2NH_{3(g)}$$

Both the Contact and Haber processes are **economically important**.

## The **Hydrogen-Iodine** Reaction Is **Reversible**

The table below shows the results of several experiments that investigate the hydrogen-iodine reaction in a closed system at 763 K.

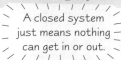 *Square brackets, [ ], mean concentration in $mol\ dm^{-3}$.*

| Experiment | Starting Concentrations | | | Equilibrium Concentrations | | |
|---|---|---|---|---|---|---|
| | $[H_{2(g)}]$ | $[I_{2(g)}]$ | $[HI_{(g)}]$ | $[H_{2(g)}]$ | $[I_{2(g)}]$ | $[HI_{(g)}]$ |
| 1 | 1.0 | 1.0 | 0.0 | 0.228 | 0.228 | 1.544 |
| 2 | 0.0 | 0.0 | 2.0 | 0.228 | 0.228 | 1.544 |
| 3 | 1.0 | 2.0 | 3.0 | 0.316 | 1.316 | 4.368 |

The **equilibrium concentrations** of the **reactants** and **products** depend on the **initial concentrations** of each **element** in the reaction — whichever side of the equilibrium they start off on. When these initial concentrations are **the same**, the equilibrium concentrations of the products and reactants will be the same. **Experiments 1 and 2** both start off with 2 mol dm⁻³ of **H atoms** and the same of **I atoms** — and both finish with the same equilibrium concentrations.

# Dynamic Equilibria

## The **Equilibrium Concentrations** of Reactants and Products are **Related**

If you calculate the ratio of **product concentration to reactant concentration** for each of the experiments on the previous page, you will **always** end up with the **same value**.

For the hydrogen-iodine reaction, the **ratio of equilibrium concentrations** can be calculated as:

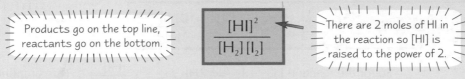

Products go on the top line, reactants go on the bottom.

$$\frac{[HI]^2}{[H_2][I_2]}$$

There are 2 moles of HI in the reaction so [HI] is raised to the power of 2.

For **experiments 1 and 2**, this ratio $= \dfrac{1.544^2}{0.228 \times 0.228} = 45.9$

For **experiment 3**, this ratio $= \dfrac{4.368^2}{0.316 \times 1.316} = 45.9$

If you repeated this experiment at 763 K using **different starting concentrations** of $H_2$, $I_2$ or HI, and then plugged the numbers into this same expression, you would **always** end up with a value of 45.9. The value of this ratio is known as the **equilibrium constant**, $K_c$, and it is always **constant** for a particular reaction when measured at the **same temperature**.

## Practice Questions

Q1 At equilibrium, what do you know about the rate of the forward reaction compared to the rate of the reverse reaction?

Q2 What is a 'closed system'?

Q3 Name two industrial processes that involve reversible reactions.

Q4 Under what conditions does the equilibrium constant of a particular reaction remain the same?

### Exam Questions

1  The table on the right shows the initial concentrations of $N_2$, $H_2$ and $NH_3$ for four experiments investigating the reaction
$$N_{2(g)} + 3H_{2(g)} \rightleftharpoons 2NH_{3(g)}$$
in a closed system. All four experiments were carried out at the same temperature. For which experiment would the concentrations of $N_2$, $H_2$ and $NH_3$ at equilibrium be different from the other three?

| Experiment | $[N_{2(g)}]$ | $[H_{2(g)}]$ | $[NH_{3(g)}]$ |
|---|---|---|---|
| A | 1.0 | 1.5 | 0.0 |
| B | 0.5 | 0.0 | 1.0 |
| C | 0.0 | 0.0 | 2.0 |
| D | 0.75 | 0.75 | 0.5 |

[1 mark]

2  a)  What is meant by dynamic equilibrium?  [2 marks]

b)  At 473 K, the equilibrium constant, $K_c$, for the reaction below has a numerical value of 125.
$$PCl_{3(g)} + Cl_{2(g)} \rightleftharpoons PCl_{5(g)}$$

i)  At 473 K, a quantity of $Cl_{2(g)}$ was added to the mixture and equilibrium was re-established. What effect would this have on the value of the equilibrium constant? Explain your answer.  [2 marks]

ii)  The temperature of the equilibrium mixture was allowed to drop to 423 K. What effect would this have on the value of the equilibrium constant? Explain your answer.  [2 marks]

iii)  At 473 K, what would be the numerical value of $K_c$ for the reaction below?  [2 marks]
$$PCl_{5(g)} \rightleftharpoons PCl_{3(g)} + Cl_{2(g)}$$

## Dynamic equilibria — the movers and shakers of the equilibrium world...

*As those of you who are a bit more on the ball might've guessed from the section title, these next few pages are all about equilibria. This has been quite a nice, gentle introduction I think — compared with what's to come anyway, mwahahahaaa. Take your time getting to grips with it all, then turn over. It'll be fine. Honestly. That mwahahahaa thing was just a joke...*

# Equilibrium Constants

*The equilibrium constant is about to become a constant presence in your life — just you wait and see...*

## $K_c$ is the **Equilibrium Constant**

You saw on the last page that $K_c$ is calculated from the **ratio** of product concentration to reactant concentration. This means that if you know the **molar concentration** of each substance **at equilibrium**, you can work out $K_c$. Your value of $K_c$ will only be true for that particular **temperature**.

For the general reaction $aA + bB \rightleftharpoons dD + eE$, $K_c = \dfrac{[D]^d[E]^e}{[A]^a[B]^b}$

*Products go on the top line.*

*The lower-case letters a, b, d and e are the number of moles of each substance.*

So for the reaction $H_{2(g)} + I_{2(g)} \rightleftharpoons 2HI_{(g)}$, $K_c = \dfrac{[HI]^2}{[H_2]^1[I_2]^1}$ . This simplifies to $K_c = \dfrac{[HI]^2}{[H_2][I_2]}$ .

1) Actually this definition of $K_c$ only applies to **homogeneous equilibria**, i.e. ones where all the products and reactants are in the **same phase**. If you've got more than one phase in there — a **heterogeneous equilibrium** — life's slightly more complicated.

2) If the mixture involves **solids and gases**, or **solids and liquids**, you still use $K_c$, but you **leave out** the concentrations of the solids. If you've got a mix of **gases and liquids**, you need to use $K_p$ instead (see pages 30-31).

## You Might Need to **Work Out** the Equilibrium Concentrations

You might have to figure out some of the **equilibrium concentrations** before you can find $K_c$:

**Example:** 0.20 moles of phosphorus(V) chloride decomposes at 600 K in a vessel of 5.00 dm³. The equilibrium mixture is found to contain 0.08 moles of chlorine. Write the expression for $K_c$ and calculate its value, including units.

$$PCl_{5(g)} \rightleftharpoons PCl_{3(g)} + Cl_{2(g)}$$

First find out how many moles of $PCl_5$ and $PCl_3$ there are at equilibrium:

The **equation** tells you that when **1 mole of $PCl_5$** decomposes, **1 mole of $PCl_3$** and **1 mole of $Cl_2$** are formed. So if 0.08 moles of chlorine are produced at equilibrium, then there will be **0.08 moles** of $PCl_3$ as well. 0.08 moles of $PCl_5$ must have decomposed, so there will be (0.2 – 0.08 =) **0.12 moles** left.

Divide each number of moles by the volume of the flask to give the molar concentrations:

$[PCl_3] = [Cl_2] = 0.08 \div 5.00 = $ **0.016 mol dm⁻³**     $[PCl_5] = 0.12 \div 5.00 = $ **0.024 mol dm⁻³**

Put the concentrations in the expression for $K_c$ and calculate it: $K_c = \dfrac{[PCl_3][Cl_2]}{[PCl_5]} = \dfrac{[0.016][0.016]}{[0.024]} = $ **0.011**

Now find the units of $K_c$: $K_c = \dfrac{(mol\ dm^{-3})(mol\ dm^{-3})}{(mol\ dm^{-3})} = $ **mol dm⁻³**     So $K_c = $ **0.011 mol dm⁻³**

## $K_c$ can be used to Find **Concentrations** in an **Equilibrium Mixture**

**Example:** When ethanoic acid was allowed to reach equilibrium with ethanol at 25 °C, it was found that the equilibrium mixture contained 2.0 mol dm⁻³ ethanoic acid and 3.5 mol dm⁻³ ethanol. The $K_c$ of the equilibrium is 4.0 at 25 °C. What are the concentrations of the other components?

$$CH_3COOH_{(l)} + C_2H_5OH_{(l)} \rightleftharpoons CH_3COOC_2H_{5\ (l)} + H_2O_{(l)}$$

Put all the values you know in the $K_c$ expression: $K_c = \dfrac{[CH_3COOC_2H_5][H_2O]}{[CH_3COOH][C_2H_5OH]} \Rightarrow 4.0 = \dfrac{[CH_3COOC_2H_5][H_2O]}{2.0 \times 3.5}$

Rearranging this gives: $[CH_3COOC_2H_5][H_2O] = 4.0 \times 2.0 \times 3.5 = 28.0$

From the equation, you know that an equal number of moles of $CH_3COOC_2H_5$ and $H_2O$ will form, so:

$[CH_3COOC_2H_5] = [H_2O] = \sqrt{28} = 5.3$ mol dm⁻³     **The concentration of $CH_3COOC_2H_5$ and $H_2O$ is 5.3 mol dm⁻³**

# Equilibrium Constants

## The **Equilibrium Constant** Can Be Calculated from **Experimental Data**

A simple experiment that can be carried out in the laboratory involves the following reaction:

$$Fe^{2+}_{(aq)} + Ag^+_{(aq)} \rightleftharpoons Fe^{3+}_{(aq)} + Ag_{(s)}$$

1) To carry out this reaction you need to add **500 cm³** of **0.1 mol dm⁻³** silver nitrate solution to **500 cm³** of **0.1 mol dm⁻³** of iron(II) sulfate solution. The **silver nitrate** provides the $Ag^+$ ions and the **iron(II) sulfate** provides the $Fe^{2+}$ ions.

2) If you leave the mixture in a stoppered flask at 298 K, it will eventually reach **equilibrium**. You can then take samples of the equilibrium mixture and **titrate** them — this will let you work out the **equilibrium concentration** of the **Fe²⁺ ions**. From this, you can work out the equilibrium concentrations of the other components.

*Example calculation:*

The **starting concentrations** of $Ag^+$ and $Fe^{2+}$ are the same and equal to **0.05 mol dm⁻³**.

*500 cm³ of each solution is diluted to 1000 cm³. The concentration of each reactant is halved*

The **titration result** gives you an **equilibrium concentration** for $Fe^{2+}$ of **0.0439 mol dm⁻³**.

The equation tells you 1 mole of $Fe^{2+}$ reacts with 1 mole of $Ag^+$ to form 1 mole of $Fe^{3+}$ and 1 mole of Ag. In this particular reaction **solid** silver is formed. The concentration of a solid is **constant**, so you **don't** need to include it in the expression for $K_c$.

The equilibrium concentration of $Ag^+$ will be the same as $Fe^{2+}$ i.e. **0.0439 mol dm⁻³**.
The equilibrium concentration of **Fe³⁺** will be 0.05 − 0.0439 = **0.0061 mol dm⁻³**.

$$So \ K_c = \frac{[Fe^{3+}]}{[Fe^{2+}][Ag^+]} = \frac{0.0061}{0.0439 \times 0.0439} = 3.17$$

The units of $K_c$ are: $\frac{mol\,dm^{-3}}{(mol\,dm^{-3})(mol\,dm^{-3})} = mol^{-1}\,dm^3$

**At 298 K, $K_c$ for this reaction = 3.17 mol⁻¹ dm³**

## Practice Questions

Q1 What do the square brackets, [ ], represent in a $K_c$ expression?

Q2 Write the expression for $K_c$ for the following equilibrium: $2SO_2 + O_2 \rightleftharpoons 2SO_3$

Q3 In the reaction $Cl_{2(g)} + PCl_{3(g)} \rightleftharpoons PCl_{5(g)}$, what are the units of $K_c$?

**Exam Questions**

1 At 723 K, the equilibrium constant for the reaction $H_{2(g)} + Cl_{2(g)} \rightleftharpoons 2HCl_{(g)}$ is 60.
If the equilibrium concentrations of $H_2$ and $Cl_2$ are 2.0 mol dm⁻³ and 0.3 mol dm⁻³ respectively, the molar concentration of HCl at equilibrium is:

A 0.1
B 0.01
C 6.0
D 36.0 [1 mark]

2 Nitrogen dioxide dissociates according to the equation $2NO_{2(g)} \rightleftharpoons 2NO_{(g)} + O_{2(g)}$.
When 42.5 g of nitrogen dioxide were heated in a vessel of volume 22.8 dm³ at 500 °C, 14.1 g of oxygen were found in the equilibrium mixture.

a) Calculate i) the number of moles of nitrogen dioxide originally. [1 mark]

ii) the number of moles of each gas in the equilibrium mixture. [3 marks]

b) Write an expression for $K_c$ for this reaction. Calculate the value for $K_c$ at 500 °C and give its units. [5 marks]

## As far as I'm concerned, equilibria are a constant pain in the *@?!

*I suppose my issue is... if they were proper constants, you wouldn't have to calculate them all the time would you? I mean, at least when Avogadro said he had a constant he flippin' well meant it. Still, since they're there to be calculated, calculate them you must — and the only way to get good at it is to practise. And then practise again, just to be on the safe side.*

# Gas Equilibria

*Gases are different from solutions — they're more floaty and less soggy. So they've got a special equilibrium constant, $K_p$.*

## The Total Pressure is Equal to the Sum of the Partial Pressures

In a mixture of gases, each individual gas exerts its own pressure — this is called its **partial pressure**.

> The **total pressure** of a gas mixture is the **sum** of all the **partial pressures** of the individual gases.

You might have to put this fact to use in pressure calculations:

**Example:** When 3.0 moles of the gas $PCl_5$ is heated, it decomposes into $PCl_3$ and $Cl_2$.

$$PCl_{5(g)} \rightleftharpoons PCl_{3(g)} + Cl_{2(g)}$$

In a sealed vessel at 500 K, the equilibrium mixture contains chlorine with a partial pressure of 263 kPa. If the total pressure of the mixture is 714 kPa, what is the partial pressure of $PCl_5$?

From the equation you know that $PCl_3$ and $Cl_2$ are produced in equal amounts, so the partial pressures of these two gases are the **same** at equilibrium — they're both 263 kPa.

Total pressure = $p(PCl_5) + p(PCl_3) + p(Cl_2)$ ⟵ $p$ just means partial pressure.
714 = $p(PCl_5) + 263 + 263$

So the partial pressure of $PCl_5$ = 714 − 263 − 263 = **188 kPa**

## Partial Pressures can be Worked Out from Mole Fractions

'**Mole fraction**' might sound a bit complicated, but it's just the **proportion** of a gas mixture that is a particular gas. So if you've got four moles of gas in total, and two of them are gas A, the mole fraction of gas A is ½.

There are two formulas you've got to know:

$$\text{Mole fraction of a gas in a mixture} = \frac{\text{number of moles of gas}}{\text{total number of moles of all gases in the mixture}}$$

Partial pressure of a gas = mole fraction of gas × total pressure of the mixture

**Example:** When 3.0 mol of $PCl_5$ is heated in a sealed vessel, the equilibrium mixture contains 1.75 mol of chlorine. If the total pressure of the mixture is 714 kPa, what is the partial pressure of $PCl_5$?

$PCl_3$ and $Cl_2$ are produced in equal amounts, so there'll be **1.75 moles** of $PCl_3$ too.

1.75 moles of $PCl_5$ must have decomposed so (3.0 − 1.75 =) **1.25 moles** of $PCl_5$ must be left at equilibrium.

This means that the total number of moles of gas at equilibrium = 1.75 + 1.75 + 1.25 = **4.75**

So the mole fraction of $PCl_5 = \dfrac{1.25}{4.75} = $ **0.263**

The partial pressure of $PCl_5$ = mole fraction × total pressure = 0.263 × 714 = **188 kPa**

## The Equilibrium Constant $K_p$ is Calculated from Partial Pressures

The expression for $K_p$ is just like the one for $K_c$ — except you use partial pressures instead of concentrations.

For the equilibrium $aA_{(g)} + bB_{(g)} \rightleftharpoons dD_{(g)} + eE_{(g)}$: $K_p = \dfrac{p(D)^d p(E)^e}{p(A)^a p(B)^b}$

> There are no square brackets because they're partial pressures, not molar concentrations.

So to **calculate $K_p$**, it's just a matter of sticking the partial pressures in the expression. You have to work out the **units** each time though, just like for $K_c$.

**Example:** Calculate $K_p$ for the decomposition of $PCl_5$ gas at 500 K (as shown above). The partial pressures of each gas are: $p(PCl_5)$ = 188 kPa, $p(PCl_3)$ = 263 kPa, $p(Cl_2)$ = 263 kPa

$$K_p = \frac{p(Cl_3) \, p(PCl_2)}{p(PCl_5)} = \frac{263 \times 263}{188} = 368$$

The units for $K_p$ are worked out by putting the units into the expression instead of the numbers, and cancelling (like for $K_c$): $K_p = \dfrac{kPa \times kPa}{kPa} = kPa$ So, $K_p$ = **368 kPa**

# Gas Equilibria

## $K_p$ can be Used to Find **Partial Pressures**

You might be given the $K_p$ and have to use it to calculate **equilibrium partial pressures**.

**Example:** An equilibrium exists between ethanoic acid monomers, $CH_3COOH$, and dimers, $(CH_3COOH)_2$.

At 160 °C the $K_p$ for the reaction $(CH_3COOH)_{2(g)} \rightleftharpoons 2CH_3COOH_{(g)}$ is 180 kPa.

At this temperature the partial pressure of the dimer, $(CH_3COOH)_2$, is 28.5 kPa.

Calculate the partial pressure of the monomer in this equilibrium and state the total pressure exerted by the equilibrium mixture.

$$K_p = \frac{p(CH_3COOH)^2}{p((CH_3COOH)_2)}$$ This rearranges to give: $p(CH_3COOH)^2 = K_p \times p((CH_3COOH)_2) = 180 \times 28.5 = 5130$

$$\Rightarrow p(CH_3COOH) = \sqrt{5130} = \textbf{71.6 kPa}$$

So the total pressure of the equilibrium mixture = 28.5 + 71.6 = **100.1 kPa**

*Add the two partial pressures together to get the total pressure.*

## $K_p$ for **Heterogenous** Equilibria Still **Only Includes Gases**

Up until now we've only thought about $K_p$ expressions for **homogeneous equilibria**.

If you're writing an expression for $K_p$ for a **heterogeneous equilibrium**, you don't include **solids** or **liquids**.

E.g. for the **heterogeneous equilibrium** $NH_4HS_{(s)} \rightleftharpoons NH_{3(g)} + H_2S_{(g)}$, $K_p = p(NH_3)\, p(H_2S)$

*There's no bottom line as the reactant is a solid.*

## Practice Questions

Q1 What is meant by partial pressure?

Q2 How do you work out the mole fraction of a gas?

Q3 Write the expression for $K_p$ for the following equilibrium: $PCl_{5(g)} \rightleftharpoons PCl_{3(g)} + Cl_{2(g)}$

Q4 Write the expression for $K_p$ for the following equilibrium: $H_2O_{(g)} + C_{(s)} \rightleftharpoons H_{2(g)} + CO_{(g)}$

### Exam Questions

1   At high temperatures, $SO_2Cl_2$ dissociates according to the equation $SO_2Cl_{2(g)} \rightleftharpoons SO_{2(g)} + Cl_{2(g)}$.
When 1.50 moles of $SO_2Cl_2$ dissociates at 700 K, the equilibrium mixture contains $SO_2$ with a partial pressure of 60.2 kPa.
The mixture has a total pressure of 141 kPa.

a)   Write an expression for $K_p$ for this reaction.                                     [1 mark]

b)   Calculate the partial pressure of $Cl_2$ and the partial pressure of $SO_2Cl_2$ in the equilibrium mixture.   [4 marks]

c)   Calculate a value for $K_p$ for this reaction and give its units.                      [3 marks]

2   When nitric oxide and oxygen were mixed in a 2:1 mole ratio, an equilibrium was set up at a
constant temperature in a sealed flask, according to the equation $2NO_{(g)} + O_{2(g)} \rightleftharpoons 2NO_{2(g)}$.
The partial pressure of the nitric oxide (NO) at equilibrium was 36 kPa and the total pressure in the flask was 99 kPa.

a)   Deduce the partial pressure of oxygen in the equilibrium mixture.                     [2 marks]

b)   Calculate the partial pressure of nitrogen dioxide in the equilibrium mixture.        [2 marks]

c)   Write an expression for the equilibrium constant, $K_p$, for this reaction and calculate its value
at this temperature.  State its units.                                                    [4 marks]

## I just can't take this constant pressure...

*Partial pressures are just like concentrations for gases.  The more of a substance you've got in a solution, the higher the concentration, and the more of a gas you've got in a container, the higher the partial pressure.  It's all to do with how many molecules you've got crashing into the sides.  With gases though, you've got to keep the lid on tight or they'll escape.*

# Equilibrium Constants and Entropy

*I've said this before — the problem with equilibrium constants is, they are constantly turning up...*

## Total Entropy Change is Related to the Equilibrium Constant, K

A **spontaneous** reaction produces lots of product so it will have a **high equilibrium constant**. Its spontaneity depends on the **total entropy change** for the reaction, $\Delta S_{total}$ (see page 22). It's not surprising then that there's an equation linking $\Delta S_{total}$ and the **equilibrium constant, K**:

$$\Delta S_{total} = R \ln K \text{ (where R is the gas constant, 8.31 J K}^{-1}\text{mol}^{-1}\text{)}$$  ln = natural log

By substituting in values for $\Delta S_{total}$ you can see how **K varies** with **increasing total entropy**.

**Example 1:** Reaction of barium hydroxide with ammonium chloride

$$Ba(OH)_2.8H_2O_{(s)} + 2NH_4Cl_{(s)} \rightarrow BaCl_{2(s)} + 10H_2O_{(l)} + 2NH_{3(g)} \quad \Delta S_{total} = 50.8 \text{ J K}^{-1}\text{mol}^{-1}$$

As we know $\Delta S_{total}$, we need to rearrange the equation to find $\ln K$:  $\ln K = \Delta S_{total} \div R$

So plugging the numbers in, we get:  $\ln K = 50.8 \div 8.31 = 6.11$

So, $\ln K = 6.11$
$K = e^{6.11} = 450.3$

For this calculation you're going to need the exponential button, $e^x$, on your calculator — it's the inverse of natural log, ln. Basically, when $\ln a = b$, $a = e^b$.

**Example 2:** The burning of hydrogen

$$H_{2(g)} + \tfrac{1}{2}O_{2(g)} \rightleftharpoons H_2O_{(l)} \quad \Delta S_{total} = 796.2 \text{ J K}^{-1}\text{mol}^{-1} \quad \ln K = 796.2 \div 8.31 = 95.8$$
$$K = e^{95.8} = 4.0 \times 10^{41}$$

*You can use either $K_c$ or $K_p$ for this calculation.*

As $\Delta S_{total}$ **increases**, the equilibrium constant, **K**, **increases**.

## The Size of K Tells You How Far a Reaction Has Progressed

The equilibrium constant is the **ratio** of products against reactants (see p28).

This means that the **higher** the value of **K**, the **greater** the concentration of **product** and the **further** the forward reaction has progressed — this would make the concentration of reactants low. A **low** value of K would mean that very **little product** had been formed.

It's generally accepted by science bods that:

1) A reaction with an equilibrium constant of **less than $10^{-10}$** does **not** take place.
2) A reaction with an equilibrium constant **greater than $10^{10}$** goes to **completion**.
3) Reactions with **intermediate values** are **reversible**.

If the total entropy change for a reaction is positive, a reaction will be spontaneous. Because there's a relationship between K and $\Delta S_{total}$, you can also look at the **value of $\Delta S_{total}$** to see **how far** a reaction progresses.

| K | $\Delta S_{total}$ | Progression of Reaction |
|---|---|---|
| > $10^{-10}$ | > –191 | Reaction doesn't go |
| > $10^{-5}$ | > –96 | Reversible reaction with equilibrium pushed well to the **left** |
| 1 | 0 | Reversible reaction **balanced** between product and reactants |
| < $10^5$ | < +96 | Reversible reaction with equilibrium pushed well to the **right** |
| < $10^{10}$ | < +191 | Reaction complete |

**Examples:**

1) The dissolution of sodium chloride — $\Delta S_{total} = +30.2$ — this is a **reversible reaction** with the equilibrium pushed to the **right**.

2) The dissolution of silver chloride — $\Delta S_{total} = -186.6$ — this reaction is reversible, with the equilibrium pushed **well to the left**. If this value were much lower, the reaction wouldn't go — only a **very small amount** of silver chloride will dissolve in water.

3) The burning of hydrogen — $\Delta S_{total} = +796.2$ — this reaction goes to **completion**.

# Equilibrium Constants and Entropy

## Changing the **Temperature** of a Reaction Affects $\Delta S_{total}$

$$\Delta S_{total} = \Delta S_{system} + \Delta S_{surroundings} \quad \text{and} \quad \Delta S_{surroundings} = -\frac{\Delta H}{T}$$

This means that: $\Delta S_{total} = \Delta S_{system} - \frac{\Delta H}{T}$

When you **increase** the temperature, the value of $\frac{\Delta H}{T}$ **decreases**.

1) For an **endothermic** reaction, **increasing** the temperature will cause an **increase** in $\Delta S_{total}$.
   For an **exothermic** reaction, increasing the temperature will **decrease** $\Delta S_{total}$.

2) Conversely, **decreasing** in temperature will **decrease** $\Delta S_{total}$ in an **endothermic** reaction
   and **increase** it in an **exothermic** reaction.

'Apparently, they were trying
to increase the entropy when
the lab exploded...'

Changing the temperature of a reaction can change its **outcome**.

*Example:* the thermal decomposition of calcium carbonate.

$$CaCO_{3(s)} \rightleftharpoons CaO_{(s)} + CO_{2(g)} \qquad \Delta H = +178 \text{ kJ mol}^{-1} \qquad \Delta S_{system} = 165.0 \text{ J K}^{-1}\text{mol}^{-1}$$

At 298 K, $\Delta S_{total} = 165.0 - (178\,000 \div 298) = 165.0 - 597.0 = -432 \text{ J K}^{-1}\text{mol}^{-1}$

$\Delta S_{total}$ is very **negative**, so the reaction doesn't happen.

To get $\Delta S_{total}$ to a **positive** value, then $\Delta S_{surroundings}$ would have to be at least **165 J K$^{-1}$ mol$^{-1}$**.
This means raising the **temperature** of the reaction system.

To calculate this temperature you need to rearrange the equation for $\Delta S_{surroundings}$:

$$T = \Delta H/\Delta S_{surroundings} = 178\,000 \div 165 = \textbf{1080 K}.$$

This is the sort of temperature
found in the lime kilns where
this reaction takes place.

## Practice Questions

Q1 Why does a spontaneous reaction have a high equilibrium constant?

Q2 For a particular reaction at 298 K, show that $K = 187.7$, when $\Delta S_{total} = 43.5$ J K$^{-1}$ mol$^{-1}$?

Q3 In terms of the extent of the reaction, how would you classify the reaction in Q2?

Q4 What happens to $\Delta S_{total}$ for an endothermic reaction when its temperature is increased?

### Exam Questions

1   What is the effect of a decrease in temperature on the value of $\Delta S_{surroundings}$ for an exothermic reaction?

    A    $\Delta S_{surroundings}$ will decrease.

    B    $\Delta S_{surroundings}$ will increase.

    C    $\Delta S_{surroundings}$ will stay the same.

    D    $\Delta S_{surroundings}$ will increase then decrease.                                    [1 mark]

2   This question relates to the equilibrium:

$$N_2O_{4(g)} \rightleftharpoons 2NO_{2\,(g)} \qquad \Delta H = +57.2 \text{ kJ mol}^{-1} \quad \Delta S_{system} = 175.8 \text{ J K}^{-1}\text{mol}^{-1}$$

    a)   Calculate $\Delta S_{total}$ at 60 °C for this reaction.                                         [2 marks]

    b)   What is the value of $K$ at 60 °C? There is no need to include the units for $K$.      [2 marks]

    c)   Recalculate $\Delta S_{total}$ and the value of K at 160 °C.                               [4 marks]

    d)   What effect does the increased temperature have on the position of equilibrium?      [2 marks]

## I've run out of 'constant' jokes now...The Equilibrium Gardener anyone?

*Entropy and the equilibrium constant — as a double act they're up there with the greats: Morecambe and Wise, Laurel and Hardy, Ant and Dec. Anyway, what you need to take away from this is that the equilibrium constant, K, and the total entropy change for a reaction are related. You don't need to take my word for it — there's an equation to prove it.*

# Le Chatelier's Principle

*"When studying equilibrium, there's only one thing you can truly rely on — the chocolate biscuit."*
*— Le Chatelier's lesser known principle on what's needed to get through Unit 4 Section 3 of A2 Chemistry.*

## Le Chatelier's Principle Predicts what will happen if Conditions are Changed

If you **change** the **pressure** or **temperature** of a reversible reaction, you're going to **alter** the **position of equilibrium**. This just means you'll end up with **different amounts** of reactants and products at equilibrium.

> If the position of equilibrium moves to the **left**, you'll get more **reactants**.
>
> $$H_{2(g)} + I_{2(g)} \rightleftharpoons 2HI_{(g)}$$

> If the position of equilibrium moves to the **right**, you'll get more **products**.
>
> $$H_{2(g)} + I_{2(g)} \rightleftharpoons \mathbf{2HI_{(g)}}$$

**Le Chatelier's principle** tells you how the **position of equilibrium** will change if a **condition changes**:

> If there's a change in **pressure** or **temperature**, the equilibrium will move to help **counteract** the change.

So, basically, if you **raise the temperature**, the position of equilibrium will shift to try to **cool things down**. And if you **raise the pressure**, the position of equilibrium will shift to try to **reduce it again**.

## Temperature Changes Alter $K_c$ and $K_p$ — Pressure Changes Don't

**PRESSURE** (changing this only really affects **equilibria involving gases**)
**Increasing** the pressure shifts the equilibrium to the side with **fewer** gas molecules — this **reduces** the pressure. **Decreasing** the pressure shifts the equilibrium to the side with **more** gas molecules. This **raises** the pressure again. $K_p$ stays the **same**, no matter what you do to the pressure.

> There are 3 moles on the left, but only 2 on the right. So an increase in pressure would shift the equilibrium to the right. $\longrightarrow$ $2SO_{2(g)} + O_{2(g)} \rightleftharpoons 2SO_{3(g)}$

**TEMPERATURE**

1) If you **increase** the temperature, you **add heat**. The equilibrium shifts in the **endothermic (positive $\Delta H$) direction** to absorb this heat.

2) **Decreasing** the temperature **removes heat**. The equilibrium shifts in the **exothermic (negative $\Delta H$) direction** to try to replace the heat.

3) If the forward reaction's **endothermic**, the reverse reaction will be **exothermic**, and vice versa.

4) If the change means **more product** is formed, $K_c$ and $K_p$ will **rise**. If it means **less product** is formed, then $K_c$ and $K_p$ will **decrease**.

> The reaction below is exothermic in the forward direction. If you increase the temperature, the equilibrium shifts to the left to absorb the extra heat. This means that less product's formed.
>
> Exothermic $\Longrightarrow$
> $$2SO_{2(g)} + O_{2(g)} \rightleftharpoons 2SO_{3(g)} \quad \Delta H = -197 \text{ kJ mol}^{-1}$$
> $\Longleftarrow$ Endothermic
>
> $$K_p = \frac{p(SO_3)^2}{p(SO_2)^2\, p(O_2)}$$
>
> There's less product, so $K_p$ decreases.

> **Catalysts** have **NO EFFECT** on the **position of equilibrium**. They **can't** increase **yield** — but they **do** mean equilibrium is approached **faster**.

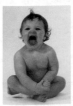

*The removal of his dummy was a change that Maxwell always opposed.*

# Le Chatelier's Principle

## Both **Temperature** and **Pressure** Affect the **Rate of a Reaction**

A lot of this depends on the good old **collision theory**. It pretty much says that particles have to **collide** in the right direction and with a minimum amount of **kinetic energy** in order to react.

Changes to temperature and pressure can affect the rate at which equilibrium is reached.

1) If you **increase** the **temperature** of a reaction system, the particles move around more and their average kinetic energy is higher. As a result, they'll collide more often and are more likely to **react** when they do — this'll **speed up** the reaction. A **decrease** in temperature will **slow down** the reaction because particles will move around less and have less energy to react.

2) A change in pressure will only affect the rate of reaction if the reagents are **gases**. If you **increase** the **pressure** of a reaction system, the gas particles will be pushed closer together — this increases the chances of the particles colliding and reacting so the reaction **speeds up**. If you **decrease** the pressure, rate of reaction will **slow down**.

## Practice Questions

Q1 In which direction does the position of equilibrium move to get more products?

Q2 How does an increase in pressure affect $K_p$?

Q3 For an exothermic reaction, in which direction would the equilibrium move when the temperature is decreased?

Q4 How does the presence of a catalyst affect the position of equilibrium?

### Exam Questions

1   This question relates to the following equilibrium:

$$CO_{(g)} + 2H_{2(g)} \rightleftharpoons CH_3OH_{(g)} \quad \Delta H = -92 \text{ kJ mol}^{-1}$$

Explain what happens to the equilibrium concentration of $CH_3OH_{(g)}$ when:

a)   The temperature of the system is increased. [2 marks]

b)   The pressure of the system is decreased. [2 marks]

c)   A catalyst is added. [2 marks]

2   The following equilibrium was established at temperature $T_1$:

$$2SO_{2(g)} + O_{2(g)} \rightleftharpoons 2SO_{3(g)} \quad \Delta H = -196 \text{ kJ mol}^{-1}.$$

$K_p$ at $T_1$ was found to be 0.67 kPa$^{-1}$.

a)   When equilibrium was established at a different temperature, $T_2$, the value of $K_p$ was found to have increased. State which of $T_1$ or $T_2$ is the lower temperature and explain why. [3 marks]

b)   The experiment was repeated exactly the same in all respects at $T_1$, except a flask of smaller volume was used. How would this change affect the yield of sulfur trioxide and the value of $K_p$? [2 marks]

## I've got a good one — an equilibrium and an industrial process walk into a bar...

*The take home point: temperature affects the value of K, pressure and catalysts don't. Easy. That's really all there is to say. I mean I could waffle on about how the position of equilibrium moves to counteract changes to temperature and pressure and how they both affect rate of reaction, but I won't. Keep it simple. That's my motto.*

# Equilibria in Industrial Processes

*Finally, the light at the end of the tunnel. I spy section 4 approaching...*

## The **Haber Process** Combines **Nitrogen** and **Hydrogen** to make **Ammonia**

$$N_{2(g)} + 3H_{2(g)} \rightleftharpoons 2NH_{3(g)} \qquad \Delta H = -92 \text{ kJ mol}^{-1}, \quad \Delta S_{system} = -201.8 \text{ J K}^{-1} \text{ mol}^{-1}$$

Businesses using the Haber process want to make **as much** ammonia as they can, as **quickly** and as **cheaply** as possible, so that they make bags of money. To do this, they've had to look carefully at choosing the **best conditions** for the job.

*Usually, the Haber process is carried out at 450 °C and a pressure of 200 atmospheres — but you **don't** need to learn this.*

## The **Temperature** Chosen is a **Compromise**

1) Because it's an **exothermic reaction**, **lower** temperatures favour the forward reaction. This means **more** hydrogen and nitrogen is converted to ammonia — you get a better **yield**.

2) The trouble is, **lower temperatures** mean a **slower rate of reaction** — and you'd be **daft** to try to get a **really high yield** of ammonia if it's going to take you 10 years. So the temperature chosen is a **compromise** between **maximum yield** and **a faster reaction**.

3) Another way of looking at this problem is to consider the **entropy changes** involved:

   You get a **balanced equilibrium** when $\Delta S_{total} = 0$.

   The temperature this happens at $= \Delta H \div \Delta S_{system} = -92000 \div 201.8 = 456 \text{ K } (183 \text{ °C})$

   Remember: the forward reaction is **exothermic**. If you **increase** the temperature, $\Delta S_{total}$ will **decrease** and the position of equilibrium will shift to the **left** — producing **less ammonia**. The temperature has to be increased though, because the reaction would be too slow at 183 °C.

## High Pressure Would Give a **Big Yield** — But It'd Be **Expensive**

1) **Higher pressures** favour the **forward reaction**. This is because the equilibrium moves to the side with **fewer molecules**. There are **four molecules** of gas on the reactant side ($N_{2(g)} + 3H_{2(g)}$) to every **two molecules** on the product side ($2NH_{3(g)}$).

2) **Increasing** the **pressure** also **increases** the **rate** of reaction.

3) Cranking up the pressure as high as you can sounds like a great idea so far. **But** very **high pressures** are really **expensive** to produce. You also need **strong pipes** and **containers** to **withstand** the **high pressure**. So the pressure chosen is a **compromise**. In the end, it all comes down to **minimising costs**.

During the **industrial production** of ammonia the reaction **never** actually **reaches equilibrium**. This is because it does not take place in a **closed system**. The gas mixture continually leaves the reactor and is liquified so that the **ammonia** can be **removed** — the unreacted nitrogen and hydrogen are then recycled.

*The Haber process does use a catalyst, but it doesn't affect how much product is made — it just makes the reaction reach equilibrium much more quickly.*

## Industrial Reactions are Designed to **Maximise Atom Economy**

$$\% \text{ atom economy} = \frac{\text{mass of atoms in product}}{\text{mass of atoms in reactants}} \times 100$$

The greater the atom economy, the less the waste. There are a couple of ways to increase it:

1) **Recycling** unreacted materials.

   Looking at the **Haber process** again, you can see that the atom economy for the conversion of nitrogen and hydrogen to ammonia is **100%** — assuming that the reaction goes to completion. But the reaction is in **equilibrium** with a **conversion rate** of only about **15%** — this means that the atom economy is also 15%. If the **unreacted gases** are continually **recycled**, then the conversion rate and atom economy are **increased** to **98%**.

2) Finding an **alternative route** for synthesis.

   **Ibuprofen**, a painkiller, was patented in the 1960s. It was manufactured in a **6 step process** with an atom economy of **40%**. In the mid-1980s a new company came along and developed an **alternative synthesis**, which converted the same starting materials to ibuprofen in just **three steps** — this increased the atom economy to **77%**.

# Equilibria in Industrial Processes

## Industrial Processes Need to be **Controlled**

If you're developing an industrial process based on a chemical reaction,
you'll need to answer a few questions before you can start.

### 1) WILL THE REACTION GO?

Analysis of equilibrium constants and **entropy changes** can answer this question.
Reactions with $\Delta S_{total}$ values of **less than −100 J K$^{-1}$ mol$^{-1}$** are unlikely to go even with changes to temperature
and pressure. Reactions with $\Delta S_{total}$ values **between −100 and 0 J K$^{-1}$ mol$^{-1}$** could be made to go with economic
and safe changes to temperature and pressure. Given that the product is removed, the equilibrium can be pushed
towards better yields. If $\Delta S_{total}$ is **greater than 0 J K$^{-1}$ mol$^{-1}$** the reaction should work without interference.

### 2) HOW FAST IS THE REACTION?

Some reactions will occur, but only **very slowly**. This doesn't make the process very **economical**. Changes to
temperature and pressure, or the introduction of a catalyst, can **speed up** the rate at which equilibrium is reached.

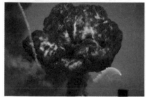

### 3) CAN THE ATOM ECONOMY OF A REACTION BE INCREASED?

This will help **reduce waste** (which is better for the environment) and **keep costs down**.

### 4) ARE THERE WAYS OF REDUCING ENERGY CONSUMPTION?

E.g. by using **heat exchangers**. This will help to keep production **costs** down.

*Joanne's industrial marshmallow-
toaster needed a few tweaks
before going on sale.*

### 5) WHAT SAFETY PROCEDURES NEED TO BE PUT IN PLACE?

If **high pressures or temperatures** are used, there need to be **safeguards** in place to protect the **workforce** and the
**environment**. The same is true if the **products** or **waste products** from the reaction are **toxic** or **highly flammable**.

Answering these questions is vital if you are going to be in control of the chemical reactions
that form part of the industrial process.

## Practice Questions

Q1 In an exothermic reaction, what sort of temperature favours the reverse reaction?

Q2 Why are the reaction conditions for the Haber process regarded as a compromise?

Q3 Why is it important to maximize the atom economy of an industrial process?

### Exam Question

1   The following reaction is part of the Contact process, which manufactures sulfuric acid:

$$2SO_{2(g)} + O_{2(g)} \rightleftharpoons 2SO_{3(g)} \quad \Delta H = -57.2 \text{ kJ mol}^{-1}$$

a)   The reaction takes place at a temperature of 450 °C.
     Explain why this might be termed a 'compromise temperature'.                    [3 marks]

b)   A vandium(V) oxide catalyst is used to speed up the reaction. How does this affect the product yield?   [1 mark]

c)   Suggest how the atom economy of this reaction might be increased.               [1 mark]

d)   A new company has decided to start manufacturing sulfuric acid.
     Suggest and explain two factors that could influence their choice of process.   [4 marks]

## For maximum atom economy, wash at 30 °C...

*These last few pages have basically taken everything you've learnt so far and told you how it gets used in the chemical
industry — so if you're planning a career as a chemical engineer I'd make sure you've read this properly. To be fair, I'd say
read it properly anyway. There is an exam at the end of all this. They're bound to ask you some questions.*

# Acids and Bases

*Remember this stuff?  Well, it's all down to Brønsted and Lowry — they've got a lot to answer for...*

## An Acid **Releases** Protons — a Base **Accepts** Protons

1) The **scientific definition** of an **acid** has changed over time — originally, the word **acid** just meant something that **tasted sour**.

2) In the late 19th century, the Swedish scientist **Svante Arrhenius** came up with a more scientific definition — he defined an acid as a substance that produces **excess hydrogen ions** when it dissolves in water.

3) In 1923, **Johannes Nicolaus Brønsted** and **Martin Lowry** refined the definition.  They said that acids and bases were to do with **donating and accepting protons**.  Here's their definition...

**Brønsted-Lowry acids** are **proton donors** — they release **hydrogen ions** ($H^+$) when they're mixed with water.  You never get $H^+$ ions by themselves in water though — they're always combined with $H_2O$ to form **hydroxonium ions, $H_3O^+$**.

HA is just any old acid. $\implies$ $HA_{(aq)} + H_2O_{(l)} \rightarrow H_3O^+_{(aq)} + A^-_{(aq)}$

**Brønsted-Lowry bases** do the opposite — they're **proton acceptors**.  When they're in solution, they grab **hydrogen ions** from water molecules.

B is just a random base.

$B_{(aq)} + H_2O_{(l)} \rightarrow BH^+_{(aq)} + OH^-_{(aq)}$

## Acids and Bases can be **Strong** or **Weak**

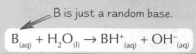
These are really all reversible reactions, but the equilibrium lies extremely far to the right.

1) **Strong acids ionise** almost **completely** in water — **nearly all** the $H^+$ ions will be released.  **Hydrochloric acid** is a strong acid — $HCl_{(g)} + \text{water} \rightarrow H^+_{(aq)} + Cl^-_{(aq)}$.
**Strong bases** (like sodium hydroxide) **ionise almost completely** in water too.  E.g. $NaOH_{(s)} + \text{water} \rightarrow Na^+_{(aq)} + OH^-_{(aq)}$.

2) **Weak acids** (e.g. ethanoic or citric) ionise only very **slightly** in water — so only small numbers of $H^+$ ions are formed.  An **equilibrium** is set up which lies well over to the **left**.  E.g. $CH_3COOH_{(aq)} \rightleftharpoons CH_3COO^-_{(aq)} + H^+_{(aq)}$.
**Weak bases** (such as ammonia) **only slightly ionise** in water too.  E.g. $NH_{3(aq)} + H_2O_{(l)} \rightleftharpoons NH_4^+_{(aq)} + OH^-_{(aq)}$.
Just like with weak acids, the equilibrium lies well over to the **left**.

## **Protons** are **Transferred** when **Acids** and **Bases** React

Acids **can't** just throw away their protons — they can only get rid of them if there's a **base** to accept them.  In this reaction the **acid**, HA, **transfers** a proton to the **base**, B:

$HA_{(aq)} + B_{(aq)} \rightleftharpoons BH^+_{(aq)} + A^-_{(aq)}$

It's an **equilibrium**, so if you add more **HA** or **B**, the position of equilibrium moves to the **right**.  But if you add more **BH$^+$** or **A$^-$**, the equilibrium will move to the **left**.  This is all down to **Le Chatelier's principle** (see page 34).

When an acid is added to **water**, the water acts as the **base** and accepts the proton:

$HA_{(aq)} + H_2O_{(l)} \rightleftharpoons H_3O^+_{(aq)} + A^-_{(aq)}$

The equilibrium's far to the left for weak acids, and far to the right for strong acids.

## Acids and Bases form **Conjugate Pairs**

So when an acid's added to water, the equilibrium shown on the right is set up.

In the **forward reaction**, HA acts as an **acid** as it **donates** a proton.  In the **reverse reaction**, A$^-$ acts as a **base** and **accepts** a proton from the $H_3O^+$ ion to form HA.

HA and A$^-$ are called a **conjugate pair** — HA is the **conjugate acid** of A$^-$ and A$^-$ is the **conjugate base** of the acid, HA.  $H_2O$ and $H_3O^+$ are a conjugate pair too.

The acid and base of a conjugate pair can be linked by an $H^+$, like this: $HA \rightleftharpoons H^+ + A^-$ or this: $H^+ + H_2O \rightleftharpoons H_3O^+$

conjugate pair

acid   base    acid   base
$HA + H_2O \rightleftharpoons H_3O^+ + A^-$
conjugate pair

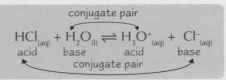
Here's the equilibrium for aqueous HCl.  
Cl$^-$ is the conjugate base of HCl$_{(aq)}$.

conjugate pair

$HCl_{(aq)} + H_2O_{(l)} \rightleftharpoons H_3O^+_{(aq)} + Cl^-_{(aq)}$
acid      base     acid     base
conjugate pair

An equilibrium with **conjugate pairs** is also set up when a **base** dissolves in water.

The base B takes a proton from the water to form **BH$^+$** — so B is the **conjugate base** of BH$^+$, and BH$^+$ is the **conjugate acid** of B.  $H_2O$ and OH$^-$ also form a **conjugate pair**.

conjugate pair

$B + H_2O \rightleftharpoons BH^+ + OH^-$
base   acid    acid   base
conjugate pair

# Acids and Bases

## Water can Behave as an Acid AND a Base

Water can act as an **acid** by **donating** a proton — but it can also act as a **base** by accepting a **proton**.
So, in water there'll always be both **hydroxonium ions** and **hydroxide ions** swimming around at the **same time**.

> The equilibrium below exists in water:
>
> $$2H_2O_{(l)} \rightleftharpoons H_3O^+_{(aq)} + OH^-_{(aq)}$$     or more simply...     $$H_2O_{(l)} \rightleftharpoons H^+_{(aq)} + OH^-_{(aq)}$$
>
> And, just like for any other equilibrium reaction, you can apply the equilibrium law and write an expression for the **equilibrium constant**:     $K_c = \dfrac{[H^+][OH^-]}{[H_2O]}$

Water only dissociates a **tiny amount**, so the equilibrium lies well over to the **left**. There's so much water compared to the amounts of $H^+$ and $OH^-$ ions that the concentration of water is considered to have a **constant** value.

So if you multiply $K_c$ (a constant) by $[H_2O]$ (another constant), you get a **constant**.
This new constant is called the **ionic product of water** and it is given the symbol $K_w$.

$$K_w = K_c \times [H_2O] = [H^+][OH^-] \Rightarrow \boxed{K_w = [H^+][OH^-]}$$

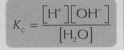
The units of $K_w$ are always $mol^2\,dm^{-6}$.

$K_w$ always has the **same value** for an aqueous solution at a **given temperature**.
It's important that you know its value at standard temperature, **25 °C**:

> At 25 °C (298 K), $K_w = 1.0 \times 10^{-14}\ mol^2\,dm^{-6}$

You need to know that $K_w$ can also be given as **p$K_w$**, where **p$K_w$ = $-\log_{10} K_w$** .
The advantage of p$K_w$ values is that they're a decent size so they're easy to work with —
for example, the p$K_w$ of water at 25 °C is $-\log_{10}(1.0 \times 10^{-14}) = $ **14**.

## A Neutral Solution has Equal H⁺ and OH⁻ Concentrations

> A neutral solution is one in which $[H^+] = [OH^-]$.

If $[H^+]$ is greater than $[OH^-]$ the solution is **acidic**, and if $[OH^-]$ is greater than $[H^+]$ the solution is **alkaline.**

## Practice Questions

Q1 Ammonia is a Brønsted-Lowry base. Write the equation for it reacting with water.

Q2 Explain the difference between strong and weak acids.

Q3 Write the equilibrium for hydrochloric acid dissolving in water and identify the conjugate pairs.

Q4 Explain how water can act as a base and as an acid.

### Exam Questions

1   Hydrocyanic acid, $HCN_{(aq)}$, is a weak acid with a faint smell of bitter almonds. It is extremely poisonous.
   a)   Write the equation for the equilibrium set up when it dissolves in water.     [1 mark]
   b)   What can you say about the position of this equilibrium?     [2 marks]
   c)   What is the conjugate base of this acid?     [1 mark]

2   Water is considered as a neutral substance.
   a)   What is meant by a neutral substance?     [1 mark]
   b)   Write an equation for the equilibrium that exists in water.     [1 mark]
   c)   Write an expression for $K_c$ for this equilibrium.     [1 mark]
   d)   Show how the constant $K_w$ is derived from this expression.     [2 marks]
   e)   Find the value of $[H^+]$ for water at 298 K.     [2 marks]

## Acids and bases — the Julie Andrews and Marilyn Manson of the chemistry world...

*Don't confuse strong acids with concentrated acids, or weak acids with dilute acids. Strong and weak are to do with how much an acid ionises, whereas concentrated and dilute are to do with the number of moles of acid you've got per $dm^3$. You can have a dilute strong acid, or a concentrated weak acid. It works the same way with bases too.*

# pH Calculations

*Get those calculators warmed up — especially the log function key.*

## The pH Scale is a Measure of the Hydrogen Ion Concentration

The **concentration of hydrogen ions** can vary enormously, so some clever chemists decided to express the concentration on a **logarithmic scale**.

$$pH = -\log_{10}[H^+]$$

The pH scale normally goes from **0** (very acidic) to **14** (very alkaline). **pH 7** is regarded as being **neutral**.

## For Strong Monoprotic Acids, Hydrogen Ion Concentration = Acid Concentration

Hydrochloric acid and nitric acid ($HNO_{3(aq)}$) are **strong acids** so they ionise fully. They're also **monoprotic**, so each mole of acid produces **one mole of hydrogen ions**. This means the $H^+$ concentration is the **same** as the acid concentration. So for 0.1 mol dm$^{-3}$ hydrochloric acid, $[H^+]$ is **0.1 mol dm$^{-3}$**. Its pH = $-\log_{10}[H^+] = -\log_{10}(0.1) = $ **1.0**.

Here's an example:

1) Calculate the pH of 0.05 mol dm$^{-3}$ nitric acid. $[H^+] = 0.05 \Rightarrow pH = -\log_{10}(0.05) = $ **1.30**

You also need to be able to work out $[H^+]$ if you're given the **pH** of a solution. You do this by finding the **inverse log of –pH**, which is **10$^{-pH}$**.

2) If an acid solution has a pH of 2.45, what is the hydrogen ion concentration, or $[H^+]$, of the acid?

$$[H^+] = 10^{-2.45} = 3.55 \times 10^{-3} \text{ mol dm}^{-3}$$

*Watch out for $H_2SO_4$ which dissociates to give $2H^+$. This means the $[H^+]$ will be twice the $[H_2SO_4]$.*

## Use $K_w$ to Find the pH of a Base

Sodium hydroxide (NaOH) and potassium hydroxide (KOH) are **strong bases** that **fully ionise** in water. They each have **one hydroxide ion**, so they donate **one mole of OH$^-$ ions** per mole of base. This means that the concentration of OH$^-$ ions is the **same** as the **concentration of the base**. So for 0.02 mol dm$^{-3}$ sodium hydroxide solution, $[OH^-]$ is also **0.02 mol dm$^{-3}$**.

But to work out the **pH** you need to know $[H^+]$ — luckily this is linked to $[OH^-]$ through the **ionic product of water**, $K_w$:

$$K_w = [H^+][OH^-] = 1.0 \times 10^{-14} \text{ at } 298 \text{ K}$$

So if you know $K_w$ and $[OH^-]$ for a **strong aqueous base** at a certain temperature, you can work out $[H^+]$ and then the **pH**.

Find the pH of 0.1 mol dm$^{-3}$ NaOH at 298 K.

$$[OH^-] = 0.1 \text{ mol dm}^{-3} \Rightarrow [H^+] = \frac{K_w}{[OH^-]} = \frac{1.0 \times 10^{-14}}{0.1} = 1.0 \times 10^{-13} \text{ mol dm}^{-3}$$

So pH = $-\log_{10}(1.0 \times 10^{-13}) = $ **13.0**

## To Find the pH of a Weak Acid you Use $K_a$ (the Acid Dissociation Constant)

Weak acids **don't** ionise fully in solution, so the $[H^+]$ **isn't** the same as the acid concentration. This makes it a **bit trickier** to find their pH. You have to use yet another **equilibrium constant**, $K_a$.

For a weak aqueous acid, HA, you get the following equilibrium: $HA_{(aq)} \rightleftharpoons H^+_{(aq)} + A^-_{(aq)}$
You have to make a **couple of assumptions**:

1) Only a **tiny amount** of HA dissociates, so you can assume that $[HA_{(aq)}]_{start} = [HA_{(aq)}]_{equilibrium}$.

So if you apply the equilibrium law, you get: $K_a = \dfrac{[H^+][A^-]}{[HA]}$

2) You also assume all the **H$^+$ ions** come from the **acid**, so $[H^+_{(aq)}] = [A^-_{(aq)}]$... So $K_a = \dfrac{[H^+]^2}{[HA]}$

*The units of $K_a$ are mol dm$^{-3}$.*

Here's an example of how to use $K_a$ to find the **pH** of a weak acid:

Calculate the hydrogen ion concentration and the pH of a 0.02 mol dm$^{-3}$ solution of propanoic acid ($CH_3CH_2COOH$). $K_a$ for propanoic acid at this temperature is $1.30 \times 10^{-5}$ mol dm$^{-3}$.

$$K_a = \frac{[H^+]^2}{[CH_3CH_2COOH]} \Rightarrow [H^+]^2 = K_a[CH_3CH_2COOH] = 1.30 \times 10^{-5} \times 0.02 = 2.60 \times 10^{-7}$$

$$\Rightarrow [H^+] = \sqrt{2.60 \times 10^{-7}} = 5.10 \times 10^{-4} \text{ mol dm}^{-3} \quad \text{So pH} = -\log_{10}(5.10 \times 10^{-4}) = 3.29$$

# pH Calculations

## You Might Have to Find the **Concentration** or $K_a$ of a **Weak Acid**

You don't need to know anything new for this type of calculation. You usually just have to find **[H+]** from the pH, then fiddle around with the $K_a$ **expression** to find the missing bit of information.

1) The pH of an ethanoic acid ($CH_3COOH$) solution was 3.02 at 298 K. $K_a$ for ethanoic acid is $1.75 \times 10^{-5}$ mol dm$^{-3}$ at 298 K. Calculate the molar concentration of this solution.

$$[H^+] = 10^{-pH} = 10^{-3.02} = 9.55 \times 10^{-4} \text{ mol dm}^{-3}$$

$$K_a = \frac{[H^+]^2}{[CH_3COOH]} \Rightarrow [CH_3COOH] = \frac{[H^+]^2}{K_a} = \frac{(9.55 \times 10^{-4})^2}{1.75 \times 10^{-5}} = \textbf{0.0521 mol dm}^{-3}$$

2) A solution of propanoic acid ($CH_3CH_2COOH$) was prepared containing 0.185g of the acid in 250 ml. The solution had a pH of 3.44 at 298 K. What is the value of $K_a$ for propanoic acid at 298 K?

Moles = mass ÷ $M_r$ = 0.185 ÷ 74 = 0.0025 moles per 250 ml

So $[CH_3CH_2COOH]$ = 0.0025 × (1000 ÷ 250) = 0.01 mol dm$^{-3}$

*Don't forget 1000 ml = 1 dm³*

$$[H^+] = 10^{-pH} = 10^{-3.44} = 3.63 \times 10^{-4} \text{ mol dm}^{-3} \quad K_a = \frac{[H^+]^2}{[CH_3CH_2COOH]} = \frac{(3.63 \times 10^{-4})^2}{0.01} = \textbf{1.32} \times \textbf{10}^{-5} \text{ mol dm}^{-3}$$

## $pK_a = -log_{10} K_a$ and $K_a = 10^{-pK_a}$

$pK_a$ is calculated from $K_a$ in exactly the same way as pH is calculated from [H+] — and vice versa. So if an acid has a $K_a$ value of $1.50 \times 10^{-7}$, its **$pK_a$ = $-log_{10}(1.50 \times 10^{-7})$ = 6.82**. And if an acid has a $pK_a$ value of 4.32, its **$K_a$ = $10^{-4.32}$ = $4.79 \times 10^{-5}$**.

*Notice how $pK_a$ values aren't annoyingly tiny like $K_a$ values.*

Just to make things that bit more complicated, there might be a **$pK_a$** value in a question. If so, you need to convert it to $K_a$ so that you can use the **$K_a$ expression**.

Calculate the pH of 0.050 mol dm$^{-3}$ methanoic acid (HCOOH). Methanoic acid has a $pK_a$ of 3.75 at this temperature.

$$K_a = 10^{-pK_a} = 10^{-3.75} = 1.78 \times 10^{-4} \text{ mol dm}^{-3} \quad \longleftarrow \text{First you have to convert the } pK_a \text{ to } K_a.$$

$$K_a = \frac{[H^+]^2}{[HCOOH]} \Rightarrow [H^+]^2 = K_a[HCOOH] = 1.78 \times 10^{-4} \times 0.050 = 8.9 \times 10^{-6}$$

$$\Rightarrow [H^+] = \sqrt{8.9 \times 10^{-6}} = 2.98 \times 10^{-3} \text{ mol dm}^{-3}$$

$$pH = -log(2.98 \times 10^{-3}) = \textbf{2.53}$$

Sometimes you have to give your answer as a **$pK_a$** value. In this case, you just work out the $K_a$ value as usual and then convert it to **$pK_a$** — and Bob's your pet hamster.

## The **pH** of Equimolar Solutions can give you **Information** about the Substances

You can learn quite a lot about the nature of a chemical just by looking at its **pH**.

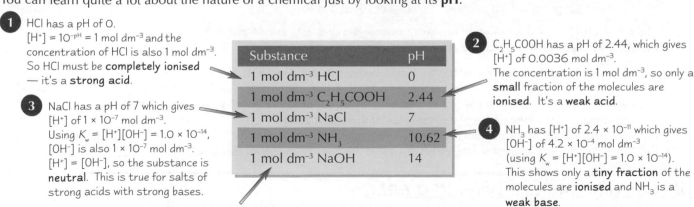

**1** HCl has a pH of 0.
$[H^+] = 10^{-pH} = 1$ mol dm$^{-3}$ and the concentration of HCl is also 1 mol dm$^{-3}$. So HCl must be **completely ionised** — it's a **strong acid**.

**3** NaCl has a pH of 7 which gives $[H^+]$ of $1 \times 10^{-7}$ mol dm$^{-3}$. Using $K_w = [H^+][OH^-] = 1.0 \times 10^{-14}$, $[OH^-]$ is also $1 \times 10^{-7}$ mol dm$^{-3}$. $[H^+] = [OH^-]$, so the substance is **neutral**. This is true for salts of strong acids with strong bases.

| Substance | pH |
|---|---|
| 1 mol dm$^{-3}$ HCl | 0 |
| 1 mol dm$^{-3}$ $C_2H_5COOH$ | 2.44 |
| 1 mol dm$^{-3}$ NaCl | 7 |
| 1 mol dm$^{-3}$ $NH_3$ | 10.62 |
| 1 mol dm$^{-3}$ NaOH | 14 |

**2** $C_2H_5COOH$ has a pH of 2.44, which gives [H+] of 0.0036 mol dm$^{-3}$. The concentration is 1 mol dm$^{-3}$, so only a **small** fraction of the molecules are **ionised**. It's a **weak acid**.

**4** $NH_3$ has [H+] of $2.4 \times 10^{-11}$ which gives $[OH^-]$ of $4.2 \times 10^{-4}$ mol dm$^{-3}$ (using $K_w = [H^+][OH^-] = 1.0 \times 10^{-14}$). This shows only a **tiny fraction** of the molecules are **ionised** and $NH_3$ is a **weak base**.

**5** NaOH has [H+] of $1 \times 10^{-14}$ mol dm$^{-3}$ which means $[OH^-]$ is 1 mol dm$^{-3}$. The concentration of NaOH is also 1 mol dm$^{-3}$ so NaOH is **completely ionised** — it's a **strong base**.

# pH Calculations

## When Acids are Diluted their pH Changes

Diluting an acid reduces the **concentration of H⁺** in the solution. This **increases the pH**. The table shows the pH of a strong and a weak acid at different concentrations.

| Concentration of Acid (mol dm⁻³) | HCl pH at 298 K | C₂H₅COOH pH at 298 K |
|---|---|---|
| 1 | 0 | 2.44 |
| 0.1 | 1 | 2.94 |
| 0.01 | 2 | 3.44 |
| 0.001 | 3 | 3.94 |

### Strong Acid — HCl

Diluting a **strong acid** by a **factor of 10** increases the pH by **1**.

It's easy to see this for yourself. Remember that for a strong acid, $[H^+] = [acid]$, so $pH = -\log_{10}[acid]$.

Just try sticking $[acid]$ = 1, 0.1, 0.01, .... into this formula.

*These results may seem a bit random, but they're true. It's all in the maths...*

### Weak Acid — Propanoic acid

Diluting a **weak acid** by a **factor of 10** increases the pH by **0.5**.

Again, you can see this for yourself if you like by sticking numbers into the right formula, but it's a lot more fiddly this time...

Rearranging $K_a = \dfrac{[H^+]^2}{[acid]}$ gives $[H^+] = \sqrt{K_a[acid]}$, and then $pH = -\log_{10}[H^+]$

Stick $[acid]$ = 1, 0.1, 0.01, ... into the rearranged $[H^+]$ formula and find the pH each time. The pH will always change by 0.5, no matter what value you use for $K_a$.

E.g. To get the figures in the table above, $K_a$ of propanoic acid is $1.31 \times 10^{-5}$.

So $[C_2H_5COOH]$ = 1 mol dm⁻³ gives $[H^+] = 3.6 \times 10^{-3}$ which gives pH = 2.44
$[C_2H_5COOH]$ = 0.1 mol dm⁻³ gives $[H^+] = 1.14 \times 10^{-3}$ which gives pH = 2.94

## Practice Questions

Q1 Explain how to calculate the pH of a strong acid.
Q2 How do you calculate the pH of a strong base?
Q3 Explain how to calculate the pH of a weak acid.
Q4 The pH of a 1 mol dm⁻³ solution of nitric acid is 0 at 298 K. What does this tell you about the amount nitric acid is ionised? Is nitric acid a strong or weak acid?

### Exam Questions

1 The value of $K_a$ for the weak acid HA, at 298 K, is $5.60 \times 10^{-4}$ mol dm⁻³.
 a) Write an expression for $K_a$. [1 mark]
 b) Calculate the pH of a 0.280 mol dm⁻³ solution of HA at 298 K. [3 marks]

2 The pH of a 0.150 mol dm⁻³ solution of a weak monoprotic acid, HX, is 2.65 at 298 K.
 Calculate the value of $K_a$ for the acid HX at 298 K. [5 marks]

3 The pH of a 0.1 mol dm⁻³ solution of the weak acid, benzoic acid, C₆H₅COOH, is 2.60 at 298 K
 a) Calculate a value for $K_a$ for the acid at this temperature. [5 marks]
 b) Use the value of $K_a$ that you have calculated to find the [H⁺] of a 0.01 mol dm⁻³ solution of this acid. [2 marks]
 c) Calculate the pH of the 0.01 mol dm⁻³ solution of the acid at 298 K. [1 mark]
 d) Show that the pH of a 1 mol dm⁻³ solution of the acid is 2.1. [2 marks]
 e) What rule can you suggest for the effect of 10 fold dilutions on the pH of this acid? [1 mark]

## pH calculations are pH–ing great...

*No, I really like them. Honestly. Although they can be a bit tricky. Just make sure you learn all the key formulas and assumptions made for this topic. If something's got a p in front of it, like pH, pK_w or pK_a, it'll mean $-\log_{10}$ of whatever. Oh and not all calculators work the same way, so make sure you know how to work logs out on your calculator.*

# Titration Curves and Indicators

*If you add alkali to acid the pH changes in a squiggly sort of way.*

## Use **Titration** to Find the **Concentration** of an **Acid** or **Alkali**

**Titrations** allow you to find out **exactly** how much alkali is needed to **neutralise** a quantity of acid.

1) You start by measuring out some **acid** of known concentration using a pipette and putting it in a flask with an **appropriate indicator** (see below).

2) First do a rough titration — add the **alkali** to the acid fairly quickly using a **burette** to get an approximate idea of where the solution changes colour (the **end point**). Give the flask a regular **swirl**.

3) Now do an **accurate** titration. Run the alkali in to within 2 cm³ of the end point, then add it **drop by drop**. If you don't notice exactly when the solution changes colour you've **overshot** and your result won't be accurate.

4) **Record** the amount of alkali needed to **neutralise** the acid. It's best to **repeat** this process a few times, making sure you get very similar answers each time (within about 0.2 cm³ of each other).

You can also find out how much **acid** is needed to neutralise a quantity of **alkali**. It's exactly the same as above, but you add **acid to alkali** instead.

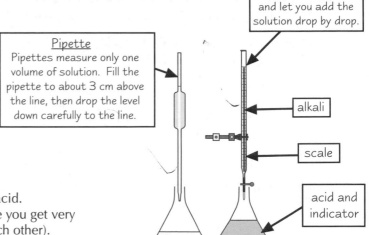

Pipette
Pipettes measure only one volume of solution. Fill the pipette to about 3 cm above the line, then drop the level down carefully to the line.

Burette
Burettes measure different volumes and let you add the solution drop by drop.

alkali

scale

acid and indicator

## pH Curves Plot pH Against Volume of Acid or Alkali Added

The graphs below show the pH curves for the **different combinations** of **strong and weak** monoprotic acids and alkalis.

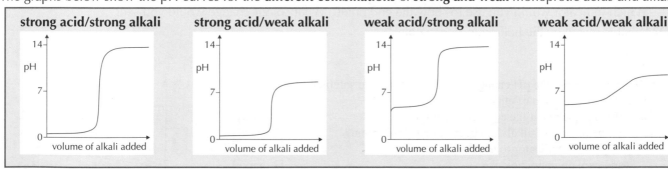

| strong acid/strong alkali | strong acid/weak alkali | weak acid/strong alkali | weak acid/weak alkali |

*(pH plotted against volume of alkali added for each curve; pH axis marked at 0, 7, 14)*

All the graphs apart from the weak acid/weak alkali graph have a bit that's almost vertical — this is the **equivalence point** or **end point**. At this point, a tiny amount of alkali causes a sudden, big change in pH — it's here that all the acid is just **neutralised**. The equivalence point varies depending on the acid and alkali used.

You don't get such a sharp change in a **weak acid/weak alkali** titration. The indicator colour changes **gradually** and it's tricky to see the exact end point. You're usually better off using a **pH meter** for this type of titration.

## pH Curves can Help you Decide which Indicator to Use

**Methyl orange** and **phenolphthalein** are **indicators** that are often used for acid-base titrations. They each change colour over a **different pH range**:

| Name of indicator | Colour at low pH | Approx. pH of colour change | Colour at high pH |
|---|---|---|---|
| Methyl orange | red | 3.1 – 4.4 | yellow |
| Phenolphthalein | colourless | 8.3 – 10 | pink |

For a **strong acid/strong alkali** titration, you can use **either** of these indicators — there's a rapid pH change over the range for **both** indicators.

For a **strong acid/weak alkali** only **methyl orange** will do. The pH changes rapidly across the range for methyl orange, but not for phenolphthalein.

For a **weak acid/strong alkali**, **phenolphthalein** is the stuff to use. The pH changes rapidly over phenolphthalein's range, but not over methyl orange's.

For **weak acid/weak alkali** titrations there's no sharp pH change, so **neither** of these indicators will work.

# Titration Curves and Indicators

You can work out $pK_a$ of a weak acid using the pH curve for a **weak acid/strong base titration**. It involves finding the **pH** at the **half-equivalence point**.

**Half-equivalence** is the stage of a titration when **half** of the acid has been neutralised — it's when half of the equivalence volume of **strong base** has been added to the **weak acid**.

A weak acid, HA, dissociates like this: $HA \rightleftharpoons H^+ + A^-$.
At the half-equivalence point, $[HA] = [A^-]$.

[HA] and [A⁻] cancel.

So for the weak acid HA, $K_a = \dfrac{[H^+][A^-]}{[HA]} \Rightarrow K_a = [H^+]$ and $pK_a = pH$.

$pK_a = -\log_{10}[H^+]$ (which is pH)

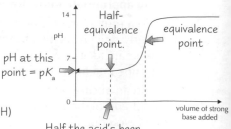

pH at this point = $pK_a$

Half the acid's been neutralised when this much base has been added.

So the pH at half equivalence is actually the $pK_a$ value for the weak acid.
And if you know the $pK_a$ value you can work out $K_a$ ($K_a = 10^{-pK_a}$ — see page 41).

## Practice Questions

Q1 What piece of equipment is used in a titration to accurately measure the amount of alkali being added to a fixed amount of acid?

Q2 Sketch the pH curve for adding ammonia solution slowly to hydrochloric acid.
Which indicator would you use to show the end point? What colour change would you see?

Q3 What is meant by the half-equivalence point?

### Exam Questions

1 This curve shows the pH change as sodium hydroxide solution is added to a solution of ethanoic acid.
  a) What is the pH at the equivalence point? [1 mark]
  b) What volume of alkali had been added at this point? [1 mark]
  c) Suggest an indicator to use for the titration and explain your choice. [2 marks]
  d) Sketch the curve you would get if the titration was repeated using ammonia solution as the base. [1 mark]
  e) How would you need to change the method in this titration if you were using ammonia as the base? [1 mark]

2 This curve shows the pH change when sodium hydroxide is added to a 0.1 mol dm⁻³ solution of methanoic acid, HCOOH.
  a) What is the pH of
     i) the equivalence point, [1 mark]
     ii) the half-equivalence point? [1 mark]
  b) Write an expression for $K_a$ for the dissociation of this acid. [1 mark]
  c) At the half-equivalence point what is the concentration of the acid? [1 mark]
  d) Calculate the value of $pK_a$ and $K_a$ for the acid [2 marks]

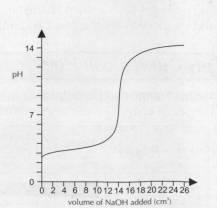

## Drip, Drip, Drop little acid shower...

*Titrations involve playing with big bits of glassware that you're told not to break as they're really expensive — so you instantly become really clumsy. If you manage to not smash the burette, you'll find it easier to get accurate results if you use a dilute acid or alkali — drops of dilute acid or alkali contain fewer particles so you're less likely to overshoot.*

# Buffers

*How can a solution resist becoming more acidic if you add acid to it? Here's where you find out...*

## Buffers **Resist** Changes in pH

> A **buffer** is a solution that **resists** changes in pH when **small** amounts of acid or alkali are added.

A buffer **doesn't** stop the pH from changing completely — it does make the changes **very slight** though.
Buffers only work for small amounts of acid or alkali — put too much in and they'll go "Waah" and not be able to cope.

## Acidic Buffers are Made from a **Weak Acid** and one of its **Salts**

**Acidic buffers** have a pH of less than 7 — they're made by mixing a **weak acid** with one of its **salts**.
**Ethanoic acid** and **sodium ethanoate** ($CH_3COO^-Na^+$) is a good example:

The salt **fully** dissociates into its ions when it dissolves: $CH_3COO^-Na^+_{(aq)} \rightarrow CH_3COO^-_{(aq)} + Na^+_{(aq)}$.
Sodium ethanoate    Ethanoate ions

The ethanoic acid is a **weak acid**, so it only **slightly** dissociates: $CH_3COOH_{(aq)} \rightleftharpoons H^+_{(aq)} + CH_3COO^-_{(aq)}$

So in the solution you've got heaps of **ethanoate ions** from the salt, and heaps of **undissociated ethanoic acid molecules**.

**Le Chatelier's principle** (see page 34)
explains how buffers work:

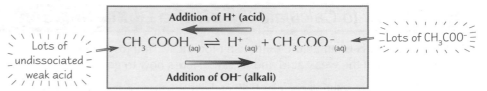

Lots of undissociated weak acid

Addition of H⁺ (acid)
$$CH_3COOH_{(aq)} \rightleftharpoons H^+_{(aq)} + CH_3COO^-_{(aq)}$$
Addition of OH⁻ (alkali)

Lots of $CH_3COO^-$

| | |
|---|---|
| If you add a **small** amount of **acid**, the H⁺ concentration increases. Most of the extra H⁺ ions combine with $CH_3COO^-$ ions to form $CH_3COOH$. This shifts the equilibrium to the **left**, reducing the H⁺ concentration to near its original value. So the **pH** doesn't change much. | If a **small** amount of **alkali** (e.g. NaOH) is added, the **OH⁻** concentration increases. Most of the extra OH⁻ ions react with H⁺ ions to form water — removing H⁺ ions from the solution. This causes more $CH_3COOH$ to **dissociate** to form H⁺ ions — shifting the equilibrium to the **right**. The H⁺ concentration increases until it's close to its original value, so the **pH** does not change much. |

## Alkaline Buffers are Made from a **Weak Base** and one of its **Salts**

A mixture of **ammonia solution** (a base) and **ammonium chloride** (a salt of ammonia) acts as an **alkaline** buffer.
It works in a similar way to acidic buffers:

The **salt** is fully ionised in solution: $NH_4Cl_{(aq)} \rightarrow NH_4^+_{(aq)} + Cl^-_{(aq)}$.
ammonium chloride    ammonium ions

An equilibrium is set up between the **ammonium ions and ammonia**.

Addition of H⁺ (acid)
$$NH_4^+_{(aq)} \rightleftharpoons H^+_{(aq)} + NH_3_{(aq)}$$
Addition of OH⁻ (alkali)

Lots of $NH_4^+$

Lots of weak base

If a small amount of **acid** is added, the H⁺ concentration **increases** — most of the added H⁺ reacts with $NH_3$ and the equilibrium shifts **left**. This reduces the H⁺ concentration to near its original value. So the pH **doesn't** change much.

If a small amount of **alkali** is added, the OH⁻ concentration **increases**. OH⁻ ions react with the H⁺ ions, removing them from the solution. There's plenty of $NH_4^+$ molecules around that can dissociate to generate replacement **H⁺ ions** — so the equilibrium shifts **right**, stopping the pH from changing much.

## Buffer Action can be Seen on a **Titration Curve**

The **titration curves** for weak acids with strong bases, and for strong acids with weak bases, have a **distinctive shape** due to the formation of **buffer solutions** as the reaction proceeds.

The pH changes quickly to start with as the alkali is strong and contains a lot of hydroxide ions to react with hydrogen ions

Then the curve levels off. This is because a buffer solution of sodium ethanoate in ethanoic acid is formed which resists further dramatic change in pH.

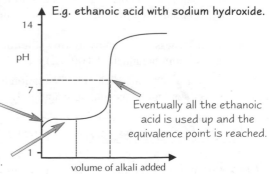

E.g. ethanoic acid with sodium hydroxide.

Eventually all the ethanoic acid is used up and the equivalence point is reached.

volume of alkali added

# Buffers

## Buffer Solutions are Important in Biological Environments

1) **Cells** need a constant pH to allow the **biochemical reactions** to take place. The pH is controlled by a buffer based on the equilibrium between **dihydrogen phosphate** and **hydrogen phosphate**.

$$H_2PO_4^- \rightleftharpoons H^+ + HPO_4^{2-}$$

Nobody's gonna change my pH.

2) **Blood** needs to be kept at pH 7.4. It is buffered using carbonic acid ($H_2CO_3$). The levels of **$H_2CO_3$** are controlled by the body. By **breathing out $CO_2$** the level of $H_2CO_3$ is reduced as it moves this **equilibrium** to the **right**. The levels of $HCO_3^-$ are controlled by the **kidneys** with excess being **excreted** in the urine.

$$H_2CO_{3(aq)} \rightleftharpoons H^+_{(aq)} + HCO^-_{3\ (aq)}$$
and
$$H_2CO_{3(aq)} \rightleftharpoons H_2O_{(l)} + CO_{2(g)}$$

Acids and alkalis didn't mess with Jeff after he became buffer.

3) Buffers are used in **food products** to control the pH. Changes in pH can be caused by **bacteria** and **fungi** and cause food to **deteriorate**. A common buffer is **sodium citrate**, which sets up an equilibrium between citrate ions and citric acid. **Phosphoric acid/ phosphate ions** and **benzoic acid/benzoate** ions are also used as buffers.

## Here's How to Calculate the pH of a Buffer Solution

Calculating the **pH** of an acidic buffer isn't too tricky. You just need to know the $K_a$ of the weak acid and the **concentrations** of the weak acid and its salt. Here's how to go about it:

**Example:** A buffer solution contains 0.40 mol dm$^{-3}$ methanoic acid, HCOOH, and 0.6 mol dm$^{-3}$ sodium methanoate, HCOO$^-$Na$^+$. For methanoic acid, $K_a = 1.6 \times 10^{-4}$ mol dm$^{-3}$. What is the pH of this buffer?

Firstly, write the expression for $K_a$ of the weak acid:

$$HCOOH_{(aq)} \rightleftharpoons H^+_{(aq)} + HCOO^-_{(aq)} \Rightarrow K_a = \frac{[H^+][HCOO^-]}{[HCOOH]}$$

Remember — these all have to be equilibrium concentrations.

Then rearrange the expression and stick in the data to calculate [H$^+_{(aq)}$]:

$$[H^+] = K_a \times \frac{[HCOOH]}{[HCOO^-]} = 1.6 \times 10^{-4} \times \frac{0.4}{0.6} = 1.07 \times 10^{-4} \text{ mol dm}^{-3}$$

You have to make a **few assumptions** here:
• HCOO$^-$Na$^+$ is fully dissociated, so assume that the equilibrium concentration of HCOO$^-$ is the same as the initial concentration of HCOO$^-$Na$^+$.
• HCOOH is only slightly dissociated, so assume that its equilibrium concentration is the same as its initial concentration.

Finally, convert [H$^+$] to pH: $pH = -\log_{10}[H^+] = -\log_{10}(1.07 \times 10^{-4}) = \mathbf{3.97}$ And that's your answer.

## Practice Questions

Q1 What's a buffer solution?
Q2 How can a mixture of ethanoic acid and sodium ethanoate act as a buffer?
Q3 Describe how to make an alkaline buffer.

**Exam Questions**

1 A buffer solution contains 0.40 mol dm$^{-3}$ benzoic acid, $C_6H_5COOH$, and 0.20 mol dm$^{-3}$ sodium benzoate, $C_6H_5COO^-Na^+$. At 25 °C, $K_a$ for benzoic acid is $6.4 \times 10^{-5}$ mol dm$^{-3}$.
   a) Calculate the pH of the buffer solution. [3 marks]
   b) Explain the effect on the buffer of adding a small quantity of dilute sulphuric acid. [3 marks]

2 A buffer was prepared by mixing solutions of butanoic acid, $CH_3(CH_2)_2COOH$, and sodium butanoate, $CH_3(CH_2)_2COO^-Na^+$, so that they had the same concentration.
   a) Write a balanced chemical equation to show butanoic acid acting as a weak acid. [1 mark]
   b) Given that $K_a$ for butanoic acid is $1.5 \times 10^{-5}$ mol dm$^{-3}$, calculate the pH of the buffer solution. [3 marks]

## Old buffers are often resistant to change...

*So that's how buffers work. There's a pleasing simplicity and neatness about it that I find rather elegant. Like a fine wine with a nose of berry and undertones of... OK, I'll shut up now.*

# Isomerism

*'You say potato and I say potato' — that doesn't seem to work very well when its written down.*
*Anyway, isomerism is all about things that are the same but different...*

## Structural Isomers have Different Structural Arrangements of Atoms

**Structural isomers** have the same **molecular formula**, but their atoms are **arranged** in different ways.
The molecules below are all structural isomers of each other — they all have the **molecular formula** $C_4H_{10}O$:

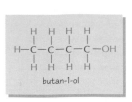
butan-1-ol

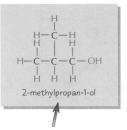
2-methylpropan-1-ol

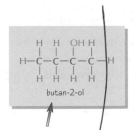
butan-2-ol

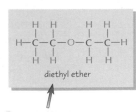
diethyl ether

Structural isomers can have...

...different arrangements of the carbon skeleton...

...different positions of the functional groups...

...or different functional groups.

## Stereoisomers are Arranged Differently in Space

**Stereoisomers** have the same molecular formula and their atoms are arranged in the same way.
The only difference is the **orientation** of the bonds in **space**.
There are two types of stereoisomerism — **E/Z isomerism** and **optical isomerism**.

## E/Z Isomerism Happens Because there's no Rotation about the Double Bond

E/Z isomerism **only** happens if —

- there's a C=C **double bond**, like in alkenes.  C–C single bonds can rotate, but C=C double bonds **can't**
  — so the groups attached to the carbons are fixed in position.

- two **different** groups are attached to **each** of the double bonded carbon atoms.

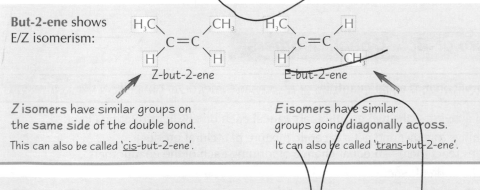

**But-2-ene** shows E/Z isomerism:

Z-but-2-ene

E-but-2-ene

*Z* isomers have similar groups on the **same side** of the double bond.
This can also be called '<u>cis</u>-but-2-ene'.

*E* isomers have similar groups going diagonally across.
It can also be called '<u>trans</u>-but-2-ene'.

\\\\| | | | | | | | | | | | | | | //
E stands for the German word
'entgegen' which means opposite
and Z stands for 'zusammen'
which means together.
If that doesn't help you remember
which is which, you can spot a
**Z**-isomer because they have the
groups on the **zame zide**.
//// | | | | | | | | | | | | | \\\

But **but-1-ene** doesn't:   identical groups

but-1-ene

\\\| | | | | | | | | | | | | | //
If there are two identical groups
attached to a double bonded carbon,
then there is no E/Z isomerism.
/// | | | | | | | | | | | | | \\\

E/Z isomerism is sometimes called **geometric** or **cis-trans isomerism** —
where '**cis**' is the **Z-isomer**, and '**trans**' is the **E-isomer**.

The trouble with the cis-trans naming system is that it doesn't work if there are 4 **different** groups involved.
The E/Z system keeps working though, because each group linked to the double-bonded carbons is given a **priority**.

If the two carbon atoms have their 'higher priority group' on **opposite** sides, then it's an **E isomer**.
If the two carbon atoms have their 'higher priority group' on the **same** side, then it's a **Z isomer**.

(Thankfully, you don't need to know how to work out the priority of the groups — this is just why the E/Z naming system was developed.)

# Isomerism

## *Optical Isomers* are *Mirror Images* of Each Other

**Optical isomerism** is another type of stereoisomerism.

A **chiral** (or **asymmetric**) carbon atom is one that has **four different groups** attached to it. It's possible to arrange the groups in two different ways around the carbon atom so that two different molecules are made — these molecules are called **enantiomers** or **optical isomers**.

The enantiomers are **mirror images** and no matter which way you turn them, they can't be **superimposed**.

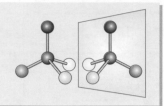

*If the molecules can be superimposed, they're achiral — and there's no optical isomerism.*

You have to be able to draw optical isomers. But first you have to identify the chiral centre...

**Example**

**Locating the chiral centre:**
Look for the carbon atom with four different groups attached. Here it's the carbon with the four groups H, OH, COOH and CH₃ attached.

2-hydroxypropanoic acid
chiral centre

**Drawing isomers:**
Once you know the chiral carbon, draw one enantiomer in a tetrahedral shape. Don't try to draw the full structure of each group — it gets confusing. Then draw a mirror image beside it.

optical isomers of 2-hydroxypropanoic acid

*A **solid wedge** means that a bond is coming out of the page **towards** you. A **dotted line** means that it's going into the page **away** from you.*

Optical isomers are **optically active** — they **rotate plane-polarised light**. One enantiomer rotates it in a **clockwise** direction, and the other rotates it in an **anticlockwise** direction.

*Normal light vibrates in all directions, but plane-polarised light only vibrates in one direction.*

## A *Racemate* is a *Mixture* of Both *Optical Isomers*

A **racemate** (or **racemic mixture**) contains **equal quantities** of each enantiomer of an optically active compound.

Racemates **don't** show any optical activity — the two enantiomers **cancel** each other's light-rotating effect.

Chemists often react two **achiral** things together and get a **racemic** mixture of a **chiral** product. This is because when two molecules react there's an **equal chance** of forming each of the enantiomers.

Look at the reaction between butane and chlorine:

Butane $+ Cl_2 \longrightarrow$ HCl + Enantiomer 1 or Enantiomer 2 → Enantiomer 1  Enantiomer 2

A **chlorine atom** replaces one of the H atoms, to give **2-chlorobutane**.
**Either** of the H atoms can be replaced, so the reaction produces a **mixture** of the **two possible enantiomers**.
Each hydrogen has a **fifty-fifty chance** of being replaced, so the two optical isomers are formed in **equal amounts**.

# Isomerism

## You Can Use **Optical Activity** to **Work Out** a Reaction **Mechanism**

Optical activity can give you some insight into how the **mechanism** of a reaction works.
For example, **nucleophilic substitution** (see page 14) can take place by one of two mechanisms.

### S$_N$1 mechanism

If it's an S$_N$1 mechanism and you start with a **single enantiomer** reactant,
the product will be a **racemic mixture** of **two optical isomers** of each other.

In step 1, a group breaks off, leaving a **planar** (flat) ion.
In step 2, the planar ion can be **attacked** by a nucleophile from **either side** — this results in two optical isomers.

### S$_N$2 mechanism

In an S$_N$2 mechanism, a **single enantiomer** reactant produces a **single enantiomer** product.

There's only **one step** in this mechanism — the nucleophile always attacks the **opposite side** to the leaving group, so only
**one product** is produced. During the reaction, the molecule is **inverted**, which causes the product to rotate polarised light
in the **opposite direction** from the reactant.

So if you know the **optical activity** of the **reactant** and **products**, you can sometimes work out the reaction **mechanism**.

## Practice Questions

Q1  Draw three isomers of butan–1–ol.
Q2  What feature must a molecule have for E/Z isomerism to occur?
Q3  What is meant by a chiral carbon atom?
Q4  What is a racemic mixture?

### Exam Questions

1   There are many possible structural isomers with the molecular formula C$_3$H$_6$O$_2$, four of which show stereoisomerism.

　　a)  Explain the meaning of the term *stereoisomerism*. [2 marks]
　　b)  Draw a pair of geometric isomers of C$_3$H$_6$O$_2$, with hydroxyl groups. Label them E and Z. [3 marks]
　　c)  i)  There are two chiral isomers of C$_3$H$_6$O$_2$. Draw the enantiomers of one of the chiral isomers. [2 marks]
　　　　ii)  What structural feature in the molecule gives rise to optical isomerism? [1 mark]
　　　　iii)  State how you could distinguish between the enantiomers. [2 marks]

2   The molecule 2-bromobutane displays optical isomerism.

　　a)  Draw the structure of 2-bromobutane, and mark the chiral centre of the molecule on the diagram. [2 marks]

　　A sample of a single, pure enantiomer of 2-bromobutane is dissolved in an
　　ethanol and water solvent and mixed with dilute sodium hydroxide solution.
　　This mixture is gently heated under reflux. The product of the reaction is a racemic mixture of butan-2-ol.

　　b)  Explain why the butan-2-ol solution produced will not rotate plane-polarised light. [2 marks]

　　c)  Has the substitution reaction proceeded via an S$_N$1 mechanism or an S$_N$2 mechanism?
　　　　Explain your answer. [2 marks]

## Time for some quiet reflection...

*This optical isomer stuff's not all bad — you get to draw pretty little pictures of molecules. If you're having difficulty
picturing them as 3D shapes, you could always make some models with matchsticks and clay. It's easier to see the mirror
image structure with a solid version in front of you. And if you become a famous artist, you can sell them for millions...*

# Aldehydes and Ketones

*The sun is shining outside, it's a glorious day. The birds are singing, flowers are in bloom. Alas, you have to stay in and learn about the properties and reactions of organic compounds... it's tough, but that's the life you've chosen, my friend.*

## Aldehydes and Ketones Contain a Carbonyl Group

Aldehydes and ketones are **carbonyl compounds** — they contain the **carbonyl** functional group, **C=O**.

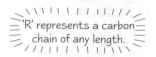
'R' represents a carbon chain of any length.

**Aldehydes** have their carbonyl group at the **end** of the carbon chain. Their names end in **–al**.

methanal    propanal

**Ketones** have their carbonyl group in the middle of the carbon chain. Their names end in **–one**, and often have a number to show which **carbon** the carbonyl group is on.

propanone    pentan-2-one

## Aldehydes and Ketones Don't Hydrogen Bond with Themselves...

Aldehydes and ketones **don't** have a **polar** $O^{\delta-}$–$H^{\delta+}$ **bond**, so they can't form **hydrogen bonds** with other aldehyde or ketone molecules.

This lack of hydrogen bonding means **solutions** of aldehydes and ketones have **lower boiling points** than their equivalent alcohols (which **can** form hydrogen bonds because they **do** have a polar O–H bond).

Propanone —
Boiling temperature 56 °C

Propanal —
Boiling Temperature 48 °C

Propan-1-ol —
Boiling Temperature 97 °C

## ...But Aldehydes and Ketones can Hydrogen Bond with Water

Although aldehydes and ketones don't have polar OH groups, they do have a **polar** $C^{\delta+}=O^{\delta-}$ **bond**.

This polarity means that the oxygen can use its lone pairs to form **hydrogen bonds** with $H^{\delta+}$ atoms on **water** molecules. So **small** aldehydes and ketones will **dissolve** in water.

Large aldehydes and ketones have **long** carbon chains. The intermolecular forces between these long chains are relatively large. So if an aldehyde or ketone is **large enough**, the intermolecular forces will be stronger than the hydrogen bonds that could form and the compound **won't dissolve**.

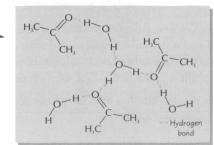

Look back at your AS notes if you're rusty on polar bonds, intermolecular forces or hydrogen bonding.

# Aldehydes and Ketones

Here's the first of the reactions you need to know for aldehydes and ketones. It's a good 'un.

## Hydrogen Cyanide will React with Carbonyls by Nucleophilic Addition

Hydrogen cyanide reacts with carbonyl compounds to produce **hydroxynitriles** (molecules with a CN and OH group). It's a **nucleophilic addition reaction** — a **nucleophile** attacks the molecule, and an extra group is **added** to it.

Hydrogen cyanide is a **weak acid** — it partially dissociates in water to form **H⁺** and **CN⁻** ions.  $HCN \rightleftharpoons H^+ + CN^-$

1) The CN⁻ ion **attacks** the slightly positive carbon atom and **donates** a pair of electrons to it. Both electrons from the double bond transfer to the oxygen.

2) H⁺ (from either hydrogen cyanide or water) bonds to the oxygen to form the **hydroxyl group** (OH).

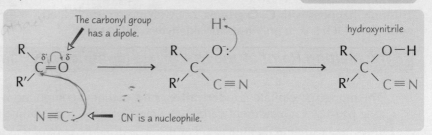

The carbonyl group has a dipole.

CN⁻ is a nucleophile.

hydroxynitrile

> **Hydrogen cyanide** is a **highly toxic** gas. When this reaction is done in the laboratory, a solution of **acidified potassium cyanide** is used instead, to reduce the risk. Even so, the reaction should be done in a **fume cupboard**.

Information about the optical activity of the **hydroxynitrile** can provide **evidence** for the reaction mechanism.

The carbonyl group in a ketone or aldehyde is **planar**. The nucleophile (CN⁻ ion) can attack it from **either side**.

When you react an aldehyde or asymmetric ketone with CN⁻, you get a **racemic mixture** of **two optical isomers**. This is exactly what you'd expect from the mechanism — the carbonyl group gets attacked equally from **each side**, producing **equal amounts** of the two products, which are optical isomers.

## Practice Questions

Q1  Why do aldehydes and ketones have lower boiling points than alcohols?
Q2  Why do small aldehydes and ketones dissolve in water like alcohols do?
Q3  Explain why a racemic mixture of two optical isomers is produced by reacting an aldehyde with hydrogen cyanide.

### Exam Questions

1  $C_3H_6O$ is the molecular formula of both an aldehyde and a ketone.
   a)  Draw the aldehyde and ketone isomers.                                                [2 marks]
   b)  Name the type of reaction that occurs when hydrogen cyanide reacts with carbonyl compounds.  [1 mark]
   c)  Draw the products obtained when hydrogen cyanide reacts with the aldehyde and the ketone with the formula $C_3H_6O$.   [2 marks]
   d)  Show the mechanism of the reaction between HCN and the aldehyde.                      [2 marks]
   e)  Which of the products in c) will be formed as a racemic mixture? Explain your answer. [3 marks]

2  The molecular formula $C_5H_{10}O$ can represent three isometric straight chain carbonyl compounds.
   a)  Draw the three isomers. Circle the isomer that will not produce a racemic mixture when it reacts with hydrogen cyanide.   [4 mark]
   b)  The carbonyl compound, hexanal, boils at around 120 °C. The isomer hexan–1–ol boils at 150 °C. Explain this relatively large difference.   [2 marks]

## Spot the difference...

*If you can't remember which is aldehyde and which is ketone, this might help — 'a' comes at one end of the alphabet, so CO is at the end of the molecule, 'k' is in the middle of the alphabet, so the CO is in the middle. Maybe you could make it into a poem or even better a song. Maybe try the chord sequence Am, Cm, Fm7, G#m, Bm. Just an idea.*

# More on Aldehydes and Ketones

*Knowing what an aldehyde and a ketone look like isn't going to help you tell them apart in the lab. Unless the bottle is labelled with a picture of them. But if it's not labelled, you are going to need to know these tests...*

## Brady's Reagent Tests for a Carbonyl Group

**Brady's reagent** is **2,4-dinitrophenylhydrazine** (2,4-DNPH) dissolved in methanol and concentrated sulfuric acid.

The **2,4-dinitrophenylhydrazine** forms a **bright orange precipitate** if a carbonyl group is present.

This only happens with **C=O groups**, not with more complicated ones like COOH, so it only tests for **aldehydes** and **ketones**.

*You have to be careful when handling Brady's reagent — it's harmful, flammable and can be explosive when dry, eek!*

### The Melting Point of the Precipitate Identifies the Carbonyl Compound

The orange precipitate is a **derivative** of the carbonyl compound which can be purified by **recrystallisation** (see p114). Each different carbonyl compound gives a crystalline derivative with a **different melting point**.

If you measure the melting point of the crystals and compare it to a table of **known** melting points of the possible derivatives, you can **identify** the carbonyl compound.

## There are a Few Ways of Testing for Aldehydes

These tests let you distinguish between an aldehyde and a ketone.
They all work on the idea that an **aldehyde** can be **easily oxidised** to a carboxylic acid, but a ketone can't.
As an aldehyde is oxidised, another compound is **reduced** — so a reagent is used that **changes colour** as it's reduced.

### Tollens' Reagent

Tollens' reagent is a **colourless** solution of **silver nitrate** dissolved in **aqueous ammonia**.
If it's heated in a test tube with an aldehyde, a **silver mirror** forms after a few minutes.

*You shouldn't heat the test tube directly over a flame — most organic compounds are flammable. Use a water bath or heating mantle instead.*

$$\underset{\text{colourless}}{Ag(NH_3)_2^+{}_{(aq)}} + e^- \longrightarrow \underset{\text{silver}}{Ag_{(s)}} + 2NH_{3(aq)}$$

### Fehling's solution or Benedict's solution

Fehling's solution is a **blue** solution of complexed **copper(II) ions** dissolved in **sodium hydroxide**.
If it's heated with an aldehyde the copper(II) ions are reduced to a **brick-red precipitate** of **copper(I) oxide**.

$$\underset{\text{blue}}{Cu^{2+}{}_{(aq)}} + e^- \longrightarrow \underset{\text{brick-red}}{Cu^+{}_{(s)}}$$

*(Don't forget — heat the test tube in a water bath or heating mantle.)*

Benedict's solution is exactly the same as Fehling's solution except the copper(II) ions are dissolved in **sodium carbonate** instead. You still get a **brick-red precipitate** of copper(I) oxide though.

## Aldehydes Oxidise to Carboxylic Acids — Ketones Don't

1) If you **heat** an **aldehyde** with **acidified dichromate(VI) ions** you get a carboxylic acid.

   The **dichromate(VI) ions** are the oxidising agent [O].
   Potassium dichromate(VI) with dilute sulfuric acid is often used.

   *(During this reaction you should see the solution change colour — from orange to green.)*

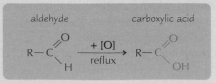

2) Ketones won't oxidise with acidified **dichromate(VI) ions**.
   It's not a strong enough oxidising agent.

# More on Aldehydes and Ketones

## You can **Reduce** Aldehydes and Ketones Back to **Alcohols**

Using a **reducing agent** [H] you can:

1) reduce an **aldehyde** to a **primary alcohol**.  2) reduce a **ketone** to a **secondary alcohol**.

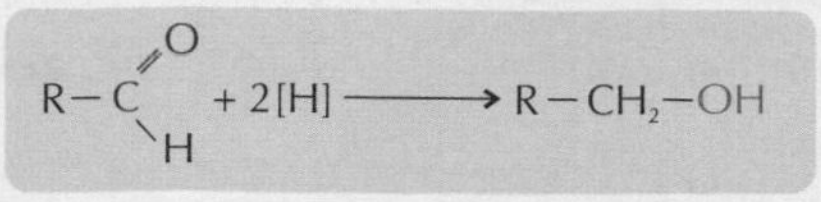

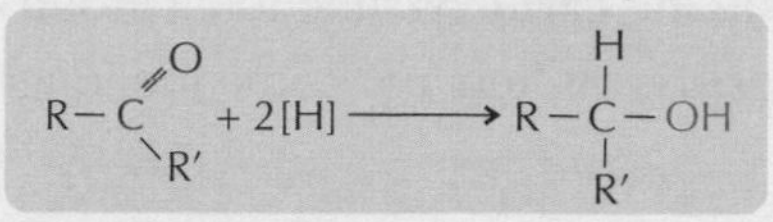

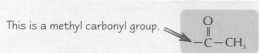

$$R-\underset{\underset{H}{|}}{\overset{\overset{O}{\|}}{C}} + 2[H] \longrightarrow R-CH_2-OH$$

$$R-\underset{\underset{R'}{|}}{\overset{\overset{O}{\|}}{C}} + 2[H] \longrightarrow R-\underset{\underset{R'}{|}}{\overset{\overset{H}{|}}{C}}-OH$$

*These are nucleophilic addition reactions — the reducing agent supplies an H⁻ that acts as a nucleophile and attacks the δ+carbon.*

For the **reducing agent,** you could use **LiAlH₄** (lithium tetrahydridoaluminate(III) or lithium aluminium hydride) in **dry diethyl ether** — it's a very powerful reducing agent, which reacts violently with water, bursting into flames. Eeek.

## Some Carbonyls will react with **Iodine**

Carbonyls that contain a **methyl carbonyl** group react when heated with **iodine** in the presence of an alkali. If there's a methyl carbonyl group you'll get a **yellow precipitate** of triiodomethane (CHI₃) and an antiseptic smell.

This is a methyl carbonyl group. → $-\overset{\overset{O}{\|}}{C}-CH_3$

*You can also use potassium iodide solution and sodium chlorate(I).*

If something contains a **methyl carbonyl** group, it must be:

Ethanal $H-\overset{\overset{O}{\|}}{C}-CH_3$  or  A **ketone** with **at least one** methyl group $R-\overset{\overset{O}{\|}}{C}-CH_3$

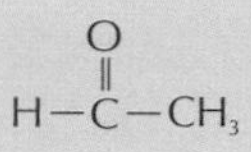

*Iodoform.*

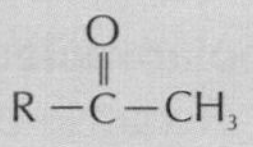

## Practice Questions

Q1 Describe the use of Brady's reagent.
Q2 Describe the use of Tollens' reagent.
Q3 How can an aldehyde be converted into a carboxylic acid?
Q4 How can an aldehyde be converted into an alcohol?

$Ag^+ + e^- \rightarrow Ag_{(s)}$

### Exam Questions

1  Compound A has the molecular formula C₃H₆O. It can be converted into an alcohol with the molecular formula C₃H₈O. When A is warmed with Fehling's solution a brick-red precipitate forms.
  a) Using the information given identify A and draw its structure. [2 marks]
  b) Draw the structure of the alcohol that can be made from A. [1 mark]
  c) Suggest suitable reagents and conditions for the reaction to convert A into an alcohol. [2 marks]
  d) What would you see if A was heated with iodine in alkaline solution? Explain your answer. [2 marks]

2  Substance Q gives an orange precipitate with Brady's reagent. It has no reaction when warmed with Tollens' reagent. It reacts with iodine to give a yellow precipitate. The molecular formula of Q is C₇H₁₄O.
  a) Use the information to draw a structure for Q. Explain how each piece of information is useful. [4 marks]
  b) Explain how the precipitate formed when Q reacts with Brady's reagent could be used to confirm your suggested structure. [2 marks]
  c) Draw the structure of the substance produced when Q reacts with LiAlH₄ in dry diethyl ether. [1 mark]

## It's all crystal clear — unless it's a precipitate or a silver mirror...

*I wonder what it's like to have a reagent named after you. Could be a great conversation starter at parties. 'So Professor Brady, what do you do?' — 'Well I make scientific reagents.' — '......' — 'My most famous one tests for carbonyl groups.' — '......' — 'It turns orange' — 'Oooo... orange is my favourite, both the colour and the fruit, which is much nicer than celery.'*

# Carboxylic Acids

*Carboxylic acids are more interesting than cardboard boxes — as you're about to discover...*

## Carboxylic Acids contain –COOH

> A <u>carb</u>oxyl group contains a <u>carb</u>onyl group and a hyd<u>roxyl</u> group.

1) **Carboxylic acids** contain the **carboxyl** functional group **–COOH**.

2) To name a carboxylic acid, you find and name the longest alkane chain, take off the 'e' and add **'–oic acid'**.

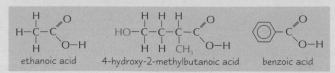

ethanoic acid     4-hydroxy-2-methylbutanoic acid     benzoic acid

3) The carboxyl group is always at the **end** of the molecule and when naming it's more important than any other functional groups — so all the other functional groups in the molecule are numbered starting from this carbon.

4) Carboxylic acids are **weak acids** — in water they partially dissociate into **carboxylate ions** and **H⁺ ions**.

> This equilibrium lies to the **left** because most of the molecules don't dissociate.

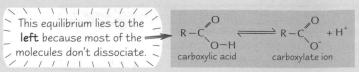

carboxylic acid     carboxylate ion

## Carboxylic Acids are Very Soluble

1) Carboxylic acids are **polar molecules**, since electrons are drawn towards the O atoms. Because of their polar nature, carboxylic acids have relatively **high boiling points**.

2) The polar bonds make small carboxylic acids **very soluble** in water, as they form **hydrogen bonds** with the water molecules — $H^{\delta+}$ and $O^{\delta-}$ atoms on different molecules are attracted to each other.

···· Hydrogen bond

3) The solubility **decreases** as the length of the chain **increases**. Longer chains have stronger intermolecular forces between them — if these intermolecular forces are stronger than the hydrogen bonds would be, the carboxylic acid won't dissolve.

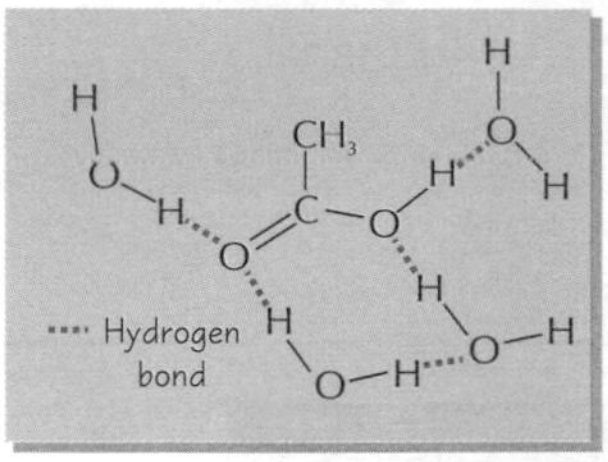

In pure, liquid carboxylic acids, **dimers** can also form. This is when a molecule hydrogen bonds with just **one** other molecule. This effectively **increases** the **size** of the molecule, **increasing** the intermolecular forces, and so the boiling point.

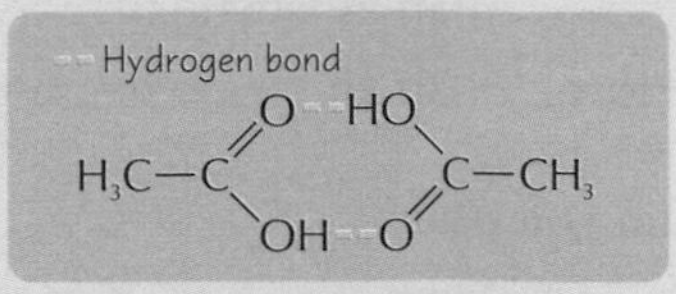

Hydrogen bond

## Carboxylic Acids Can Be Formed from Alcohols, Aldehydes and Nitriles

### Oxidation of primary alcohols and aldehydes

You can make a carboxylic acid by **oxidising** a **primary alcohol** to an **aldehyde**, and then to a carboxylic acid.

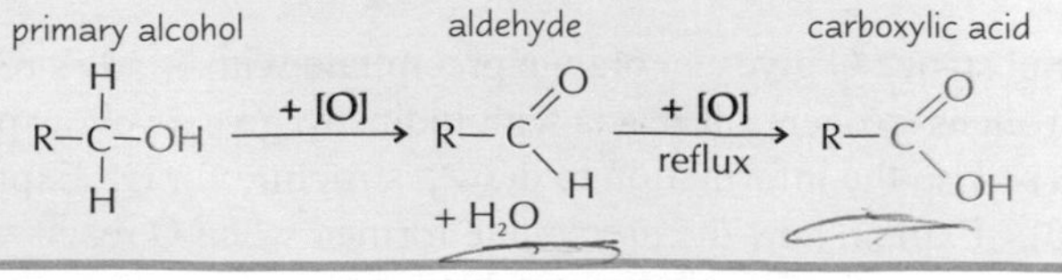

primary alcohol    aldehyde    carboxylic acid

### Hydrolysis of nitriles

Carboxylic acids can also be made by **hydrolysing** a **nitrile**. You reflux the nitrile with dilute hydrochloric acid, and then distil off the carboxylic acid.

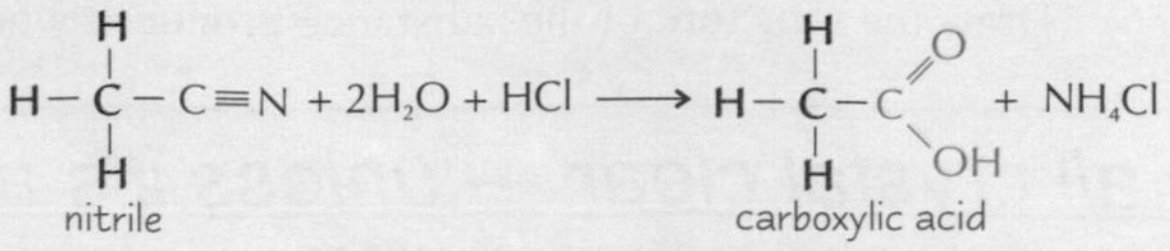

$$H-\overset{\displaystyle H}{\underset{\displaystyle H}{C}}-C\equiv N + 2H_2O + HCl \longrightarrow H-\overset{\displaystyle H}{\underset{\displaystyle H}{C}}-C\overset{O}{\underset{OH}{\diagup}} + NH_4Cl$$

nitrile     carboxylic acid

# Carboxylic Acids

## Carboxylic Acids React with **Alkalis** and **Carbonates** to Form **Salts**

1) Carboxylic acids are **neutralised** by **aqueous alkalis** to form **salts** and **water**.

ethanoic acid            sodium ethanoate

$$CH_3COOH + NaOH \rightarrow CH_3COONa + H_2O$$

*Salts of carboxylic acids are called carboxylates and their names end with –oate.*

2) Carboxylic acids react with **carbonates $CO_3^{2-}$** or **hydrogencarbonates $HCO_3^-$** to form a **salt**, **carbon dioxide** and **water**.

*In these reactions, carbon dioxide fizzes out of the solution.*

ethanoic acid            sodium ethanoate

$$2CH_3COOH_{(aq)} + Na_2CO_{3(s)} \rightarrow 2CH_3COONa_{(aq)} + H_2O_{(l)} + CO_{2(g)}$$

$$CH_3COOH_{(aq)} + NaHCO_{3(s)} \rightarrow CH_3COONa_{(aq)} + H_2O_{(l)} + CO_{2(g)}$$

## Other Reactions You'll Need to Know

It's quite **hard** to reduce a carboxylic acid, so you have to use a **powerful reducing agent** like <u>LiAlH$_4$</u> in **dry diethyl ether**. It reduces the carboxylic acid right down to an alcohol in one go — you can't get the reduction to stop at the aldehyde.

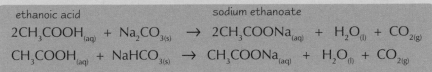

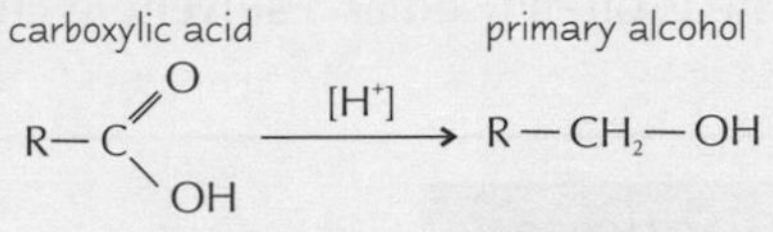

carboxylic acid         primary alcohol

$$R-C{\overset{O}{\underset{OH}{}}} \xrightarrow{[H^+]} R-CH_2-OH$$

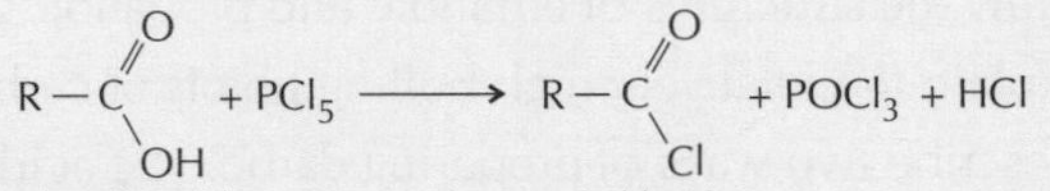

*Acyl chlorides are covered on page 59.*

Mix a carboxylic acid with **phosphorus(V) chloride** and you'll get an **acyl chloride**.

$$R-C{\overset{O}{\underset{OH}{}}} + PCl_5 \longrightarrow R-C{\overset{O}{\underset{Cl}{}}} + POCl_3 + HCl$$

carboxylic acid         acyl chloride

## Carboxylic Acid **Concentration** can be **Estimated** Using **Titration**

Citric acid is found in fruit juices. It has not one, not two, but **three** –COOH groups. Crazy. You can use the reaction between carboxylic acids and alkalis above to find out **how much citric acid** there is in a fruit juice.

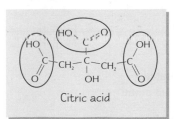

Citric acid

1) A measured amount of the fruit juice is placed in a flask and the indicator **phenolphthalein** is added — this turns **pink** in **alkaline** conditions. If the fruit juice is too dark to see the indicator change colour you can dilute it with a known amount of water first.

2) **Sodium hydroxide** solution with a known concentration is **added slowly** from a burette.

3) The –COOH groups are neutralised by the NaOH. The **end point** is when the indicator has turned pink for at least 30 seconds. Citric acid is a **weak acid** so the reaction is relatively slow.

Once you know how much NaOH is needed to neutralise the carboxylic acid you can work out the concentration of the citric acid in the fruit juice. Here's an example:

**Example**: 12.5 ml of 0.1 mol dm$^{-3}$ sodium hydroxide exactly neutralises 25 ml of orange juice. What is the concentration of citric acid in the juice?

*Look at pages 43 and 78 for more titration fun.*

1) The equation for this reaction is...

$$3NaOH + C_6H_8O_7 \rightarrow Na_3C_6H_5O_7 + 3H_2O$$

*Don't forget to convert ml to dm$^3$*

2) The 12.5 ml of sodium hydroxide contains $(12.5 \div 1000) \times 0.1 = 0.00125$ moles

3) From the equation 3 moles of NaOH neutralise 1 mole of citric acid so the 25 ml of juice must contain $0.00125 \div 3$ moles $= 0.000417$ moles

4) So the concentration of acid in the juice is $(1000 \div 25) \times 0.000417 = 0.017$ mol dm$^{-3}$

# Carboxylic Acids

## Alcohols React with Carboxylic Acids to form Esters

1) If you heat a **carboxylic acid** with an **alcohol** in the presence of an **acid catalyst**, you get an ester. The reaction is imaginatively called **esterification**.

2) For example, to make **ethyl ethanoate** you reflux ethanoic acid with ethanol and concentrated sulfuric acid as the catalyst:

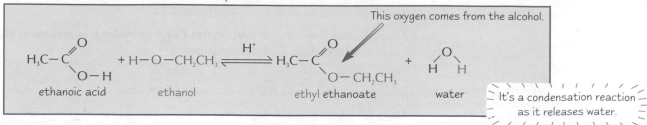

This oxygen comes from the alcohol.

ethanoic acid        ethanol        ethyl ethanoate        water

It's a condensation reaction as it releases water.

3) The reaction is **reversible**, so you need to separate out the product **as it's formed**. You do this by **distillation**, collecting the liquid that comes off just **below** 80 °C.

4) The product is then mixed with **sodium carbonate** solution to react with any **acid** that might have snuck in. The **ethyl ethanoate** forms a layer on the **top** of the aqueous layer and can be easily separated using a separating funnel.

5) Ethyl ethanoate is often used as a **solvent** in chromatography and as a **pineapple flavouring**.

## Practice Questions

Q1  Draw the structures of ethanoic and propanoic acids.

Q2  Explain the relatively high boiling points of carboxylic acids.

Q3  Describe two ways of preparing carboxylic acids.

Q4  How can you make an acyl chloride from a carboxylic acid?

### Exam Questions

1  Propanol and propanoic acid both contain three carbon atoms.
   a)  Explain why propanoic acid behaves as an acid, but propanol does not.  [2 marks]
   b)  Describe a simple test tube reaction to distinguish between propanol and propanoic acid.
       Give the reagent(s) and state the observations expected.  [3 marks]
   c)  A student refluxes propanol with propanoic acid and a little concentrated sulfuric acid.
       i) Write an equation for the reaction, showing the structures clearly.  [2 marks]
       ii) Name the organic product formed.  [1 mark]

2  25 ml of mango juice was mixed with 75 ml of deionised water. 25 ml of this mixture was titrated
   with 0.5 mol dm$^{-3}$ sodium hydroxide solution. 17.5 ml of the alkali was needed to reach the end point.
   The equation for the reaction is as follows:

   $$3NaOH + C_6H_8O_7 \rightarrow Na_3C_6H_5O_7 + 3H_2O$$

   a)  Suggest why the juice was mixed with water.  [1 mark]
   b)  Calculate the concentration of citric acid in the original juice (assume citric acid is the only acid present).  [5 marks]

3  Tartaric acid is found in unripe grapes.
   a)  The systematic name of tartaric acid is 2,3-dihydroxybutanedioic acid. Draw its structure.  [1 mark]
   b)  Draw the structure of the compound formed if tartaric acid is completely reduced.
       Suggest a reducing agent for the reaction.  [3 marks]
   c)  Potassium bitartrate crystals form in wine casks after fermentation.
       Suggest a reagent to make potassium bitartrate from tartaric acid in the laboratory.  [1 mark]

## Alright, so maybe cardboard boxes do have the edge after all...

*So many reactions — it's enough to make your head swim. When you think about it though, the reactions with bases and carbonates are just the same as they would be for any old acid. And learning the last section about how to make an ester will really put you ahead of the curve for the next page. Guess what it's about... no, go on, guess...*

# Esters

*OK, well I've kind of spoilt the surprise now, but anyway here are esters... ta da!*

## Esters have the Functional Group –COO–

So esters are made by reacting an **alcohol** with a **carboxylic acid**, as you saw on the last page. The **name** of an **ester** is made up of **two parts** — the **first** bit comes from the **alcohol**, and the **second** bit from the **carboxylic acid**.

1) Look at the **alkyl group** that came from the **alcohol**. This is the first bit of the ester's name.

This is an **ethyl** group.

2) Now look at the part that came from the **carboxylic acid**. Swap its '-oic acid' ending for '-oate' to get the second bit of the name.

This came from ethanoic acid, so it is an **ethanoate**.

3) Put the two parts together.

It's **ethyl ethanoate** $CH_3COOCH_2CH_3$

The name's written the opposite way round from the formula.

This goes for molecules with benzene rings too — react methanol with benzoic acid, and you get methyl benzoate, $C_6H_5COOCH_3$.

If either of the carbon chains is **branched** you need to name the attached groups too.

For an ester, number the carbons starting from the C atoms in the C–O–C bond.

1-methylpropyl methanoate $HCOOCH(CH_3)CH_2CH_3$

ethyl 2-methylbutanoate $CH_3CH_2CH(CH_3)COOCH_2CH_3$

## Esters are Hydrolysed to Form Alcohols

As it's a reversible reaction, you need to use lots of water to push the equilibrium over to the right.

### Acid Hydrolysis

**Acid hydrolysis** splits the ester into an **acid** and an **alcohol** — it's just the **reverse** of the condensation reaction on the previous page. You have to **reflux** the ester with a **dilute acid**, such as hydrochloric or sulfuric. For example:

ethyl ethanoate + $H_2O$ $\xrightarrow{H^+ \text{ reflux}}$ ethanoic acid + ethanol

### Base Hydrolysis

This time you have to **reflux** the ester with a **dilute alkali**, such as sodium hydroxide. You get a carboxylate ion and an alcohol. For example:

ethyl ethanoate + $OH^-$ $\xrightleftharpoons{reflux}$ ethanoate + ethanol

## Base Hydrolysis of Esters is Used to Make Soaps

1) **Vegetable oils and animal fats** are actually **triesters** (or 'triglycerides').
2) They're made from the esterification of **glycerol** (propane-1,2,3-triol) with **fatty acids** (long chain carboxylic acids). Each OH group on the glycerol is replaced with a fatty acid joined by an ester bond.
3) As with other esters, you can **hydrolyse** fats and oils by heating them with NaOH. The sodium salt that you get is a **soap**:

fat + 3NaOH → glycerol + 3 $CH_3(CH_2)_{16}COO^-Na^+$ sodium salt (soap)

4) So if you want to make a soap, **heat** a fat or oil with a **concentrated** solution of **NaOH**, and allow it to **cool**. Then add some saturated NaCl solution and the soap will **separate** out as a crust on the **surface** of the liquid. Amazing.

# Esters

## Esters React With **Alcohols** to Make **New Esters**

You can react an **ester** with an **alcohol** to get a **new ester** in a process called **transesterification**. It allows you to **swap** a different alcohol for the alcohol part of the ester.

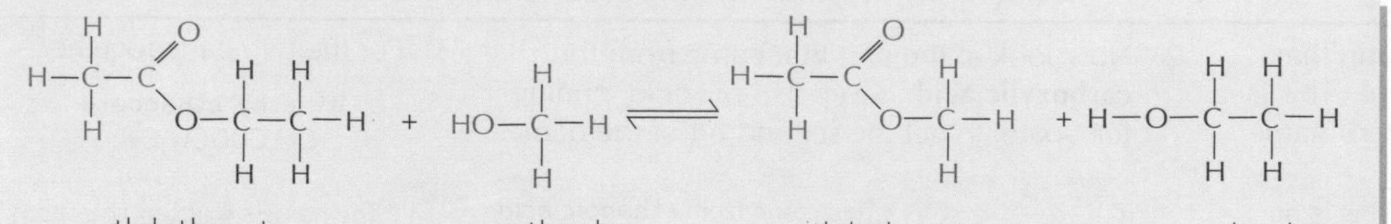

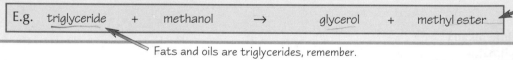

ethyl ethanoate          methanol          methyl ethanoate          ethanol

Ester's reaction with alcohol often led to the making of new Esters.

This reaction comes in handy for a couple of things:

### Making low fat spreads to replace butter

1) **Saturated** fats have **no double bonds** in their fatty acid chains. **Unsaturated** fats have at least one **double bond.**

2) **Saturated** fats have **higher melting temperatures** — their molecules are straighter which lets them to pack closer together, giving greater **intermolecular** forces.

3) Low fat spreads used to be made by **hydrogenation** — in this process, **unsaturated vegetable oil** is reacted with **hydrogen** to **remove** its double bonds. This increases the melting point and produces a **solid fat** that spreads easily like butter.

4) The problem with this method is that it also produces **trans** isomers of the fatty acids — these trans isomers have been linked with various **diseases**.

5) So now, manufacturers are using **transesterification** to convert the vegetable oils (which are triesters, remember) into **different** esters with higher melting temperatures — this avoids the hydrogenation process that produces the nasty trans isomers.

> Remember — **fatty acids** are long chain carboxylic acids, **fats and oils** are esters of fatty acids and glycerol.

### Making biodiesel from vegetable oils

1) Biodiesel is a renewable fuel for diesel engines made from **vegetable oils** or **animal fats**. It's gaining popularity as an alternative to crude-oil based diesel.

2) It's also made by a **transesterification** reaction — oils or fats are reacted with **methanol** or **ethanol** to produce methyl or ethyl esters.

E.g.  triglyceride  +  methanol  →  glycerol  +  methyl ester

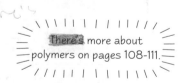

Biodiesel is a mixture of methyl and ethyl esters.

Fats and oils are triglycerides, remember.

## Reactions Between **Dicarboxylic Acids** and **Diols** Make **Polyesters**

**Carboxyl** groups react with **hydroxyl** groups to form **ester links**.

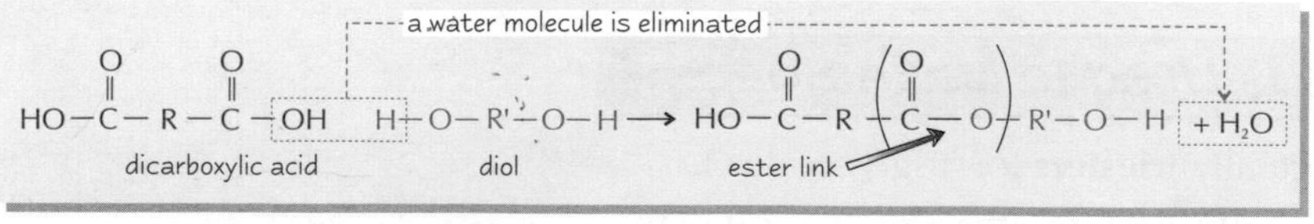

a water molecule is eliminated

$$HO-\overset{O}{\underset{}{C}}-R-\overset{O}{\underset{}{C}}-OH \quad H-O-R'-O-H \longrightarrow HO-\overset{O}{\underset{}{C}}-R-\left(\overset{O}{\underset{}{C}}-O\right)-R'-O-H \quad + H_2O$$

dicarboxylic acid          diol          ester link

> There's more about polymers on pages 108-111.

Example **Terylene™ (PET)** — formed from **benzene-1,4-dicarboxylic acid** and **ethane-1,2-diol.**

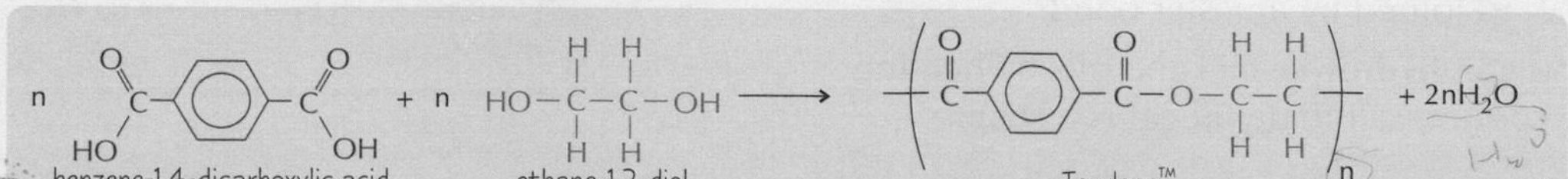

benzene-1,4-dicarboxylic acid          ethane-1,2-diol          Terylene™          $+ 2nH_2O$

Polyester fibres are **strong**, **flexible** and **abrasion-resistant**.

Terylene™ is used in **clothes** to keep them crease-free and make them last longer. Polyesters are also used in **carpets**.

You can treat polyesters (by stretching and heat-treating them) to make them stronger. Treated terylene™ is used to make fizzy drink bottles and food containers.

# Acyl Chlorides

And what better way to end the section than with acyl chlorides... other than ice cream.

## Acyl Chlorides have the Functional Group –COCl

Acyl (or acid) chlorides have the functional group **COCl** — their general formula is $C_nH_{2n-1}OCl$.
All their names end in '**–oyl chloride**'.

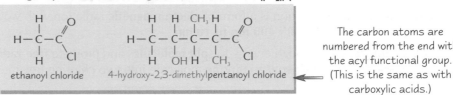

ethanoyl chloride    4-hydroxy-2,3-dimethylpentanoyl chloride

The carbon atoms are numbered from the end with the acyl functional group. (This is the same as with carboxylic acids.)

## Acyl Chlorides Easily Lose Their Chlorine

Acyl chlorides react with...

This irreversible reaction is a much easier, faster way to produce an ester than esterification.

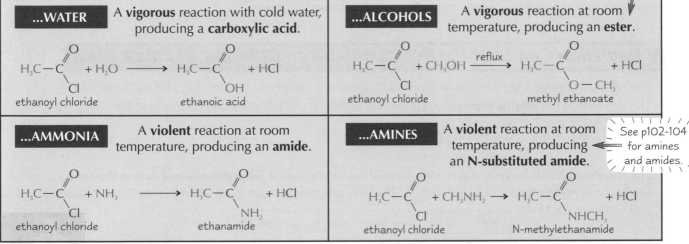

| **...WATER** A **vigorous** reaction with cold water, producing a **carboxylic acid**. | **...ALCOHOLS** A **vigorous** reaction at room temperature, producing an **ester**. |
|---|---|
| $H_3C-C$ $\begin{smallmatrix}O\\Cl\end{smallmatrix}$ + $H_2O$ ⟶ $H_3C-C$ $\begin{smallmatrix}O\\OH\end{smallmatrix}$ + HCl<br>ethanoyl chloride    ethanoic acid | $H_3C-C$ $\begin{smallmatrix}O\\Cl\end{smallmatrix}$ + $CH_3OH$ ─reflux→ $H_3C-C$ $\begin{smallmatrix}O\\O-CH_3\end{smallmatrix}$ + HCl<br>ethanoyl chloride    methyl ethanoate |
| **...AMMONIA** A **violent** reaction at room temperature, producing an **amide**. | **...AMINES** A **violent** reaction at room temperature, producing an **N-substituted amide**. |
| $H_3C-C$ $\begin{smallmatrix}O\\Cl\end{smallmatrix}$ + $NH_3$ ⟶ $H_3C-C$ $\begin{smallmatrix}O\\NH_2\end{smallmatrix}$ + HCl<br>ethanoyl chloride    ethanamide | $H_3C-C$ $\begin{smallmatrix}O\\Cl\end{smallmatrix}$ + $CH_3NH_2$ → $H_3C-C$ $\begin{smallmatrix}O\\NHCH_3\end{smallmatrix}$ + HCl<br>ethanoyl chloride    N-methylethanamide |

See p102-104 for amines and amides.

Each time, **Cl** is **substituted** by an oxygen or nitrogen group and **hydrogen chloride** fumes are given off.

## Practice Questions

Q1  Draw the structure of 2-methylpropyl ethanoate.
Q2  Describe how to make a soap from olive oil.
Q3  What is meant by transesterification?
Q4  Name the products formed when methyl ethanoate undergoes acid hydrolysis.

### Exam Questions

1  Compound C, shown on the right, is found in raspberries.
   a)  Name compound C.                                                              [1 mark]
   b)  Draw and name the structures of the products formed
       when compound C is refluxed with dilute sulfuric acid.
       What kind of reaction is this?                                               [5 marks]
   c)  If compound C is refluxed with excess sodium hydroxide, a similar reaction occurs.
       Give a difference between the products of this reaction and the reaction described in b).   [1 mark]

2  Waste vegetable oil can be converted into biodiesel.
   a)  Name the process used for the conversion.                                    [1 mark]
   b)  Explain how the process works.                                               [2 marks]
   c)  What is the advantage of biodiesel over ordinary diesel?                     [2 marks]

## Transesterification lets your car run on chip oil — a good excuse for chips...

*Transesterification is like a returns policy on your ester. If you don't like one you've got you can react it with an alcohol and get a new one. But this approach doesn't work for everything. If you don't like your neighbour's cat you can't give it vodka-laced cat food and hope they will get a new one. Instead you just get angry neighbours and a court order...*

# UV and Microwave Radiation

*You're gonna like this: straightforward, simple, a smattering of amusing graphics... What more could you ask for? That was a rhetorical question by the way. There's no need to start a list.*

## Ultraviolet Radiation Can Initiate Reactions

1) Ultraviolet (UV) radiation is a form of **electromagnetic** radiation with wavelengths between those of visible light and X-rays — that's **400 nm to 10 nm**.

2) UV radiation has enough energy to **split molecules** and produce **free radicals**.
   For example, you can split a chlorine molecule into two chlorine free radicals using UV radiation:

$$Cl{-}Cl \xrightarrow{UV} Cl\bullet \ + \ Cl\bullet$$

   Each chlorine atom takes **one electron** from the covalent bond. This is called **homolytic fission**.
   A chlorine free radical is exactly the same as a chlorine atom and is **very reactive**.

3) The production of free radicals is an important **first step** in many reactions — particularly the substitution reactions that can take place between **halogens** and **alkanes** (or **arenes**).

## UV Radiation Can Start the Reaction Between Chlorine and Methane

1) **Sunlight** has enough UV radiation in it to initiate a reaction between chlorine, $Cl_2$, and methane, $CH_4$.

2) The production of **chlorine radicals** by UV light is known as the **initiation step** in this reaction.

$$Cl_2 \xrightarrow{UV} 2Cl\bullet$$

3) The chlorine radicals go on to react with the methane in a series of **propagation steps**, where they get used up and **re-created** in a chain reaction. The new free radicals can react with more methane molecules and continue the **cycle**.

$$CH_4 \ + \ Cl\bullet \ \rightarrow \ CH_3\bullet \ + \ HCl$$
$$CH_3\bullet \ + \ Cl_2 \ \rightarrow \ CH_3Cl \ + \ Cl\bullet$$

4) These two reactions continue very rapidly until two free radicals **combine** in a **termination step**:

$$Cl\bullet \ + \ Cl\bullet \ \rightarrow \ Cl_2$$
$$Cl\bullet \ + \ CH_3\bullet \ \rightarrow \ CH_3Cl$$
$$CH_3\bullet \ + \ CH_3\bullet \ \rightarrow \ C_2H_6$$

*All three of these termination steps are very exothermic.*

Brian was something of a free radical when it came to dressing for the office.

## UV Radiation Can Create Chlorine Free Radicals from CFCs

You also get this type of reaction at the **outer edge** of the atmosphere.
UV from sunlight reacts with chlorine molecules and **CFCs** to produce chlorine free radicals.

*This is the initiation step.* 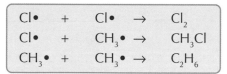 E.g. $\quad CF_3Cl \xrightarrow{UV} CF_3 \ + \ Cl\bullet$

The **ozone** ($O_3$) layer that protects the Earth's surface, and us, from harmful UV radiation is **broken down** by the chlorine free radicals:

$$Cl\bullet \ + \ O_3 \ \rightarrow \ O_2 \ + \ ClO\bullet$$
$$ClO\bullet \ + \ O_3 \ \rightarrow \ Cl\bullet \ + \ 2O_2$$

*These are the propagation steps.*

**One** chlorine free radical causes the destruction of **two** ozone molecules, and makes another chlorine radical, which continues the process. This cycle of reactions is repeated **many times** before the chlorine free radical is removed from the system when it combines with another free radical. One chlorine free radical can end up **destroying thousands of ozone molecules**.

# UV and Microwave Radiation

## Microwaves Are Used for Heating Things

Microwaves are a form of **electromagnetic** radiation with a longer wavelength than infrared radiation — between **1 mm and 1 m**. They are widely used in communications, but also for **heating** stuff up.

In a **microwave oven**, the microwaves used have a **wavelength** of **12.24 cm**.
To understand how one of these ovens works, you need to know about **polar molecules**.

1) In a covalent bond between two atoms of **different** electronegativities, the bonding electrons are **pulled towards** the more **electronegative** atom. This makes the bond **polar**.
   (If you need a reminder on electronegativity and polar molecules, have a look back at your AS notes.)

2) In a water molecule, the **oxygen** atom is **more electronegative** than the hydrogens. It pulls the bonding electrons from both O–H bonds towards it, making itself slightly negative, and both hydrogens slightly positive. This makes water a **polar** molecule.

3) The **fats and sugars** found in foods are also polar, but they're **less polar** than water.

In a microwave oven, microwaves are **passed through** food. The microwave radiation creates an **electric field**, and any polar molecules in the food try to **line up** with the field by **rotating**. This makes them **collide** with other molecules, generating **heat energy**.

The **speed** of heating depends on the **thickness** and **density** of the food. Microwaves will penetrate foods to a depth of several centimetres depending on their **water content**. The surface is often **dryer** than the inside so doesn't heat up so quickly. **Frozen** water molecules can't move so easily, so they also heat up slower.

The heating effect of microwaves is used in lots of other applications too:

1) **Surgeons** can use narrow beams of microwaves to **kill cancer cells**.

2) In the **chemical industry**, microwaves can be used to heat reactants **directly** without having to **waste energy** on heating the container the chemicals are in.

3) Microwave heating is used to **dry wood**, **paper** and **textiles**. — it's a more efficient method of heating than conventional ovens.

Liam didn't care how 'safe' his microwave was — he wasn't taking any chances.

## Practice Questions

Q1 How can UV radiation initiate a reaction?

Q2 Explain how chlorine in the upper atmosphere leads to the destruction of ozone.

Q3 What types of molecules are affected by microwaves?

Q4 Why does liquid water heat up more quickly than ice?

### Exam Questions

1 Microwaves can be used to cook food and to heat chemicals in industrial processes. Which one of the following types of chemical cannot be heated using microwaves?

   A Carboxylic acids      B Esters      C Alkanes      D Ketones                    [1 mark]

2 Explain how water is heated when microwaves are passed through it.                 [3 marks]

3 A mixture of dry chlorine and hydrogen gases will explode if exposed to sunlight.

   a) Which part of the sunlight is responsible for causing the reaction?            [1 mark]

   b) Explain what the sunlight does to the chlorine molecules.                       [2 marks]

   c) The product of the reaction is HCl.
      Write equations for the initiation, propagation and termination steps of this reaction.   [6 marks]

## Note: Microwaving the cat is NOT an acceptable use of radiation...

*Neither is microwaving your little sister — I got into big trouble for that one. That's just a joke, promise. Well, this is all rather nice isn't it? A neat little story about UV radiation and the chlorine radical, and a chunk on the science behind TV dinners. Unfortunately the ozone layer gets systematically destroyed and no-one lives happily ever after. But you can't have it all, eh?*

# Mass Spectrometry

*Ah mass spectrometry. You gotta love it. No seriously — it was abandoned at birth and raised by wolves. Had to chew its own leg off to survive. Terribly sad.*

## Mass Spectrometry can be used to Find Out Relative Molecular Mass ($M_r$)

Electrons in the spectrometer **bombard** the sample molecules and **break electrons off**, forming ions. A **mass spectrum** is produced, showing the **relative amounts** of ions with different mass-to-charge ratios.

The molecular ion $M^+_{(g)}$ gives the peak in the spectrum with the **second highest mass-to-charge ratio** — so it's the last peak but one on the spectrum. This peak's called the **M peak**. The mass/charge (m/e) value of the M peak is the **molecular mass** of the molecule.

The little peak to the right of the M peak is called the M+1 peak — it's due to carbon isotope, $^{13}C$. But luckily you don't have to know about it.

The mass spectrum for ethanol ($CH_3CH_2OH$) is shown below. Ethanol has the molecular ion $CH_3CH_2OH^+$, and a molecular mass of 46.

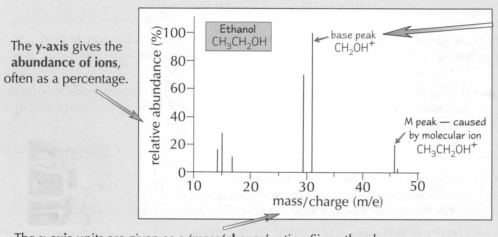

The **y-axis** gives the **abundance of ions**, often as a percentage.

base peak
$CH_2OH^+$

M peak — caused by molecular ion
$CH_3CH_2OH^+$

The highest peak is called the **base peak**, and its **relative abundance** is set at **100%**.

It's due to a particularly **stable fragment** ion, such as **carbocations** and **acylium** ($RCO^+$) ions. All the other peak heights are given as percentages of it.

The **x-axis** units are given as a '**mass/charge**' ratio. Since the charge on ions is mostly **+1**, you can assume the x-axis simply shows the **mass**.

## The Molecular Ion can be Broken into Smaller Fragments

The bombarding electrons make some of the molecular ions break up into **fragments**. These all show up on the mass spectrum, making a **fragmentation pattern**. Fragmentation patterns are actually pretty cool because you can use them to identify **molecules** and even their **structure**.

For propane, the molecular ion is $CH_3CH_2CH_3^+$, and the fragments it breaks into include $CH_3^+$ ($M_r = 15$) and $CH_3CH_2^+$ ($M_r = 29$).

Only the **ions** show up on the mass spectrum — the **free radicals** are 'lost'.

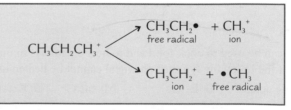

These are some common fragments to look out for:

| Fragment | Molecular Mass ($M_r$) |
|----------|------------------------|
| $CH_3$ | 15 |
| $C_2H_5$ | 29 |
| $C_3H_7$ | 43 |
| OH | 17 |
| CHO | 29 |
| COOH | 45 |

Fragment (consider revising)

Mr Clippy's grammar advice also applies to chemistry.

# Mass Spectrometry

## Mass Spectrometry can be used to Identify a Molecule

Here's an example of how to use a mass spectrum to work out what molecule you're dealing with:

Use this mass spectrum to work out the structure of the molecule:

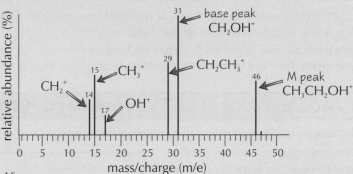

The $M_r$ of this molecule is 46.

To work out the structural formula, you've got to **guess** what **ions** could have made the other peaks from their **m/e values**. The m/e value of a peak matches the **mass** of the ion that made it (assuming it's got a 1+ charge).

For instance, this molecule's got a peak at 15 m/e, so it's likely to have a $CH_3$ **group**. It's also got a peak at 17 m/e, so it's likely to have an **OH group**. Other ions are matched to the peaks on the spectrum above.

Once you think you know what the structure is, draw it out, and work out its **molecular mass**. It should be the same as the m/z value of the M peak.

Make sure you can find a fragment in the molecule that could make **every** peak in the spectrum.

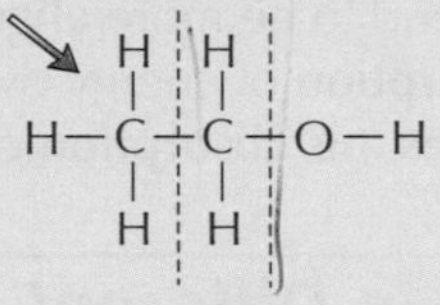

ethanol's molecular formula

## Practice Questions

Q1 Where on a mass spectrum is the peak corresponding to the molecular ion?

Q2 On a mass spectrum, what is the 'base peak'?

Q3 What are fragment ions?

Q4 What fragment ion of an alkane molecule would correspond to a peak of m/e ratio 57?

**Exam Questions**

1   The mass spectrum of propanal ($C_2H_5CHO$) has a base peak of 29.   What is the mass of its molecular ion?

   A  59       B  29       C  43       D  58                                                                [1 mark]

2   The mass spectrum of a carboxylic acid is shown on the right.
    Use the spectrum to answer this question.

   a)   What is the molecular mass of this acid?              [1 mark]

   b)   Suggest the formulae of the fragment ions that are
        responsible for the peaks labelled A, B and C.         [3 marks]

   c)   Use your answers from parts (a) and (b) to draw
        the structure of the acid, and give its name.          [2 marks]

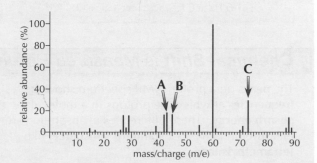

## Mass spectrometry — weight watching for molecules

*So mass spectrometry's a bit like weighing yourself, then taking bits off your body, weighing them separately, then trying to work out how they all fit together.  Luckily you won't get anything as complicated as a body, and you won't need to cut yourself up either.  Good news all round.  Now all you've got left to do is learn it.  Those exam questions'll help.*

# NMR Spectroscopy

*NMR isn't the easiest of things, so ingest this information one piece at a time — a bit like eating a bar of chocolate...*

## NMR *Gives You Information About a Molecule's* Structure

Any atomic nucleus with an **odd** number of nucleons (protons and neutrons) has a **nuclear spin**. This causes it to have a weak **magnetic field** — a bit like a bar magnet.

Nuclear magnetic resonance (NMR) spectroscopy looks at how this tiny magnetic field reacts when you put it in a much larger external magnetic field.

**Hydrogen** nuclei are **single protons**, which means that they do have a spin. So you can use **proton NMR** (or **¹H NMR**) to find out **how many hydrogens** there are in an organic molecule and how they're **arranged**.

## Protons *Align in Two Directions in an* External Magnetic Field

1) Normally, **protons** (**hydrogen nuclei**) are spinning in **random directions** — so their magnetic fields **cancel out**.

2) But when a strong **external** magnetic field is applied, the protons **align** themselves either **with** the direction of the field, or **against** the field (**opposing** it).

3) The **aligned protons** are at a **lower** energy level than the opposing protons. If they **absorb radio waves** of the right frequency, they can **flip** to the **higher** energy level. The **opposing protons** can **emit** radio waves and **flip** to the **lower energy** level.

4) There tend to be more **aligned** protons, so there's an **absorption** of energy overall. NMR spectroscopy **measures** this **absorption** of energy.

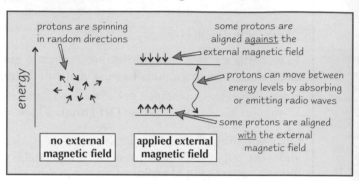

protons are spinning in random directions

some protons are aligned against the external magnetic field

protons can move between energy levels by absorbing or emitting radio waves

some protons are aligned with the external magnetic field

**no external magnetic field**    **applied external magnetic field**

## Protons in *Different Environments Absorb* Different Amounts of Energy

1) Protons are partly **shielded** from the effects of external magnetic fields by **surrounding electrons**.

2) Any **other atoms** and **groups of atoms** that are near a nucleus will also affect its amount of electron shielding.
   *E.g. If a carbon atom bonds to a more electronegative atom (like oxygen) the amount of electron shielding around its nucleus will decrease.*

3) How the protons in a molecule interact with magnetic fields depends on their **environments**. They will absorb **different amounts** of energy at **different frequencies** — and it's these **differences in absorption** between environments that you're looking for in **NMR spectroscopy**.

4) An atom's **environment** depends on **all** the groups it's connected to, going **right along the molecule** — not just the atoms it's actually bonded to. To be in the **same environment**, two atoms must be joined to **exactly the same things**.

**2-chloropropane** has **2** hydrogen environments:
• **1 H** in a CHCl group, bonded to (CH₃)₂
• **6 Hs** in CH₃ groups, bonded to CHCl(CH₃)

**1-chlorobutane** has **4** hydrogen environments.
(The H atoms in the three CH₂ groups are **different distances** from the **electronegative** Cl atom — so their **environments** are **different**.)

## Chemical Shift *is Measured Relative to* Tetramethylsilane

The **peaks** on a proton NMR spectrum show the **frequencies** at which the protons in a molecule **absorb energy**. These differences in absorption are **measured** relative to a **standard substance**, like **tetramethylsilane**.

Tetramethylsilane, or **TMS**, has the formula **Si(CH₃)₄**. It has 12 protons in **identical environments**, so it gives a **single peak** that's well away from most peaks produced by protons in other molecules.

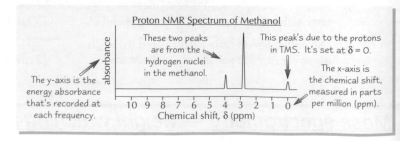

Proton NMR Spectrum of Methanol

These two peaks are from the hydrogen nuclei in the methanol.

This peak's due to the protons in TMS. It's set at δ = 0.

The y-axis is the energy absorbance that's recorded at each frequency.

The x-axis is the chemical shift, measured in parts per million (ppm).

Chemical shift, δ (ppm)

The difference in absorption of a proton relative to TMS is called its **chemical shift** (δ). The TMS peak is given a chemical shift value of 0. Spectra often have a peak at δ = 0 because some TMS is added to the test sample for **calibration** purposes.

# NMR Spectroscopy

## Proton NMR Tells you About a Molecule's **Hydrogen Environments**

**Each peak** on a proton NMR spectrum is due to one or more protons in a **particular proton environment**.
The **relative area** under each peak tells you how many protons are in that environment.

**Example:** The proton NMR spectrum of ethanoic acid, $CH_3COOH$

1) The spectrum has **two peaks** — so there are **two environments**.

2) The area ratio is **1:3** — so there must be 1 H in the environment at $\delta = 10.5$ ppm to every 3 Hs in the environment at $\delta = 2.2$ ppm.

3) This fits the structure of ethanoic acid.

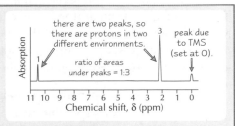

there are two peaks, so there are protons in two different environments.

ratio of areas under peaks = 1:3

peak due to TMS (set at 0).

peak at $\delta$=2.2

peak at $\delta$=10.5

## Use a **Table** to Identify the **Proton** Causing the **Chemical Shift**

You can use a table like this one to **identify** which functional group is causing each peak:

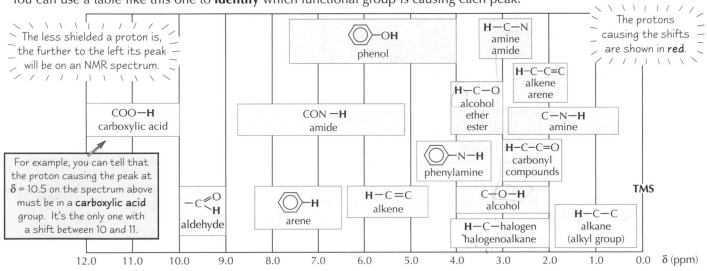

The less shielded a proton is, the further to the left its peak will be on an NMR spectrum.

The protons causing the shifts are shown in **red**.

For example, you can tell that the proton causing the peak at $\delta = 10.5$ on the spectrum above must be in a **carboxylic acid** group. It's the only one with a shift between 10 and 11.

Don't worry — **you don't need to learn it**. You'll be given one in your exam.

(Your exam copy might look a little different, and have slightly different values — they depend on the solvent, temperature and concentration.)

## Practice Questions

Q1 Which part of the electromagnetic spectrum is absorbed by hydrogen nuclei in proton NMR spectroscopy?

Q2 How many proton environments are there in a molecule of butanone, $CH_3COCH_2CH_3$?

Q3 Why is tetramethylsilane used as a standard substance in proton NMR?

**Exam Questions**

1 A chemist has samples of two chemicals labelled A and B. She analyses them using proton NMR spectroscopy.

a) Substance A is propanoic acid. How many peaks will there be on the NMR spectrum of substance A? [1 mark]

b) The NMR spectrum of substance B has a peak at $\delta = 9.6$. What does this tell you about substance B? [1 mark]

2 The low resolution proton NMR spectrum of a primary alcohol is shown on the right.

a) Give the approximate $\delta$ values of the peaks produced by each of the three proton environments in the molecule. [1 mark]

b) Suggest a possible structure for the alcohol, and explain your suggestion with reference to the NMR spectrum. Use the table of chemical shifts shown above, if necessary. [4 marks]

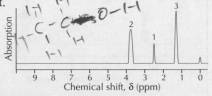

## Why did the proton flip?  Because it saw the radio wave...

*Now I don't want you to panic, but there's more NMR coming up on the next page. I'm not trying to make you cry here, I'm just flagging up a potential issue — if you haven't got your head around this lot, then turning over is only going to make things worse. So make sure that you're fully fluent in proton environments and chemical shifts before proceeding...*

# More About NMR

*Oooh, this NMR malarkey hasn't half got me in a spin...*

## Spin-Spin Coupling Splits the Peaks in an NMR Spectrum

In high resolution proton NMR spectra, the peaks are often **split** into **smaller peaks**. This is down to the **magnetic fields** of **neighbouring protons** interacting with each other — and it's called **spin-spin coupling**. Only protons that are on **adjacent** carbon atoms will affect each other.

These **multiple peaks** are called **multiplets**. They always split into the number of neighbouring protons plus one — it's called the **n+1 rule**. For example, if there are **2 protons** on the next-door carbon, the peak will be split into 2 + 1 = 3.

> You can work out the **number** of **neighbouring protons** by looking at how many the peak splits into:
> If a peak's split into **two** (a **doublet**) then there's **one** neighbouring single proton.
> If a peak's split into **three** (a **triplet**) then there are **two** neighbouring single protons.
> If a peak's split into **four** (a **quartet**) then there are **three** neighbouring single protons.

For example, here's the high resolution proton NMR spectrum for **1,1,2-trichloroethane**:

The peak due to the green protons is split into **two** because there's **one proton** on the adjacent carbon atom.

The peak due to the red proton is split into **three** because there are **two protons** on the adjacent carbon atom.

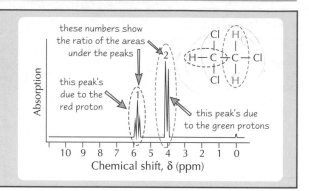

When the peaks are split, it's not as easy to see the ratio of the **areas**, so an **integration trace** is often shown. The **height increases** at each peak are proportional to the areas under the peaks.

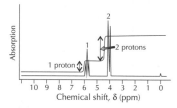

## An NMR Spectrum Gives You a Lot of Information

A proton NMR spectrum can tell you about:

1) The **different proton environments** in the molecule (from the **chemical shifts**).
2) The **relative number** of **protons** in each environment (from the **relative peak area**).
3) The **number of protons adjacent** to a particular proton (from the **splitting pattern**).

Using all this information you can predict **possible structures**, and sometimes the actual structure.

**EXAMPLE**

This is the proton NMR spectrum for a carbonyl compound. You can use it to predict the compounds structure.

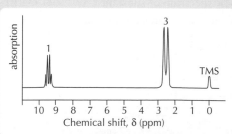

1) There are only **two sets of peaks**, so there can only be **two proton environments** in the compound.
2) The peaks at $\delta \approx 9.5$ **ppm** is likely to be due to an **R–CHO** group. So, the compound must be an aldehyde.
3) The peaks at $\delta \approx 2.5$ **ppm** can also be from a carbonyl compound. It has an area of 3 so, the group must be **R–COCH$_3$**.
4) The quartet's got **three** neighbouring protons, and the doublet's got **one** — so it's likely these two groups are next to each other.

Now you know the molecule's got to contain... and ...all you need to do is fit them together. So the compound is ethanal.

# More About NMR

## Magnetic Resonance Can See Inside You

In hospitals **MRI scanners** are used to study the **internal structures** of the body.
MRI stands for **Magnetic Resonance Imagery** and it uses the same principle as NMR spectroscopy — the word nuclear puts people off a bit, so it's been dropped from the name.

Basically, when you have an MRI scan, you're put inside a very **large magnet** and **irradiated** with radio waves. The **hydrogen nuclei** in the water molecules in your body **interact** with the radio waves.

**Different frequencies** of wave are absorbed depending on what sort of tissue the water molecules are in. This allows an image of the body to be built up **without** the **potential damage** caused by X-rays.

By moving the beam of radio waves, a **series of images** are produced which can be added together by a computer to build up a **3-D** picture.

The technique is used in cancer treatment, bone and joint treatment, and studies of the brain and cardiovascular systems.

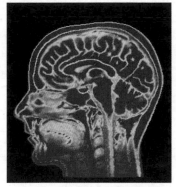

This is an MRI scan of a human head — it's been coloured to make it look nice.

## NMR Has Other Important Uses Too

In the **pharmaceutical industry** NMR is used to monitor the products to make sure they are **pure**. The NMR spectrum is like the **fingerprint** of a molecule, so if there were impurities in the product they would be **easy to spot** on the spectrum.

It's obviously pretty important that pharmaceuticals are pure — you wouldn't want to take a drug that had been **contaminated** with anything nasty.

## Practice Questions

Q1 What causes peaks to split in high resolution proton NMR?

Q2 What causes a quartet of peaks?

Q3 What three pieces of information can a proton NMR spectrum give you?

Q4 Give an advantage of MRI scanning over X-ray scanning.

### Exam Questions

1   The proton NMR spectrum shown on the right is that of a chloroalkane.
    Use the table of chemical shifts on page 65 to answer the following:

    a)  Predict the environment of the two protons with a shift of 3.6 ppm.   [1 mark]

    b)  Predict the environment of the three protons with a shift of 1.3 ppm.   [1 mark]

    c)  Suggest a possible structure for the chloroalkane molecule.   [1 mark]

    d)  Explain the splitting of the two peaks.   [2 marks]

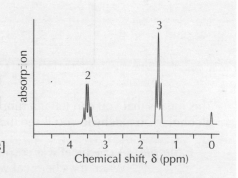

2   The proton NMR spectrum of compound Z is shown on the right.
    Z is an isomer of $C_3H_8O$.

    a)  Draw the displayed formulae of the three possible isomers of $C_3H_8O$.   [3 marks]

    b)  Suggest which of the three isomers is compound Z. Explain your reasoning with reference to the NMR spectrum.   [3 marks]

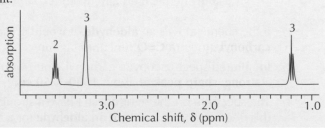

## Never mind splitting peaks — this stuff's likely to cause splitting headaches...

*Is your head spinning yet? I know mine is. Round and round like a merry-go-round. It's a hard life when you're tied to a desk trying to get NMR spectroscopy firmly fixed in your head. You must be looking quite peaky by now... so go on, learn this stuff, take the dog around the block, then come back and see if you can still remember it all.*

# Infrared Spectroscopy

*Eeek... more spectroscopy. Infrared (IR to its friends) radiation has less energy than visible light, and a longer wavelength.*

## Infrared Spectroscopy Lets You Identify Organic Molecules

Infrared spectroscopy produces **scary** looking graphs. Just learn the basics and you'll be fine.

1) In infrared (IR) spectroscopy, a beam of **IR radiation** goes through the sample.

2) The IR energy is absorbed by the **bonds** in the molecules, increasing their **vibrational** energy.

3) **Different bonds** absorb **different wavelengths**. Bonds in different **places** in a molecule absorb different wavelengths too — so the O–H group in an **alcohol** and the O–H in a **carboxylic acid** absorb different wavelengths.

4) This is a simplified table of the **frequencies** different groups absorb — the one in your data sheet shows a lot more detail. You don't need to learn it but you do need to understand how to use it.

\ \ \ \ | | / / /
~ This tells you what ⁓
⁓ the trough on the ⁓
⁓ graph will look like. ⁓
/ / | | | \ \ \

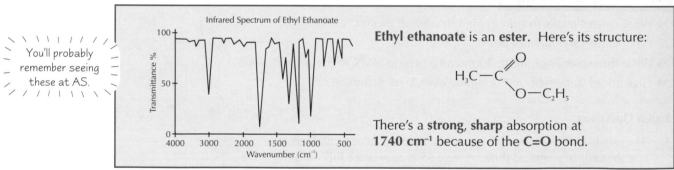

| Functional group | Where it's found | Frequency/ Wavenumber (cm⁻¹) | Type of absorption |
|---|---|---|---|
| C–H | most organic molecules | 2800 – 3100 | strong, sharp |
| O–H | alcohols | 3200 – 3550 | strong, broad |
| O–H | carboxylic acids | 2500 – 3300 | medium, broad |
| N–H | amines (e.g. methylamine, $CH_3NH_2$) | 3200 – 3500 | strong, sharp |
| C=O | aldehydes, ketones, carboxylic acids | 1680 – 1750 | strong, sharp |
| C–O | esters and carboxylic acids | 1100 – 1310 | strong, sharp |
| C–X | haloalkanes | 500 – 1000 | strong, sharp |

⁓ \ \ \ | | / / ⁓
⁓ O–H groups tend to have ⁓
⁓ broad absorptions — ⁓
⁓ it's because they take ⁓
⁓ part in hydrogen bonding. ⁓
/ / / | | \ \ \

The infrared spectrometer produces a **graph** that shows you what **wavelengths** of radiation the molecule is **absorbing**.

Infrared Spectrum of Ethyl Ethanoate

\ \ \ \ | / / / ⁓
⁓ You'll probably ⁓
⁓ remember seeing ⁓
⁓ these at AS. ⁓
/ / | | | \ \

**Ethyl ethanoate** is an **ester**. Here's its structure:

$$H_3C-C \overset{O}{\underset{O-C_2H_5}{}}$$

There's a **strong**, **sharp** absorption at **1740 cm⁻¹** because of the **C=O** bond.

This means that you can tell if a functional group has **changed** during a reaction. For example, if you **oxidise** an **alcohol** to an **aldehyde** you'll see the O–H absorption **disappear** from the spectrum, and a C=O absorption **appear**.

**Example:** A chemical was suspected to be a pure sample of an unknown aldehyde. When the chemical was tested using infrared spectroscopy, the spectrum below was obtained. Is the chemical an aldehyde? Explain your answer.

1) If the chemical was an **aldehyde**, it would contain a **carbonyl** group (a **C=O** functional group).

2) In infrared spectroscopy, a carbonyl group would show a **strong, sharp peak** at about **1680-1750 cm⁻¹**.

3) The spectrum on the right doesn't have a strong peak at this frequency, and so is **not** an **aldehyde** (or a ketone or a carboxylic acid).

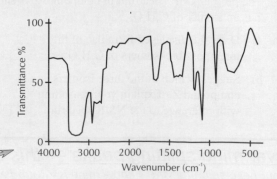

⁓ Actually, this is the infrared spectrum of ethanol. ⁓
⁓ / | | \ \ \ \ |

# Infrared Spectroscopy

## Infrared Spectroscopy Has Several Commercial Uses

1) One important use of infrared spectroscopy is in the **chemical industry**, where a reaction can be followed so that the point where one functional group **changes to another** can be measured.

   E.g. in the oxidation of a **secondary alcohol** to a **ketone**, the point at which all the **OH groups** in the alcohol have gone can be seen as well as the point when the first **C=O groups** in the ketone appear.

2) The degree of **polymerisation** that has occurred in polymer manufacture can also be measured with IR spectroscopy.

   Modern instruments can take readings up to **32 times a second**. The machine is set up so that you just record the **absorption** at the frequency of the **double bond** in the monomer. You can watch the number of double bonds change as the polymerisation takes place.

3) Polymers can be **attacked by oxygen** during the processes used to make them into useful objects. This is **invisible to the eye** but can be identified using IR spectroscopy. Absorption at about **1700cm⁻¹** is seen corresponding to a **carbonyl group** where the polymer has been oxidised. This is the first step in the formation of **cracks** in the polymer.

## Practice Questions

Q1 Which parts of a molecule absorb IR radiation?

Q2 What do the troughs on the spectrum correspond to?

Q3 Why do the troughs corresponding to OH groups appear very broad?

Q4 Explain the usefulness of IR spectroscopy in following industrial reactions.

### Exam Questions

1 The infrared spectrum of molecule X is shown on the right.
   Using the table of absorption values on page 68, which of the following compounds is molecule X most likely to be?

   A   Methane

   B   Methanol

   C   Ethene

   D   Methanoic acid                                          [1 mark]

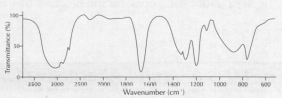

2 A molecule with a molecular mass of 74 gives the following IR spectrum. Use the table on p68 to answer the following:

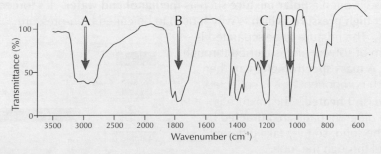

   a)   Which functional groups produce the troughs labelled A–D?                    [4 marks]

   b)   Suggest a molecular formula and name for this molecule. Explain your suggestion.    [3 marks]

## Ooooh — I'm picking up some good vibrations...

*OK. So you need to know: a) how IR spectroscopy works, b) how to interpret an IR spectrum, c) what practical and commercial uses IR spectroscopy can be put to, and d) what to do in case aliens from a far flung galaxy get bored of their home planet and bring their spaceships to take over Earth. Don't think I'm joking about that last bit. I've seen Dr Who.*

# Chromatography

*I love a bit of chromatography. Honestly, it's fascinating — all that mobile phase, stationary phase stuff. Brilliant. Had you going for a moment there, didn't I?*

## Chromatography is Good for **Separating** and **Identifying** Things

Chromatography is used to **separate** stuff in a mixture — once it's separated out, you can often **identify** the components.

There are quite a few different types of chromatography — but the ones you need to know about are **gas chromatography** (GC) and HPLC (which stands for high-pressure or performance liquid chromatography). They both have two phases:

1) A **mobile phase** — where the molecules can move. This is always a liquid or a gas.
2) A **stationary phase** — where the molecules can't move. This must be a solid, or a liquid held in a solid.

The components in the mixture separate out as the mobile phase moves through the stationary phase.

## Gas Chromatography is very **High-Tech**

In **gas chromatography** (GC) the stationary phase is a **viscous liquid**, such as an oil, which coats the inside of a long tube.

The tube's **coiled** to save space, and built into an **oven**. The mobile phase is an **unreactive carrier gas** such as nitrogen.

The **sample** gets **injected** into the carrier gas stream as either **a gas or a liquid**. If it is a liquid, the inlet is heated to **vaporise** it.

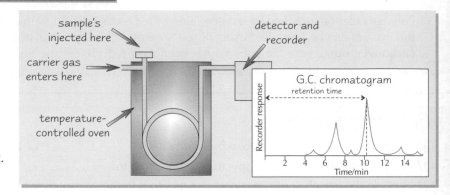

The amount that each component in the sample **adsorbs** to the stationary phase is **different**. This means each component takes a different amount of time from being **injected** into the tube to being **recorded** at the other end. This is the **retention time** — it's what's used to **identify** the component.

At the end of the tube is a **detector** — the most common sort measures the thermal conductivity of gases leaving the tube. The detector is connected to a **recorder** which gives a **peak** on a graph that shows the retention time.

The **area** under each peak (or the height if they're very sharp peaks) tells you the relative **amount** of each component.

## HPLC is a **Useful Alternative** to GC

1) In **high-performance liquid chromatography** (HPLC) the stationary phase is small particles of a **solid** packed into a tube. This is often **silica** bonded to various **hydrocarbons**.

2) The **liquid** mobile phase is often a **polar mixture** such as **methanol and water**. It's forced through the tube under **high pressure**, which is why it used to be called high-pressure liquid chromatography. The mixture to be separated is injected into the stream of solvent and is carried through the tube as a **solution**. A **mass spectrometer** can then be used to analyse each component as it is collected.

3) Unlike in GC, the tube **isn't heated**. The mixture is separated because the different parts are **attracted** by **different amounts** to the solid, so they take different lengths of time to travel through the tube.

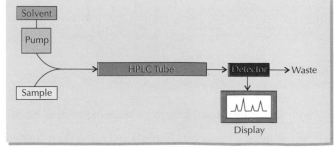

Claire was going through a bit of a stationery phase.

4) The **retention time** is measured using a detector that shines **UV light** through the stream of liquid leaving the tube. The UV is **absorbed** by the parts of the mixture as they come through. A graph is produced in the same way as in GC.

5) HPLC can be used where GC can't, for example when the sample is **heat sensitive** or has a **high boiling point**.

# Chromatography

## Both **GC** and **HPLC** Can be Used to **Check Purity** of Samples

### Gas Chromatography

GC is used in the **chemical industry** to routinely check the **purity** of products in a **continuous process**.

A small amount of the product is **diverted** by valves into a GC apparatus at regular intervals. The **chromatogram** produced will show the presence, or lack of, impurities. The likely impurities — **unused reactants** for example — can be looked for **automatically** by computer controlled detectors. These can be linked to valves that **shut down** the process if the level of impurities is too high.

### High-Performance Liquid Chromatography

A very important use of HPLC is in checking that **equipment** used in drug manufacture is **clean**. Very **strict levels** of impurities and residues are permitted, and HPLC can be used to check whether these have been exceeded as it is a very **sensitive** method of analysis.

## Practice Questions

Q1 Explain what is meant by 'mobile phase' and 'stationary phase'.

Q2 What is meant by 'retention time'?

Q3 How can you tell the relative amounts of substance from the peaks produced on the chromatogram?

Q4 In what situations is HPLC preferable to GC?

### Exam Questions

1 Which one of the following applies to gas chromatography, but not high-performance liquid chromatography?

    A   The sample passes through a tube containing the stationary phase.

    B   A detector at the end of the tube is used to measure retention time.

    C   The stationary phase is a liquid.

    D   The components in the sample separate out as the mobile phase moves through the stationary phase.   [1 mark]

2 Gas chromatography is not suitable for use when

    A   the sample is a gas.

    B   the sample is heat sensitive.

    C   the sample contains alcohol.

    D   the results of the analysis are needed quickly.   [1 mark]

3 HPLC chromatography is a useful technique for separating mixtures.

    a)   Describe the key features of HPLC apparatus.   [3 marks]

    b)   Explain how the resulting chromatogram may be used to identify the components of the mixture
         and the relative amount of each component.   [4 marks]

## GC, HPLC, YMCA — 3 acronyms for a happy and fulfilling life...

*Finished? Great stuff. Next time you want to identify what's in your milkshake, you'll know what to do. Just flicking through reading the 'funny' bits at the bottom? You'll have to do some work sooner or later. Make sure you know the differences between GC and HPLC, 'cause it'll be dead handy in the exam. Make sure you know the moves to YMCA too — it's a life skill.*

# Redox Reactions

*Redox — it's the snappy abbreviation for reactions involving reduction and oxidation.*

## If Electrons are Transferred, it's a **Redox Reaction**

1) A **loss** of electrons is called **oxidation**. A **gain** of electrons is called **reduction**.
2) Reduction and oxidation happen **simultaneously** — hence the term "**redox**" reaction.
3) An **oxidising agent accepts** electrons and gets **reduced**.
4) A **reducing agent donates** electrons and gets **oxidised**.

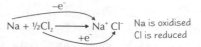

$$Na + \tfrac{1}{2}Cl_2 \xrightarrow{\phantom{xx}-e^-\phantom{xx}} Na^+ Cl^-$$
$$\underset{+e^-}{\phantom{xxxxxx}}$$

Na is oxidised
Cl is reduced

I couldn't find a red ox, so you'll have to make do with a multicoloured donkey instead.

## Sometimes it's Easier to Talk About **Oxidation Numbers** ◄ (They're also called oxidation <u>states</u>.

There are lots of rules. Take a deep breath...

1) All atoms are treated as **ions** for this, even if they're covalently bonded.

2) Uncombined **elements** have an oxidation number of **0**.

3) Elements just bonded to **identical atoms**, like $O_2$ and $H_2$, also have an oxidation number of **0**.

4) The oxidation number of a simple **monatomic ion**, e.g. $Na^+$, is the same as its **charge**.

5) In **compounds** or **compound ions**, the **overall oxidation number** is just the ion charge.

$SO_4^{2-}$ — **overall oxidation number = –2**,
 oxidation number of **O = –2** (total = –8), ◄
 so oxidation number of **S = +6**

> Within an ion, the most electronegative element has a negative oxidation number (equal to its ionic charge). Other elements have more positive oxidation numbers.

6) The sum of the oxidation numbers for a **neutral compound** is 0.

$Fe_2O_3$ — **overall oxidation number = 0**, oxidation number of **O = –2**
(total = –6), so oxidation number of **Fe = +3**

7) Combined **oxygen** is nearly always –2, except in peroxides, $H_2O_2$ where it's –1, and in the fluorides $OF_2$, where it's +2, and $O_2F_2$, where it's +1 (and $O_2$, where it's 0).

In $H_2O$, oxidation number of **O = –2**, but in $H_2O_2$, oxidation number of **H** has to be **+1** (an H atom can only lose one electron), so oxidation number of **O = –1**

8) Combined **hydrogen** is +1, except in metal hydrides where it is –1 (and $H_2$ where it's 0).

In **HF**, oxidation number of **H = +1**, but in **NaH**, oxidation number of **H = –1**

## **Roman Numerals** Give Oxidation Numbers

Sometimes, oxidation numbers aren't clear from the formula of a compound.
If you see **Roman numerals** in a chemical name, it's an **oxidation number**.
E.g. copper has oxidation number **+2** in **copper(II) sulfate**, and manganese has
oxidation number **+7** in a **manganate(VII) ion** ($MnO_4^-$).

## Oxidation States go **Up** or **Down** as Electrons are **Lost** or **Gained**

1) The oxidation state for an atom will **increase by 1** for each **electron lost**.
2) The oxidation state will **decrease by 1** for each **electron gained**.
3) An element can also be **oxidised and reduced** at the same time — this is called **disproportionation**.

Oxidation No.     0    0       +1   –1

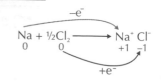

$$Na + \tfrac{1}{2}Cl_2 \xrightarrow{\phantom{xx}-e^-\phantom{xx}} Na^+ Cl^-$$
$$\underset{+e^-}{\phantom{xxxxxx}}$$

# Redox Reactions

## You can Separate Redox Reactions into Half-Equations

1) **Ionic half-equations** show oxidation or reduction.

2) An oxidation half-equation can be **combined** with a reduction half-equation to make a **full equation**.

3) The number of electrons lost and gained in the reaction must **balance**. This means that changes in **oxidation number** must also balance.

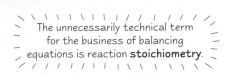
The unnecessarily technical term for the business of balancing equations is reaction **stoichiometry**.

**Example:** **Zinc metal** displaces **silver ions** from silver nitrate solution to form **zinc nitrate** and a deposit of **silver metal**.

The **zinc atoms** each lose 2 electrons (oxidation). Their oxidation number **increases** from 0 to +2.
$$Zn_{(s)} \rightarrow Zn^{2+}_{(aq)} + 2e^-$$

The **silver ions** each gain 1 electron (reduction). Their oxidation number **decreases** from +1 to 0.
$$Ag^+_{(aq)} + e^- \rightarrow Ag_{(s)}$$

**Two silver ions** are needed to accept the **two electrons** released by each zinc atom. So you need to double the silver half-equation before the two half-equations can be combined: $\quad 2Ag^+_{(aq)} + 2e^- \rightarrow 2Ag_{(s)}$

Now the number of electrons lost and gained **balance**, so the half-equations can be combined: $\quad Zn_{(s)} + 2Ag^+_{(aq)} \rightarrow Zn^{2+}_{(aq)} + 2Ag_{(s)}$

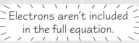
Electrons aren't included in the full equation.

## Practice Questions

Q1  What is the oxidation number of sulfur in the $S_2O_3^{2-}$ ion?

Q2  What is the oxidation number of manganese in $KMnO_4$?

Q3  State the 8 rules for oxidation numbers.  Yes, all of 8 of them please.

Q4  When zinc metal reacts with $Fe^{3+}$ ions, a mixture of iron metal and $Zn^{2+}$ ions are formed. Write a balanced equation for this reaction.

**Exam Questions**

1  Chlorine reacts with sodium hydroxide solution to give a mixture of sodium chloride (NaCl), sodium hypochlorite (NaClO) and water.  The balanced equation for the reaction is:
$$2NaOH + Cl_2 \rightarrow NaCl + NaClO + H_2O$$
What are the oxidation numbers for chlorine in the two sodium compounds formed during the reaction?

|   | NaCl | NaClO |
|---|------|-------|
| A | +1   | −1    |
| B | +2   | −2    |
| C | −1   | +1    |
| D | −2   | +2    |

[1 mark]

2  Acidified manganate(VII) ions will react with aqueous iodide ions to form iodine. The two half-equations for the changes that occur are:
$$MnO_4^-{}_{(aq)} + 8H^+_{(aq)} + 5e^- \rightarrow Mn^{2+}_{(aq)} + 4H_2O_{(l)} \qquad and \qquad 2I^-_{(aq)} \rightarrow I_{2(aq)} + 2e^-$$

a)  Write a balanced equation to show the reaction taking place.  [2 marks]

b)  Use oxidation numbers to explain the redox processes which have occurred.  [4 marks]

c)  Suggest why a fairly reactive metal such as zinc will not react with aqueous iodide ions in a similar manner to manganate(VII) ions.  [2 marks]

## They tried to make me study redox — I said no, no, no...

*Now some of this may seem vaguely familiar to you from AS.  If so, great stuff — you're ahead of the game.  If not, never fear, everything you need to know about redox is right here on this very page.  All those rules might seem daunting, but believe me once you've learnt 'em they'll make life a whole lot easier.  So I'd suggest you get cracking...*

# Electrode Potentials

*There's electrons toing and froing in redox reactions. And when electrons move, you get electricity.*

## Electrochemical Cells Make Electricity

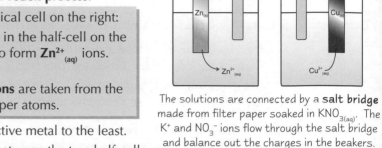

wire — the external circuit    voltmeter

salt bridge

$Zn_{(s)}$    $Cu_{(s)}$

$Zn^{2+}_{(aq)}$    $Cu^{2+}_{(aq)}$

Electrochemical cells can be made from **two different metals** dipped in salt solutions of their **own ions** and connected by a wire (the **external circuit**).

There are always **two** reactions within an electrochemical cell — one's an oxidation and one's a reduction — so it's a **redox process**.

Here's what happens in the **zinc/copper** electrochemical cell on the right:

1) Zinc **loses electrons** more easily than copper. So in the half-cell on the left, zinc (from the zinc electrode) is **OXIDISED** to form $Zn^{2+}_{(aq)}$ ions. This releases electrons into the external circuit.

2) In the other half-cell, the **same number of electrons** are taken from the external circuit, **REDUCING** the $Cu^{2+}$ ions to copper atoms.

So **electrons** flow through the wire from the most reactive metal to the least.

A voltmeter in the external circuit shows the **voltage** between the two half-cells. This is the **cell potential** or **emf**, $E_{cell}$.

The solutions are connected by a **salt bridge** made from filter paper soaked in $KNO_{3(aq)}$. The $K^+$ and $NO_3^-$ ions flow through the salt bridge and balance out the charges in the beakers.

The boys tested the strength of the bridge, whilst the girls just stood and watched.

You can also have half-cells involving **solutions of two aqueous ions of the same element**, such as $Fe^{2+}_{(aq)}/Fe^{3+}_{(aq)}$.

The conversion from $Fe^{2+}$ to $Fe^{3+}$, or vice versa, happens on the surface of the **electrode**.

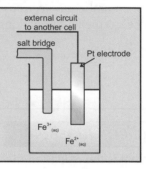

external circuit to another cell

salt bridge

Pt electrode

$Fe^{3+}_{(aq)}$

$Fe^{2+}_{(aq)}$

## Electrode Potentials are Measured Against a Standard Hydrogen Electrode

The **standard electrode potential** of a half-cell is the **voltage measured** under **standard conditions** when the **half-cell** is connected to a **standard hydrogen electrode**.

A **standard hydrogen electrode** contains a piece of **platinum foil** submerged in a **1 mol dm⁻³** solution of $H^+$ ions (i.e. an acid). $H_2$ **gas** is bubbled through at a pressure of **101 kPa**. The platinum electrode is **platinized** — which means the surface of the foil is covered in very finely powdered platinum, increasing its **surface area**. The platinized surface **adsorbs** hydrogen gas and an **equilibrium** is set up:

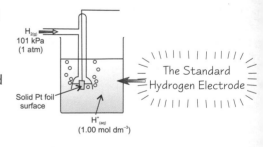

$H_{2(g)}$
101 kPa
(1 atm)

The Standard Hydrogen Electrode

Solid Pt foil surface

$H^+_{(aq)}$
(1.00 mol dm⁻³)

$$H_{2(g)} \rightleftharpoons 2H^+_{(aq)} + 2e^-$$

The **electrode potential** of this half-cell is defined as **zero**. It is known as a **reference cell**. All other standard electrode potentials are measured against it in a set-up like the one below:

1) The standard hydrogen electrode is **always** shown on the **left**.

2) $E^{\ominus}$ represents the **standard electrode potential** of a half-cell.

The whole cell potential $= E^{\ominus}_{\text{right-hand side}} - E^{\ominus}_{\text{left-hand side}}$.

3) $E^{\ominus}_{\text{left-hand side}} = \textbf{0.00 V}$

This means that the **measured cell voltage** will be the standard electrode potential for the **right-hand** half-cell. It could be **negative or positive** depending on which way the electrons flow.

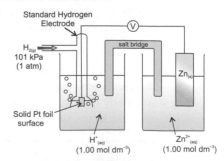

Standard Hydrogen Electrode

salt bridge

$H_{2(g)}$
101 kPa
(1 atm)

$Zn_{(s)}$

Solid Pt foil surface

$H^+_{(aq)}$
(1.00 mol dm⁻³)

$Zn^{2+}_{(aq)}$
(1.00 mol dm⁻³)

Carried out under standard conditions:
1) All solutions have a concentration of 1 mol dm⁻³
2) Temperature is at 298 K
3) Pressure is 101 kPa

# Electrode Potentials

## To Find The Standard Cell Potential, Combine The Two Half-Cells

The **standard electrode potentials** can be used to calculate the **standard cell potential** of the whole cell.
This is the equation:

$$E^\ominus_{cell} = E^\ominus_{right\text{-}hand\ side} - E^\ominus_{left\text{-}hand\ side}$$

By convention we make the half-cell with the **more negative** standard electrode potential
the **left-hand** one. In the case of the zinc/copper half-cell on page 74, that's zinc.

Now you can **calculate** the **cell potential** by doing the calculation above:

$$E^\ominus_{cell} = E^\ominus_{right\text{-}hand\ side} - E^\ominus_{left\text{-}hand\ side} = +0.34 - (-0.76) = \mathbf{+1.10\ V}$$

| Half-cell | $E^\ominus$ (V) |
|---|---|
| $Zn^{2+}_{(aq)}/Zn_{(s)}$ | −0.76 |
| $Cu^{2+}_{(aq)}/Cu_{(s)}$ | +0.34 |

The cell potential will always be a **positive voltage**, because the more negative $E^\ominus$ value is being subtracted from
the more positive $E^\ominus$ value. If the positions of the half-cells were **swapped** over, then the **size** of the voltage would
have the **same value**, but would be **negative**.

## To Write the Overall Cell Equation, Combine the Half-Equations

For electrochemical cell reactions, it's the done thing to always write
the **oxidised substance first**. In this case, **zinc** is being oxidised:

$$Zn^{2+}_{(aq)} + 2e^- \rightleftharpoons Zn_{(s)}$$
$$Cu^{2+}_{(aq)} + 2e^- \rightleftharpoons Cu_{(s)}$$

So the top reaction here goes **backwards** and the bottom reaction goes **forwards**.

This gives you two half-equations: $Zn_{(s)} \rightleftharpoons Zn^{2+}_{(aq)} + 2e^-$ and $Cu^{2+}_{(aq)} + 2e^- \rightleftharpoons Cu_{(s)}$.

These can be combined to give the overall equation: $Zn_{(s)} + Cu^{2+}_{(aq)} \rightleftharpoons Zn^{2+}_{(aq)} + Cu_{(s)}$

## Practice Questions

Q1 What is the definition of standard electrode potential?
Q2 List the three standard conditions needed when measuring standard electrode potentials.
Q3 Calculate the standard cell potential for this system:

$$Fe^{3+} + e^- \rightleftharpoons Fe^{2+}, \quad E^\ominus = +0.77\ V \qquad Mn^{3+} + e^- \rightleftharpoons Mn^{2+}, \quad E^\ominus = +1.48\ V$$

Q4 In the cell in Q3, which half-cell will release electrons to the circuit?

### Exam Questions

1   A cell is made up of a lead plate and an iron plate, dipped in solutions of lead(II) nitrate and iron(II) nitrate
    respectively, and connected by a salt bridge. The electrode potentials for the two electrodes are:

$$Fe^{2+}_{(aq)} + 2e^- \rightleftharpoons Fe_{(s)} \quad E^\ominus = -0.44\ V$$
$$Pb^{2+}_{(aq)} + 2e^- \rightleftharpoons Pb_{(s)} \quad E^\ominus = -0.13\ V$$

   What is the standard cell potential of this cell?
   A   +0.31 V
   B   −0.57 V
   C   −0.31 V
   D   +0.57 V

[1 mark]

2   An electrochemical cell containing a zinc half-cell and a silver half-cell was set up using a potassium nitrate salt bridge.

$$Zn^{2+}_{(aq)} + 2e^- \rightleftharpoons Zn_{(s)} \qquad E^\ominus = -0.76\ V$$
$$Ag^+_{(aq)} + e^- \rightleftharpoons Ag_{(s)} \qquad E^\ominus = +0.80\ V$$

   a)   Use the standard electrode potentials given to calculate the standard cell potential for a zinc-silver cell.   [1 mark]
   b)   Write an equation for the overall cell reaction.   [1 mark]
   c)   Which half-cell released the electrons into the circuit? Explain your answer.   [1 mark]

## Exam potential = hours revising – hours on the PlayStation®...

*You've just got to think long and hard about this stuff. The metal on the left-hand electrode disappears off into the solution,
leaving its electrons behind. This makes the left-hand electrode the negative one. So the right-hand electrode's got to be
the positive one. It makes sense if you think about it. This electrode gives up electrons to turn the positive ions into atoms.*

# The Electrochemical Series

*If you put lots of half-equations in order of their standard electrode potentials, you get the electrochemical series.*

## The Electrochemical Series Shows You What's Reactive and What's Not

1) The **more reactive** a **metal** is, the **more** it wants to **lose electrons** to form a **positive ion**.
   More reactive metals have **more negative standard electrode potentials**.

   > **Example:** Magnesium is **more reactive** than zinc — so it's more eager to form 2+ ions than zinc is.
   > The list of standard electrode potentials shows that $Mg^{2+}/Mg$ has a **more negative** value than $Zn^{2+}/Zn$.
   >
   > In terms of oxidation and reduction, magnesium would **reduce** $Zn^{2+}$ (or $Zn^{2+}$ would **oxidise** magnesium).

2) The more reactive a **non-metal** is, the **more** it wants to **gain electrons** to form a **negative ion**.
   More reactive non-metals have **more positive standard electrode potentials**.

   > **Example:** Chlorine is **more reactive** than bromine — so it's more eager to form a negative ion than bromine is.
   > The list of standard electrode potentials shows that $Cl_2/2Cl^-$ is **more positive** than $Br_2/2Br^-$.
   >
   > In terms of oxidation and reduction, chlorine would **oxidise** $Br^-$ (or $Br^-$ would **reduce** chlorine).

3) Here's an **electrochemical series** showing some standard electrode potentials:

Chestnut wondered if his load was hindering his pulling potential.

| Half-reaction | $E^\circ$(V) |
|---|---|
| $Mg^{2+}_{(aq)} + 2e^- \rightleftharpoons Mg_{(s)}$ | $-2.38$ |
| $Al^{3+}_{(aq)} + 3e^- \rightleftharpoons Al_{(s)}$ | $-1.66$ |
| $Zn^{2+}_{(aq)} + 2e^- \rightleftharpoons Zn_{(s)}$ | $-0.76$ |
| $Ni^{2+}_{(aq)} + 2e^- \rightleftharpoons Ni_{(s)}$ | $-0.25$ |
| $2H^+_{(aq)} + 2e^- \rightleftharpoons H_{2(g)}$ | $0.00$ |
| $Sn^{4+}_{(aq)} + 2e^- \rightleftharpoons Sn^{2+}_{(aq)}$ | $+0.15$ |
| $Cu^{2+}_{(aq)} + 2e^- \rightleftharpoons Cu_{(s)}$ | $+0.34$ |
| $Fe^{3+}_{(aq)} + e^- \rightleftharpoons Fe^{2+}_{(aq)}$ | $+0.77$ |
| $Ag^+_{(aq)} + e^- \rightleftharpoons Ag_{(s)}$ | $+0.80$ |
| $Br_{2(aq)} + 2e^- \rightleftharpoons 2Br^-_{(aq)}$ | $+1.07$ |
| $Cr_2O_7^{2-}_{(aq)} + 14H^+_{(aq)} + 6e^- \rightleftharpoons 2Cr^{3+}_{(aq)} + 7H_2O_{(l)}$ | $+1.33$ |
| $Cl_{2(aq)} + 2e^- \rightleftharpoons 2Cl^-_{(aq)}$ | $+1.36$ |
| $MnO_4^-_{(aq)} + 8H^+_{(aq)} + 5e^- \rightleftharpoons Mn^{2+}_{(aq)} + 4H_2O_{(l)}$ | $+1.52$ |

More positive electrode potentials mean that:
1. The left-hand substances are more easily reduced.
2. The right-hand substances are more stable.

More negative electrode potentials mean that:
1. The right-hand substances are more easily oxidised.
2. The left-hand substances are more stable.

## The Anticlockwise Rule Predicts Whether a Reaction Is Likely to Happen

To figure out if a metal will react with the aqueous ions of another metal, you can use the **anticlockwise rule**.

**For example, will zinc react with aqueous copper ions?**
First you write the two half-equations down, putting the one with the **more negative** standard electrode potential on **top**.
Then you draw on some **anticlockwise arrows** — these give you the **direction** of each half-reaction.

$Zn^{2+}_{(aq)} + 2e^- \rightleftharpoons Zn_{(s)}$  $E^\circ = -0.76$ V
$Cu^{2+}_{(aq)} + 2e^- \rightleftharpoons Cu_{(s)}$  $E^\circ = +0.34$ V

The **half-equations** are:  $Zn_{(s)} \rightleftharpoons Zn^{2+}_{(aq)} + 2e^-$
$Cu^{2+}_{(aq)} + 2e^- \rightleftharpoons Cu_{(s)}$

Which combine to give:  $Zn_{(s)} + Cu^{2+}_{(aq)} \rightleftharpoons Zn^{2+}_{(aq)} + Cu_{(s)}$
So zinc **does** react with aqueous copper ions.

To find the **cell potential** you always do $E^\circ_{bottom} - E^\circ_{top}$, so the cell potential for this reaction is $+0.34 - (-0.76) = +1.10$ V.

You can also draw an **electrode potential chart**. It's the same sort of idea.
You draw an '**upside-down y-axis**' with the more negative number at the top.
Then you put both half-reactions on the chart and draw on your **anticlockwise** arrows which give you the **direction** of each half-reaction.
The **difference** between the values is the **cell potential** — in this case it's **+1.10 V**.

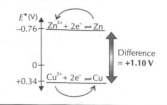

# The Electrochemical Series

## Sometimes the Prediction is Wrong

A **prediction** using $E^\circ$ and the anticlockwise rule tells you if a reaction is **feasible** under **standard conditions**.
If the cell potential is **positive** and **greater than about 0.4 V**, the reaction should go to **completion**.
If the value is **between 0.0 V and about 0.4 V** then the reaction will still happen, but it'll be reversible.

However, these predictions might be **wrong** if...

### ...the conditions are not standard

1) Changing the **concentration** (or temperature) of the solution can cause the electrode potential to **change**.
2) For example the zinc/copper cell has these half-equations in equilibrium...

$$Zn_{(s)} \rightleftharpoons Zn^{2+}_{(aq)} + 2e^-$$
$$Cu^{2+}_{(aq)} + 2e^- \rightleftharpoons Cu_{(s)}$$

3) ...if you **increase** the concentration of $Zn^{2+}$, the **equilibrium** will shift to the **left**, making **electron loss** more **difficult**. The whole cell potential will be lower.
4) ...if you **increase** the concentration of $Cu^{2+}$, the **equilibrium** will shift to the **right**, making **electron gain easier**. The whole cell potential will be higher.

### ...the reaction kinetics are not favourable

1) The **rate of a reaction** may be so **slow** that the reaction might **not appear** to happen.
2) If a reaction has a **high activation energy**, this may stop it happening.

*Gary was hopeful, but Sue's high activation energy meant it was never going to happen*

## Cell Potential is Related to Entropy and the Equilibrium Constant

The bigger the **cell potential**, the bigger the **total entropy change** taking place during the reaction in the cell.
This gives the following equations:

$$E^\circ \propto \Delta S_{total} \quad \text{and} \quad E^\circ \propto \ln K$$

This one comes from the fact that entropy change and the equilibrium constant, K, are linked — see p32.

$\propto$ means 'directly proportional'

$\Delta S_{total}$ = total entropy change

## Practice Questions

Q1 Cu is less reactive than Pb. Which half-reaction has a more negative $E^\circ$ value, $Pb^{2+} + 2e^- \rightleftharpoons Pb$ or $Cu^{2+} + 2e^- \rightleftharpoons Cu$?
Q2 Use electrode potentials to show that magnesium will reduce $Zn^{2+}$ ions.
Q3 What is the anticlockwise rule used for? Outline how you use it.
Q4 Use the table on the opposite page to predict whether or not $Zn^{2+}$ ions can oxidise $Fe^{2+}$ ions to $Fe^{3+}$ ions.

**Exam Questions**

1 Vanadium is a transition element with several oxidation states, which are differently coloured.
Vanadium(V) oxide is yellow and vanadium(IV) oxide is blue.
a) Combine the two half-equations and predict if zinc will convert vanadium from its yellow to its blue state. [2 marks]
b) Calculate the cell potential for this reaction. [1 mark]

$$Zn^{2+} + 2e^- \rightleftharpoons Zn \quad E^\circ = -0.76 \text{ V}$$
$$VO_2^+ + 2H^+ + e^- \rightleftharpoons VO^{2+} + H_2O \quad E^\circ = +1.00 \text{ V}$$

2 The standard electrode potential for manganese(IV) oxide acting as a reducing agent is:

$$MnO_2 + 4H^+ + 2e^- \rightleftharpoons Mn^{2+} + 2H_2O \quad E^\circ = +1.23 \text{ V}$$

a) Use the data on the previous page to explain why there is no reaction between manganese(IV) oxide and hydrochloric acid. [2 marks]
b) If manganese(IV) oxide is added to warm, concentrated hydrochloric acid a reaction does occur, producing chlorine gas. Explain why this is likely to be the case. [2 marks]

## Remember the anticlockwise rule — it could save your life...

*To be honest I completely made that up. Just thought I'd try and grab your attention. I imagine the chances of you actually finding yourself in the sort of situation where the anticlockwise rule saves your life are very slim. Almost nil really. James Bond certainly never found himself in that kind of pickle. But it'll help in the exam. Which is almost as good...*

# Redox Titrations

*Redox titrations are like acid-base titrations, but different. You don't need an indicator for a start.*

## Titrations Using **Transition Element Ions** are **Redox** Titrations

Titrations using transition element ions let you find out how much **oxidising agent** is needed to **exactly** react with a quantity of **reducing agent**. If you know the **concentration** of either the oxidising agent or the reducing agent, you can use the titration results to work out the concentration of the other.

1) First you measure out a quantity of **reducing agent**, e.g. aqueous $Fe^{2+}$ ions, using a pipette, and put it in a conical flask.

2) Using a **measuring cylinder**, you add about **20 cm³ of dilute sulfuric acid** to the flask — this is an excess, so you don't have to be too exact.

3) Now you add the **oxidising agent**, e.g. aqueous potassium manganate(VII), to the reducing agent using a **burette**, **swirling** the conical flask as you do so.

4) You stop when the mixture in the flask **just** becomes tainted with the colour of the oxidising agent (the **end point**) and record the volume of the oxidising agent added. This is the **rough titration**.

5) Now you do some **accurate titrations**. You need to do a few until you get **two or more** readings that are **within 0.10 cm³** of each other.

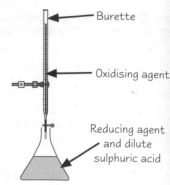

Burette

Oxidising agent

Reducing agent and dilute sulphuric acid

You can also do titrations the **other way round** — adding the reducing agent to the oxidising agent.

## The **Sharp Colour Change** Tells You when the Reaction's **Just** Been **Completed**

When the **coloured oxidising agent** is added to the reducing agent, they start reacting and the reducing agent starts to **lose its colour**. The reaction continues until **all** of the reducing agent has reacted. The **very next drop** into the flask will give the mixture the **colour of the oxidising agent**. The trick is to spot **exactly** when this happens.

The two main **oxidising agents** used are:
1) **Manganate(VII) ions** ($MnO_4^-$) in **aqueous potassium manganate(VII)** ($KMnO_4$) — these are **purple**.
2) **Dichromate(VI) ions** ($Cr_2O_7^{2-}$) in **aqueous potassium dichromate(VI)** ($K_2Cr_2O_7$) — these are **orange**.

The **acid** is added to make sure there are plenty of **H⁺ ions** to allow the oxidising agent to be reduced.

## You Can **Calculate** the **Concentration** of a Reagent from the **Titration Results**

**EXAMPLE:** 27.50 cm³ of 0.0200 mol dm⁻³ aqueous potassium manganate(VII) reacted with 25.0 cm³ of acidified iron(II) sulphate solution. Calculate the concentration of $Fe^{2+}$ ions in the solution.
$$MnO_4^-{}_{(aq)} + 8H^+{}_{(aq)} + 5Fe^{2+}{}_{(aq)} \rightarrow Mn^{2+}{}_{(aq)} + 4H_2O_{(l)} + 5Fe^{3+}{}_{(aq)}$$

1) Work out the number of **moles of $MnO_4^-$ ions** added to the flask.

Number of moles $MnO_4^-$ added $= \dfrac{\text{concentration} \times \text{volume}}{1000} = \dfrac{0.0200 \times 27.50}{1000} = 5.50 \times 10^{-4}$ moles

2) Look at the balanced equation to find how many moles of **$Fe^{2+}$** react with **every mole** of $MnO_4^-$. Then you can work out the **number of moles of $Fe^{2+}$** in the flask.

5 moles of $Fe^{2+}$ react with 1 mole of $MnO_4^-$. So moles of $Fe^{2+} = 5.50 \times 10^{-4} \times 5 = 2.75 \times 10^{-3}$ moles.

3) Work out the **number of moles of $Fe^{2+}$** in 1000 cm³ (1 dm) of solution — this is the **concentration**.

25.0 cm³ of solution contained $2.75 \times 10^{-3}$ moles of $Fe^{2+}$.

1000 cm³ of solution would contain $\dfrac{(2.75 \times 10^{-3}) \times 1000}{25.0} = 0.11$ moles of $Fe^{2+}$.

So the concentration of $Fe^{2+}$ is **0.11 mol dm⁻³**.

Manganate 007, licensed to oxidise.

# Redox Titrations

## You Can Also Estimate the Percentage of Iron in Iron Tablets

This titration can be used to find out the percentage of iron in the iron tablets that are used to treat people with the blood disorder anaemia. The iron is usually in the form of iron(II) sulfate.

**EXAMPLE**: A 2.56 g iron tablet was dissolved in dilute sulfuric acid to give 250 cm³ of solution. 25 cm³ of this solution was found to react with 12.5 cm³ of 0.025 mol dm⁻³ potassium manganate(VII) solution. Calculate the percentage of iron in the tablet.

$$MnO_4^-{}_{(aq)} + 8H^+{}_{(aq)} + 5Fe^{2+}{}_{(aq)} \rightarrow Mn^{2+}{}_{(aq)} + 4H_2O_{(l)} + 5Fe^{3+}{}_{(aq)}$$

The first two steps are the same as the example on the previous page:

1) Work out the number of moles of **manganate(VII) ions** which took part in the reaction:

$$\text{Number of moles of } MnO_4^- = \frac{\text{concentration} \times \text{volume}}{1000} = \frac{0.025 \times 12.5}{1000} = 3.125 \times 10^{-4} \text{ moles}$$

2) From the equation, you can see that **5 moles** of iron(II) ions react with **1 mole** of manganate(VII) ions.

So in **25 cm³** of the iron solution there must be: $5 \times 3.125 \times 10^{-4} = 1.5625 \times 10^{-3}$ **moles of iron(II) ions**.

3) Now you can work out the number of moles of iron in **250 cm³** of the solution — this will be the number of moles of iron in the **whole tablet**:

Number of moles of $Fe^{2+} = 1.5625 \times 10^{-3} \times 10 = 1.5625 \times 10^{-2}$

4) From this, you can work out the **mass** of iron in the tablet:

1 mole of iron weighs **56 g**, so 1 tablet contains: $1.5625 \times 10^{-2} \times 56 = 0.875$ g of iron

5) Finally, you can calculate the percentage of iron in the tablet. The total weight of the tablet is **2.56 g**.

So, the percentage of iron = $(0.875 \div 2.560) \times 100 = $ **34.18%**

## Practice Questions

Q1 Why is no indicator used when titrating potassium manganate(VII)?

Q2 What colour are dichromate(VI) ions?

Q3 How many moles of $Fe^{2+}$ ions react with 1 mole of manganate ions?

**Exam Question**

1 A 3.20 g iron tablet was dissolved in dilute sulfuric acid and made up to 250 cm³ with deionised water. 25 cm³ of this solution was found to react with 7.5 cm³ of 0.018 mol dm⁻³ potassium manganate(VII) solution.

   a) Calculate the number of moles of iron in 25 cm³ of the solution. [2 marks]
   b) Calculate the number of moles of iron in the tablet. [1 mark]
   c) What percentage, by mass, of the tablet is iron? [2 marks]

2 A 10 cm³ sample of 0.5 mol dm⁻³ $SnCl_2$ solution was titrated with acidified potassium manganate(VII) solution. Exactly 20 cm³ of 0.1 mol dm⁻³ potassium manganate(VII) solution was needed to fully oxidise the tin(II) chloride.

   a) What type of reaction is this? [1 mark]
   b) How many moles of tin(II) chloride were present in the 10 cm³ sample? [2 marks]
   c) How many moles of potassium manganate(VII) were needed to fully oxidise the tin(II) chloride? [2 marks]

The half-equation for acidified $MnO_4^-$ acting as an oxidising agent is: $MnO_4^- + 8H^+ + 5e^- \rightarrow Mn^{2+} + 4H_2O$

   d) Find the oxidation state of the oxidised tin ions present in the solution at the end of the titration. [4 marks]

## You think it's all over...

*What a lovely page of calculations. I don't know about you, but that's rounded my day off nicely. I'll let you into a secret though — you're not quite done with redox titrations yet. Just when you thought it couldn't get any better, there's more of this stuff when you turn over! It's OK, you don't have to thank me. I know I spoil you rotten. It's only because I care.*

# More Redox Titrations

*The fun just never stops, does it?*

## Iodine-Sodium Thiosulfate Titrations are Dead Handy

Iodine-sodium thiosulfate titrations are a way of finding the concentration of an **oxidising agent**.
The **more concentrated** an oxidising agent is, the **more ions will be oxidised** by a certain volume of it.
So here's how you can find out the concentration of a solution of the oxidising agent **potassium iodate(V)**:

### STAGE 1: Use a sample of oxidising agent to oxidise as much iodide as possible.

1) Measure out 25 cm³ of potassium iodate(V), $KIO_3$ — the **oxidising agent**.

2) Add this to an excess of acidic **potassium iodide** solution.
The iodate(V) ions in the potassium iodate(V) solution
**oxidise** some of the **iodide ions** to **iodine**.

$$IO_3^-{}_{(aq)} + 5I^-{}_{(aq)} + 6H^+{}_{(aq)} \rightarrow 3I_2{}_{(aq)} + 3H_2O_{(l)}$$

### STAGE 2: Find out how many moles of iodine have been produced.

You do this by **titrating** the solution produced from stage 1 with **sodium thiosulfate**,
$Na_2S_2O_3$. (You need to know the concentration of the sodium thiosulfate solution.)

The iodine in the solution reacts
with **thiosulfate ions** like this:

$$I_2{}_{(aq)} + 2S_2O_3{}^{2-}{}_{(aq)} \rightarrow 2I^-{}_{(aq)} + S_4O_6{}^{2-}{}_{(aq)}$$

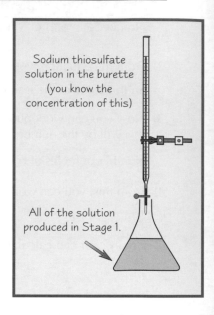

Sodium thiosulfate
solution in the burette
(you know the
concentration of this)

All of the solution
produced in Stage 1.

| | **Titration of Iodine with Sodium Thiosulfate** |
|---|---|
| 1) | Put all the solution produced in Stage 1 in a flask. |
| 2) | From the burette, add sodium thiosulfate solution to the solution in the flask. |
| 3) | It's hard to see the end point, so when the iodine colour fades to pale yellow, add 2 cm³ of starch solution (to detect the presence of iodine). The solution in the conical flask will go dark blue, showing there's still some iodine there. |
| 4) | Add sodium thiosulfate <u>one drop at a time</u> until the blue colour disappears. |
| 5) | When this happens, it means all the iodine has <u>just</u> been reacted. |
| 6) | Now you can <u>calculate</u> the number of moles of iodine in the solution. |

Here's how you'd do the titration calculation to find the **number of moles of iodine** produced in Stage 1.

Example | The iodine produced in Stage 1 reacted fully with 11.1 cm³ of 0.12 mol dm⁻³ thiosulfate solution.

$$I_2{}_{(aq)} + 2S_2O_3{}^{2-}{}_{(aq)} \rightarrow 2I^-{}_{(aq)} + S_4O_6{}^{2-}{}_{(aq)}$$
$$\text{11.1 cm}^3$$
$$\text{0.12 mol dm}^{-3}$$

Number of moles of thiosulfate $= \dfrac{\text{concentration} \times \text{volume (cm}^3)}{1000} = \dfrac{0.12 \times 11.1}{1000} = $ **1.332 × 10⁻³ moles**

**1 mole** of iodine reacts with **2 moles** of thiosulfate.
So number of **moles of iodine** in the solution $= 1.332 \times 10^{-3} \div 2 = $ **6.66 × 10⁻⁴ moles**

### STAGE 3: Calculate the concentration of the oxidising agent.

1) Now you look back at your original equation:

$$IO_3^-{}_{(aq)} + 5I^-{}_{(aq)} + 6H^+{}_{(aq)} \rightarrow 3I_2{}_{(aq)} + 3H_2O_{(l)}$$

2) 25 cm³ of potassium iodate(V) solution produced **6.66 × 10⁻⁴ moles of iodine**.
The equation shows that **one mole** of iodate(V) ions will produce **three moles** of iodine ($I_2$).

3) That means there must have been **6.66 × 10⁻⁴ ÷ 3 = 2.22 × 10⁻⁴ moles of iodate(V) ions** in the original solution.
So now it's straightforward to find the **concentration** of the potassium iodate(V) solution, which is what you're after:

$$\text{number of moles} = \frac{\text{concentration} \times \text{volume (cm}^3)}{1000} \Rightarrow 2.22 \times 10^{-4} = \frac{\text{concentration} \times 25}{1000}$$

$$\Rightarrow \textbf{concentration of potassium iodate(V) solution = 8.88 × 10}^{-3} \textbf{ mol dm}^{-3}$$

# More Redox Titrations

## You Can Use the *Titration* to Find the *Percentage of Copper* in an *Alloy*

**Copper(II) ions** will **oxidise** iodide ions to **iodine**. This can be used to find the percentage of copper in an alloy e.g. brass...

### STAGE 1:  Use a sample of oxidising agent to oxidise as much iodide as possible.

1) Dissolve a **weighed amount** of the alloy in some **concentrated nitric acid**. Pour this mixture into a **250 cm³** volumetric flask and make up to 250 cm³ with **deionised water**.

2) Pipette out a **25 cm³** portion of the diluted solution and transfer to a flask. Slowly add **sodium carbonate solution** to neutralise any remaining nitric acid. Keep going until a slight precipitate forms. This is removed if you add a few drops of **ethanoic acid**.

3) Add an excess of **potassium iodide solution** which reacts with the copper ions as follows:

$$2Cu^{2+}_{(aq)} + 4I^-_{(aq)} \rightarrow 2CuI_{(s)} + I_{2(aq)}$$

A **white precipitate** of **copper(I) iodide** forms.
The copper(II) ions have been reduced to copper(I).

### STAGE 2:  Find out how many moles of iodine have been produced.

4) Titrate the **product mixture** against **sodium thiosulphate solution** to find the number of moles of **iodine** present.

### STAGE 3:  Calculate the concentration of the oxidising agent.

5) Now you can work out the **number of moles of copper** present in both the 25 cm³ and 250 cm³ solutions (from the equation above, you can see that **2 moles** of copper ions produce **1 mole** of iodine).

6) From this you can calculate the **mass of copper** in the whole piece of brass.

7) Finally, you can work out the **percentage** of copper in the alloy.

## There are a Few *Sources of Error* in This Titration...

1) The **starch indicator** for the sodium thiosulphate titration needs to be added at the right point, when most of the iodine has **reacted**, or else the blue colour will be very **slow to disappear**.

2) The starch solution needs to be **freshly made** or else it won't behave as expected.

3) The **precipitate of copper iodide** makes seeing the **colour of the solution** quite hard.

4) The **iodine** produced in the reaction can **evaporate** from the solution, giving a **false titration reading**. The final figure for the percentage of copper would be **too low** as a result. It helps if the solution is kept **cool**.

## Practice Questions

Q1 Write the equation for iodine reacting with thiosulphate ions.
Q2 What is the indicator in iodine-sodium thiosulphate titrations?
Q3 Write the equation for copper(II) ions oxidising iodide ions.

**Exam Question**

1   A 4.20 g coin, made of a copper alloy, was dissolved in acid and the solution made up to 250 ml with deionised water. 25 cm³ of this solution was added to excess potassium iodide solution. The following reaction occurred:

$$2Cu^{2+}_{(aq)} + 4I^-_{(aq)} \rightarrow 2CuI_{(s)} + I_{2(aq)}$$

The resulting solution was neutralised and then titrated with 0.15 mol dm⁻³ sodium thiosulfate.
The iodine and thiosulfate reacted according to this equation:

$$I_{2(aq)} + 2S_2O_3^{2-}_{(aq)} \rightarrow 2I^-_{(aq)} + S_4O_6^{2-}_{(aq)}$$

The average titration result was 19.33 cm³.

a)  How many moles of iodine were present in the solution used in the titration?  [2 marks]
b)  How many moles of copper ions must have been in the 25 cm³ of solution used for the titration?  [2 marks]
c)  What percentage of the coin, by mass, was copper?  [3 marks]

## ...It is now!

*That's it, I promise. No more redox titrations. You have my permission to collapse in a heap on the living room floor — preferably with one hand placed dramatically over your forehead until someone brings you a cup of tea. Make sure you don't bump your head and forget it all though, because a) you'll hurt your head and b) you really need to know this stuff.*

# Uses of Fuel Cells

*Warning: You may find this page interesting. Do not be alarmed...*

## Fuel Cells Generate Electricity by Reacting a Fuel with an Oxidant

A **fuel cell** produces electricity by reacting a **fuel**, usually hydrogen, with an **oxidant**, which is most likely to be oxygen.

1) At the **anode** the platinum catalyst **splits** the $H_2$ into protons and electrons.

2) The **polymer electrolyte membrane** (PEM) **only** allows the $H^+$ ions across and this **forces** the $e^-$ to travel **around** the circuit to get to the cathode.

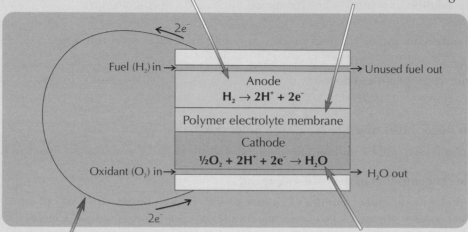

Fuel ($H_2$) in →      → Unused fuel out

$2e^-$

**Anode**
$$H_2 \rightarrow 2H^+ + 2e^-$$

Polymer electrolyte membrane

**Cathode**
$$\tfrac{1}{2}O_2 + 2H^+ + 2e^- \rightarrow H_2O$$

Oxidant ($O_2$) in →      → $H_2O$ out

$2e^-$

3) An **electric current** is created in the circuit, which is used to **power** something like a car, a bicycle, or a dancing Santa. The voltage produced is about **0.6 V**.

4) At the **cathode**, $O_2$ **combines** with the $H^+$ from the anode and the $e^-$ from the circuit to make $H_2O$. This is the only waste product.

The cell **goes on** producing a current as long as it's supplied with hydrogen and oxygen.

Hydrogen seems like the perfect fuel — the **only** waste product is **water**. No greenhouse gases are released and the supply is virtually limitless.

But the hydrogen has to be **made** first. Most hydrogen is produced by reacting **natural gas** with **steam**. This gives $CO_2$ as a waste product and needs **fossil fuels** to heat the process. You can also make hydrogen through the **electrolysis** of **water**. This uses loads of **electricity** though, which is usually generated using **fossil fuels**.

The only way to **sustainably** produce hydrogen **without** causing pollution is to generate electricity using a **renewable source** — like hydroelectric, solar, or wind power. Hydrogen is really only as clean as the method used to produce it.

## Fuel Cells Don't Just Use Hydrogen

Scientists in the car industry are developing fuel cells that use **hydrogen-rich fuels** — these have a high percentage of hydrogen in their molecules and can be converted into $H_2$ in the car by a **reformer**. Such fuels include the two simplest alcohols, **methanol** and **ethanol**.

There are also a **new generation** of fuel cells that can use alcohols **directly** without having to reform them to produce hydrogen.

In these new fuel cells, the alcohol is oxidised at the anode in the presence of water:

$$\text{E.g. } CH_3OH + H_2O \rightarrow CO_2 + 6e^- + 6H^+$$

The $H^+$ ions pass through the electrolyte and are oxidised themselves to water.

$$6H^+ + 6e^- + 1\tfrac{1}{2}O_2 \rightarrow 3H_2O$$

There are a few **advantages** of using **alcohols** instead of hydrogen in fuel cells.

1) They have a higher **hydrogen density** than liquefied hydrogen — that means more hydrogen atoms per $dm^3$.

2) There is already an **infrastructure** in place for making both methanol and ethanol on a **large scale** and they can both be produced from **renewable biomass**.

3) Alcohols are **liquids** at room temperature, so unlike hydrogen they **don't** need special **refrigerated storage**.

4) **Methanol** can be made from carbon dioxide so it offers a possible way to **reduce $CO_2$ levels** in the **atmosphere**.

# Uses of Fuel Cells

## Fuel Cell Vehicles Have Some Important Advantages over Normal Cars

1) They produce far **less pollution** than a regular car when in use.
   The only waste product of a hydrogen fuel cell is **water**, and even those that run on hydrogen-rich fuels produce a lot **less carbon dioxide** than a petrol or diesel engine.
2) A fuel cell is at least **twice as efficient** at converting fuel to power as a petrol engine.

Making the fuel cells still **isn't easy** though. They're **expensive** and have to be made using **toxic chemicals**, which then need to be **disposed of**. They also have a **limited life-span** — meaning you have to keep making new ones and getting rid of the old ones.

## Fuel Cells Have Other Uses Too

1) Fuel cells are used in **space**.
   The **Space Shuttle** uses three **fuel cell power plants**, each made up of many fuel cells, that can produce up to **12 kW** of power. The water produced is used as drinking water by the astronauts. Conventional batteries couldn't be used as they'd **weigh far too much**.

2) Some **breathalysers** use fuel cells too.
   The amount of **alcohol** (ethanol) in someone's **breath** is directly related to the amount in their **blood stream**. **Alcohol vapour** is breathed out with $CO_2$ as the blood passes through the lungs. **2100 cm³** of breath contains the same amount of alcohol as **1 cm³** of blood. The amount can be found using a **breathalyser**.

The old way of detecting alcohol in the breath was to use the **reaction** between ethanol and **potassium dichromate(VII)**. **Orange** dichromate(VII) is **reduced** to **green** chromium(III) as ethanol is oxidised to ethanoic acid. How much the colour changes is measured using a **photocell system**.
Breathalysers used in police stations use **infrared spectrometry** to detect the presence and quantity of ethanol. These machines are very **accurate** but **not** usually easily **portable**.
The most recent development is to use an **ethanol fuel cell**. The amount of alcohol is proportional to the **current produced** when the suspect's breath is fed to the **anode** of the cell. Such devices are **less susceptible** to giving **false readings** due to other substances in the suspect's breath. They're also **easily portable** and **accurate**.

## Practice Questions

Q1 What happens at each electrode in a hydrogen-oxygen fuel cell?
Q2 What particle travels through the electrolyte in a hydrogen-oxygen fuel cell?
Q3 What is meant by a hydrogen-rich fuel?
Q4 Outline the use of fuel cells in Space Shuttles.

**Exam Question**

1 Hydrogen fuel cells are used to power buses in Iceland. There are also plans to convert their fishing fleet to use them.

a) Explain the purpose of the polymer electrolyte membrane (PEM) in a hydrogen fuel cell. [2 marks]

b) Give equations for the reactions at the electrodes in a hydrogen fuel cell. [2 marks]

c) Iceland has no coal or oil reserves but plenty of geothermal and hydroelectric power.
   Suggest why they are among the first countries to use fuel cells for public transport. [2 marks]

d) Explain three advantages of hydrogen fuel cells over conventional internal combustion engines. [3 marks]

e) Outline some potential difficulties of trying to introduce hydrogen fuel cells vehicles into UK public transport. [2 marks]

## Even Back to the Future didn't predict this...

These fuel cells are pretty nifty aren't they? There are some pretty cool advantages to powering stuff using hydrogen or hydrogen-rich fuel, not least because it's potentially much better for the environment than burning fossil fuels. Plus, oil and co. will eventually run out and we'll need to replace 'em. Remember though, fuel cells aren't the perfect solution yet...

# Transition Metals — The Basics

*The transition elements are the metallic ones that sit slap bang in the middle of the periodic table. Thanks to their weird electronic structure, they make pretty-coloured solutions, and get involved in all sorts of fancy reactions.*

## Transition Elements are Found in the d-Block

1) The **d-block** is the block of elements in the middle of the periodic table.

2) Most of the elements in the d-block are **transition elements** (or transition metals). You mainly need to know about the ones in the first row of the d-block. These are the elements from **titanium to copper**.

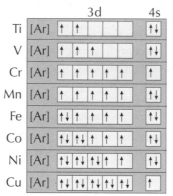

## You Have to Know the Electronic Configurations of the Transition Metals

1) The transition metals in the **first row** of the d-block all have their highest energy electrons in the **4s** and **3d** subshells.

2) To work out the electron configuration, first find the **total number of 4s and 3d electrons** by subtracting **18** (the number of electrons in the lower orbitals) from the element's **atomic number**.
   E.g. the atomic number of **cobalt** is 27, so it has 27 − 18 = **9** 4s and 3d electrons.

3) Then fill up the electron subshells. The **4s** subshell is always filled **first** — **EXCEPT** in **chromium** and **copper.**

|  |  | 3d | 4s |
|---|---|---|---|
| Ti | [Ar] | ↑ ↑ | ↑↓ |
| V | [Ar] | ↑ ↑ ↑ | ↑↓ |
| Cr | [Ar] | ↑ ↑ ↑ ↑ ↑ | ↑ |
| Mn | [Ar] | ↑ ↑ ↑ ↑ ↑ | ↑↓ |
| Fe | [Ar] | ↑↓ ↑ ↑ ↑ ↑ | ↑↓ |
| Co | [Ar] | ↑↓ ↑↓ ↑ ↑ ↑ | ↑↓ |
| Ni | [Ar] | ↑↓ ↑↓ ↑↓ ↑ ↑ | ↑↓ |
| Cu | [Ar] | ↑↓ ↑↓ ↑↓ ↑↓ ↑↓ | ↑ |

*The 3d orbitals are occupied singly at first. They only double up when they have to.*

Chromium prefers to have one electron in each orbital of the 3d subshell and just one in the 4s subshell — this gives it more stability.

Copper prefers to have a full 3d subshell and just one electron in the 4s subshell — it's more stable that way.

4) Don't forget, you can use **subshell notation** to show electronic configurations.
   In subshell notation, **vanadium** has the electronic configuration $1s^2 2s^2 2p^6 3s^2 3p^6 3d^3 4s^2$, or $[Ar]3d^3 4s^2$.
   Check back to your AS notes if this makes less than perfect sense to you.

## Sc and Zn Ain't Transition Metals

1) Here's the definition of a transition metal:

> A **transition metal** is one that can form **one or more stable ions** with a **partially filled d-subshell**.

2) d-orbitals can hold **10** electrons. So, a transition metal must form **at least one ion** that has **between 1 and 9 electrons** in the d-orbital. All the Period 4 d-block elements apart from **scandium** and **zinc** do this.

3) **Scandium** only forms one ion, $Sc^{3+}$, which has an **empty d-subshell**. Scandium has the electronic configuration $[Ar]3d^1 4s^2$, so when it loses three electrons to form $Sc^{3+}$, it ends up with the electronic configuration $[Ar]$.

4) **Zinc** only forms one ion, $Zn^{2+}$, which has a **full d-subshell**. Zinc has the electronic configuration $[Ar]3d^{10}4s^2$.
   When it forms $Zn^{2+}$ it loses 2 electrons, both from the 4s subshell. This means it keeps its full 3d subshell.

## When Ions are Formed, the s Electrons are Removed First

When transition metal atoms form **positive** ions, the **s electrons** are removed **first**, **then** d electrons.

For example, iron forms $Fe^{2+}$ ions and $Fe^{3+}$ ions.

When it forms 2+ ions, it loses **both its 4s electrons**. $Fe = [Ar]3d^6 4s^2 \rightarrow Fe^{2+} = [Ar]3d^6$

Only once the 4s electrons are removed can a **3d electron** be removed. E.g. $Fe^{2+} = [Ar]3d^6 \rightarrow Fe^{3+} = [Ar]3d^5$

# Transition Metals — The Basics

## Ionisation Energies provide Evidence for Electronic Configurations

**Ionisation energy** is the energy needed to **remove** an **electron** from an element.
The ionisation energies of transition metals can tell you a lot about their **electronic configurations**.

The **first ionisation energy** is roughly the **same** from **Sc to Cu**. This is evidence that they all have a **similar electronic structure**, and lose the first electron from the **same** shell (4s).

| Transition Element | Sc | Ti | V | Cr | Mn | Fe | Co | Ni | Cu | Zn |
|---|---|---|---|---|---|---|---|---|---|---|
| **1st ionisation energy (kJ/mol)** | 630 | 660 | 650 | 650 | 720 | 760 | 760 | 740 | 750 | 910 |
| **2nd ionisation energy (kJ/mol)** | 1240 | 1310 | 1410 | **1590** | 1510 | 1560 | 1640 | 1750 | **1960** | 1700 |
| **3rd ionisation energy (kJ/mol)** | 2390 | 2650 | 2870 | 2990 | 3260 | **2960** | 3230 | 3390 | 3560 | 3800 |

The **second** ionisation energy **increases steadily** across the elements. Cr and Cu are slightly **higher** than you'd expect. This shows that the second electron is taken from much **nearer the nucleus** (the **3d** shell) — so you need **more** energy to remove it.

*Cu [Ar] 4s¹ 3d¹⁰ full shell*
*Cr [Ar] 4s¹ 3d⁵ (half shell)*

The **third** ionisation energy also **increases** steadily but with a step down in ionisation energy at **iron**. That's because from iron onwards, the third electron removed is the one in a **paired 3d** orbital. When there are two electrons in the same orbital they repel each other slightly so it's easier to remove one of them.

## Transition Metals have Special Chemical Properties

1) They can form **complex ions** — see page 86. E.g. iron forms a **complex ion with water** — $[Fe(H_2O)_6]^{2+}$.
2) They form **coloured ions** in solution — see pages 87–88. E.g. $Fe^{2+}$ ions are **pale green** and $Fe^{3+}$ ions are **yellow**.
3) They can act as **good catalysts** — see page 94. E.g. iron is the catalyst used in the **Haber process**.
4) They can exist in **variable oxidation states**. E.g. iron can exist in the **+2** oxidation state as $Fe^{2+}$ ions and in the **+3** oxidation state as $Fe^{3+}$ ions.

## Practice Questions

Q1  Why doesn't copper have 2 electrons in its 4s subshell?

Q2  What is the definition of a transition metal?

Q3  Why is zinc not counted as a transition metal?

Q4  When vanadium forms an ion, which shell does it lose its electrons from first?

**Exam Questions**

1  Cobalt is a typical transition element.
   a)  Write the electronic configuration of a cobalt atom.  [1 mark]
   b)  Which electrons does cobalt lose when it forms a 2+ ion?  [1 mark]
   c)  Give three properties that you would expect cobalt to have.  [3 marks]

2  Iron and copper are two common transition metals.
   a)  Write the electronic configuration of an iron atom and a copper atom.  [2 marks]
   b)  Explain what is unusual about the electron configuration of copper among transition metals, and say why this feature occurs.  [2 marks]
   c)  Explain, in terms of iron's orbital and electron configuration, what happens when $Fe^{2+}$ and $Fe^{3+}$ ions are formed.  [2 marks]
   d)  What will be the most obvious difference between iron(II) and iron(III) compounds?  [1 mark]
   e)  Most naturally-occurring iron compounds are iron(III) compounds.
       Explain why they are more stable than iron(II) compounds from their electronic configurations.  [2 marks]

## That copper's gone mad — he's 1 electron short of a full 4s-orbital...

*Have a quick read of the electronic configuration stuff in your AS notes if it's been pushed to a little corner of your mind labelled, "Well, I won't be needing that again in a hurry". It should come flooding back pretty quickly. This page is just an overview of transition metal properties. Don't worry — they're all looked at in lots more detail in the coming pages...*

# Complex Ions and Colour

*Transition metals are always forming complex ions. These aren't as complicated as they sound, though. Honest.*

## Transition Metals can form Complex Ions

A **complex ion** is a **metal ion** surrounded by **dative covalently bonded ligands**.

1) A **dative covalent bond** (or coordinate bond) is a covalent bond in which **both electrons** in the shared pair come from the **same atom**.

2) So a **ligand** is an atom, ion or molecule that **donates a pair of electrons** to a central metal ion.

3) The **coordination number** is the **number** of **dative covalent bonds** that are formed with the central metal ion.

4) In most of the complex ions that you need to know about, the coordination number will be **4** or **6**. If the ligands are **small**, like $H_2O$, $CN^-$ or $NH_3$, **6** can fit around the central metal ion.

> For example: When **transition metal compounds** dissolve in water, they form **metal-aqua complex ions** which have **6 water molecules** forming dative covalent bonds with each metal ion.

But if the ligands are **larger**, like $Cl^-$, **only 4** can fit around the central metal ion.

5) One ligand can be **swapped** for another ligand — this is **ligand substitution**. It almost always causes a **colour change** (see page 89 for more on ligand substitution reactions).

### 6 DATIVE COVALENT BONDS MEAN AN <u>OCTAHEDRAL</u> SHAPE

Here are a few examples of complex ions with 6 dative covalent bonds.

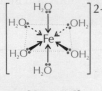 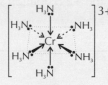 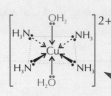

$[Fe(H_2O)_6]^{2+}$    $[Cr(NH_3)_6]^{3+}$    $[Cu(NH_3)_4(H_2O)_2]^{2+}$

> The different types of bond arrow show that the complex is 3-D. The wedge-shaped arrows represent bonds coming towards you and the dashed arrows represent bonds sticking out behind the molecule.

> The ligands don't always have to be the same.

### 4 DATIVE COVALENT BONDS USUALLY MEAN A <u>TETRAHEDRAL</u> SHAPE...

E.g.

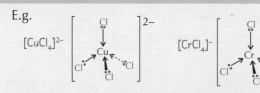

$[CuCl_4]^{2-}$    $[CrCl_4]^-$

**...BUT NOT ALWAYS**

In a **few complexes, 4 dative covalent bonds** form a **square planar** shape.

$[Pt(NH_3)_2Cl_2]$

### SOME COMPLEXES HAVE 2 DATIVE COVALENT BONDS AND FORM A <u>LINEAR</u> SHAPE

E.g.

$\left[ Cl \!:\!\longrightarrow\! Cu \!\longleftarrow\!:\! Cl \right]^-$    $[CuCl_2]^-$

$\left[ H_3N\!:\!\longrightarrow\! Ag \!\longleftarrow\!:\!NH_3 \right]^+$    $[Ag(NH_3)_2]^+$

## Complex Ions Have an *Overall Charge* or *Total Oxidation State*

The **overall charge** on the complex ion is its **total oxidation state**. It's put **outside** the **square** brackets. For example:

$$[Cu(H_2O)_6]^{2+}_{(aq)}$$ ← Overall charge is 2+.

You can use this to work out the **oxidation state of the metal**:

> **oxidation state of the metal ion = total oxidation state – sum of the oxidation states of the ligands**

E.g. $[Fe(CN)_6]^{4-}_{(aq)}$    The total oxidation state is **–4** and each $CN^-$ ligand has an oxidation state of **–1**. So in this complex, iron's oxidation state = $-4 - (6 \times -1) = +2$.

# Complex Ions and Colour

## Ligands Form Bonds Using Lone Pairs of Electrons

A ligand must have **at least one lone pair of electrons**, or it won't have anything to form a **dative covalent bond** with.

Ligands with **one lone pair** are called **monodentate** (or **unidentate**) — e.g. $H_2\ddot{O}$, $\ddot{N}H_3$, $\ddot{C}\ddot{l}^-$, $\ddot{C}N^-$.

Ligands with **two lone pairs** are called **bidentate** — e.g. ethane-1,2-diamine and ethanedioate. Bidentate ligands can each form **two dative covalent bonds** with a metal ion.

In ethane-1,2-diamine both these pairs of electrons interact with the same metal ion.

In ethanedioate it's these two.

Ethanedioate

Ethane-1,2-diamine

A haemogoblin is what carries oxygen in your blood.

Ligands with **more than two lone pairs** are called **polydentate** — e.g. EDTA$^{4-}$ has six lone pairs (so it's **hexadentate**, to be precise). It can form **six dative covalent bonds** with a metal ion.

**Haemoglobin** contains a molecule with **four nitrogens** that each forms a dative covalent bond with $Fe^{2+}$ — so this is a polydentate ligand too.

EDTA$^{4-}$

## Ligands Split the 3d Subshell into Two Energy Levels — and Create Colour

The bonding of a ligand to a transition metal has some weird effects on the metal's electrons.

1) Normally, the 3d orbitals of a transition element ion **all** have the **same energy**.

2) In a complex, there's repulsion between the electrons in the ligands and the 3d electrons of the metal. This increases the energy of all the 3d orbitals — but some are increased more than others.

3) This splits the 3d orbitals into **two different energy levels**.

4) Electrons tend to **occupy the lower orbitals** — but they can jump up to the higher orbitals by absorbing **energy** equal to the energy gap, $\Delta E$. They get this energy from **visible light**.

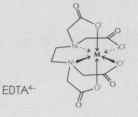

Relative Energy

$\Delta E$ (energy gap)

light energy

The 3d orbitals of a Ni$^{2+}$ ion without any ligands.

The 3d orbitals of $[Ni(H_2O)]^{2+}$

## The Colours of Compounds are the Complement of Those That are Absorbed

1) When **visible light** hits a complex transition metal ion, some frequencies are **absorbed**. Electrons use the energy to jump to the higher orbitals — the frequencies absorbed depend on the size of the **energy gap**.

2) The rest of the frequencies are **transmitted** — which means the colour you see is actually made up of all the frequencies that **aren't absorbed**. This colour is the **complement** of the absorbed colour.

A colour wheel shows complementary colours.

3) For example, $[Cu(H_2O)_6]^{2+}$ absorbs **yellow** light, so when you look at it, you see the complementary colour of yellow, which is **blue**.

4) The **central metal ion**, the **ligands** and the **coordination number** affect the size of the energy gap, so they can also affect the **colour**.

5) If there are **no** 3d electrons, there are no electrons to jump and so **no energy** is absorbed. And if the 3d subshell is **full**, there's no room in the upper orbitals for any electrons to jump to, so again, **no energy** will be absorbed. If there's no energy absorbed, the complex will look **white** or **colourless**.

# Complex Ions and Colour

## Transition Metal Complexes can be Identified by their Colour

It'd be nice if each transition metal formed ions or complexes with just one colour, but sadly it's not that simple. The **colour of a complex** can be altered by any of the factors that can affect the size of the **energy gap**.

1) **Changes in oxidation state**.

| Complex: | $[Fe(H_2O)_6]^{2+}_{(aq)}$ | $\rightarrow$ | $[Fe(H_2O)_6]^{3+}_{(aq)}$ | | $[V(H_2O)_6]^{2+}_{(aq)}$ | $\rightarrow$ | $[V(H_2O)_6]^{3+}_{(aq)}$ |
|---|---|---|---|---|---|---|---|
| Oxidation state: | +2 | $\rightarrow$ | +3 | and | +2 | $\rightarrow$ | +3 |
| Colour: | pale green | $\rightarrow$ | yellow | | violet | $\rightarrow$ | green |

2) **Changes in coordination number** — this always involves a change of ligand too.

| Complex: | $[Cu(H_2O)_6]^{2+} + 4Cl^-$ | $\rightarrow$ | $[CuCl_4]^{2-} + 6H_2O$ |
|---|---|---|---|
| Coordination number: | 6 | $\rightarrow$ | 4 |
| Colour: | blue | $\rightarrow$ | yellow |

3) **Changes in ligand** — this can cause a colour change even if the oxidation state and coordination number remain the same.

| Complex: | $[Ni(H_2O)_6]^{2+} + 6NH_3$ | $\rightarrow$ | $[Ni(NH_3)_6]^{2+} + 6H_2O$ |
|---|---|---|---|
| Oxidation state: | +2 | $\rightarrow$ | +2 |
| Colour: | green | $\rightarrow$ | blue |

## Practice Questions

Q1 Explain what a ligand is and how it bonds to a metal ion.

Q2 Explain the term 'coordination number'.

Q3 What is meant by the term 'metal-aqua complex ions'?

Q4 Why are transition metal aqua-ions coloured?

### Exam Questions

1   EDTA$^{4-}$ is a hexadentate ligand that has many industrial uses.  For example, it is used to reduce the ability of manganese(II) ions to affect the bleach used in the paper industry.

   a)   Explain the term 'hexadentate ligand'. [2 marks]

   b)   Write the formula of the complex that forms between EDTA$^{4-}$ and a manganese(II) ion. [1 mark]

2   Iron(III) can form the complex ion $[Fe(C_2O_4)_3]^{3-}$ with three ethanedioate ions. The ethanedioate ion is a bidentate ligand.  Its structure is shown on the right.

   a)   i) What kind of bond does an ethanedioate ion form with the iron? [1 mark]
      ii) What is the defining feature of this type of bond? [1 mark]

   b)   What is the coordination number of the $[Fe(C_2O_4)_3]^{3-}$ complex? [1 mark]

   c)   Use your answer from part b) to suggest what shape the $[Fe(C_2O_4)_3]^{3-}$ complex is. [1 mark]

3   Transition metal ions form a wide range of different colours when bonded to ligands. Using your knowledge of 3d orbitals, explain how ligands cause transition metals to be coloured. [5 marks]

## Put your hands up — we've got you surrounded...

You'll never get transition metal ions floating around by themselves in a solution — they'll always be surrounded by other molecules.  It's kind of like what'd happen if you put a dish of sweets in a room of eight (or eighteen) year-olds. When you're drawing a complex ion, you should always include some wedge-shaped bonds to show that it's 3-D.

# Complex Ions — Ligand Reactions

*There are more equations on this page than the number of elephants you can fit in a Mini.*

## Ligands can Exchange Places with One Another

Ligands can be **swapped** around — this is called **ligand exchange** and it pretty much always causes a **colour change**.

1) If the ligands are of **similar size**, e.g. $H_2O$ and $NH_3$, then the **coordination number** of the complex ion doesn't change, and neither does the **shape**.

$$[Cr(H_2O)_6]^{3+}_{(aq)} + 6NH_{3(aq)} \rightarrow [Cr(NH_3)_6]^{3+}_{(aq)} + 6H_2O_{(l)}$$
octahedral       octahedral
**violet**        **purple**

$$[Cu(H_2O)_6]^{2+}_{(aq)} + 4Cl^-_{(aq)} \rightleftharpoons [CuCl_4]^{2-}_{(aq)} + 6H_2O_{(l)}$$
octahedral      tetrahedral
**blue**        **yellow**

2) If the ligands are **different sizes**, e.g. $H_2O$ and $Cl^-$, there's a **change of coordination number** and a **change of shape**.

3) Sometimes the substitution is only **partial**.

$$[Cu(H_2O)_6]^{2+}_{(aq)} + 4NH_{3(aq)} \rightarrow [Cu(NH_3)_4(H_2O)_2]^{2+}_{(aq)} + 4H_2O_{(l)}$$
octahedral       elongated octahedral
**blue**        **deep blue**

$$[Cr(H_2O)_6]^{3+}_{(aq)} + SO_4^{2-}_{(aq)} \rightarrow [Cr(H_2O)_5(SO_4)]^+_{(aq)} + H_2O_{(l)}$$
octahedral       distorted octahedral
**violet**        **green**

## Different Ligands Form Different Strength Bonds

Ligand exchange reactions can be easily **reversed**, **EXCEPT** if the new complex ion is much **more stable** than the old one.

1) If the new ligands form **stronger** bonds with the central metal ion than the old ligands did, the change is **harder** to reverse. E.g. $CN^-$ ions form stronger dative covalent bonds with $Fe^{3+}$ ions than $H_2O$ molecules, so it's hard to reverse this reaction: $$[Fe(H_2O)_6]^{3+}_{(aq)} + 6CN^-_{(aq)} \rightarrow [Fe(CN)_6]^{3-}_{(aq)} + 6H_2O_{(l)}$$

2) **Bidentate** ligands form more stable complexes than monodentate ligands, so a change like the one below is hard to reverse: $$[Ni(H_2O)_6]^{2+}_{(aq)} + 3H_2NCH_2CH_2NH_{2(aq)} \rightarrow [Ni(H_2NCH_2CH_2NH_2)_3]^{2+}_{(aq)} + 6H_2O_{(l)}$$

3) A **polydentate** ligand, like EDTA, forms even more stable complexes. So a change like this one is **very** hard to reverse: $$[Cu(H_2O)_6]^{2+}_{(aq)} + EDTA^{4-}_{(aq)} \rightarrow [Cu(EDTA)]^{2-}_{(aq)} + 6H_2O_{(l)}$$

When **bidentate** ligands take the place of **monodentate** ligands there are generally **more product** molecules than **reactant** molecules. This means the **total entropy change** for the reaction is likely to be **positive**, so the reaction would be expected to "go". The same happens when a polydentate ligand replaces monodentate or bidentate ligands.

*See p19 for more on entropy.*

## Adding Alkali to Metal Aqua-Ions Forms Precipitates

Adding **OH$^-$ ions** to solutions of **metal aqua-ions** produces **insoluble metal hydroxides**. Here's why:

*M might be Fe, Al or Cr.*

1) In water, **metal aqua 3+ ions** form the equilibrium: $[M(H_2O)_6]^{3+}_{(aq)} + H_2O_{(l)} \rightleftharpoons [M(H_2O)_5(OH)]^{2+}_{(aq)} + H_3O^+_{(aq)}$. If you add **OH$^-$ ions** to the equilibrium $H_3O^+$ ions are removed — this shifts the equilibrium to the **right**.

2) Now another equilibrium is set up in the solution: $[M(H_2O)_5(OH)]^{2+}_{(aq)} + H_2O_{(l)} \rightleftharpoons [M(H_2O)_4(OH)_2]^+_{(aq)} + H_3O^+_{(aq)}$. Again the OH$^-$ ions remove $H_3O^+$ ions from the solution, pulling the equilibrium to the right.

3) This happens one last time — now you're left with an **insoluble uncharged metal hydroxide**: $[M(H_2O)_4(OH)_2]^+_{(aq)} + H_2O_{(l)} \rightleftharpoons M(H_2O)_3(OH)_{3(s)} + H_3O^+_{(aq)}$.

The same thing happens with **metal aqua 2+ ions** (e.g. Fe, Co or Cu), except this time there are only **two** steps:
$[M(H_2O)_6]^{2+}_{(aq)} + H_2O_{(l)} \rightleftharpoons [M(H_2O)_5(OH)]^+_{(aq)} + H_3O^+_{(aq)} \Longrightarrow [M(H_2O)_5(OH)]^+_{(aq)} + H_2O_{(l)} \rightleftharpoons M(H_2O)_4(OH)_{2(s)} + H_3O^+_{(aq)}$

The colours of these precipitates can be seen on the next page.

# Complex Ions — Ligand Reactions

## Precipitates Form with Sodium Hydroxide and Ammonia Solution...

When you add $OH^-$ ions to a solution of metal aqua-ions they form precipitates. The obvious way of adding hydroxide ions is to use a strong alkali, like **sodium hydroxide solution** — but you can use **ammonia solution** too.

> When ammonia dissolves in water it sets up this **equilibrium**:
>
> $$NH_3 + H_2O \rightleftharpoons NH_4^+ + OH^-$$
>
> Hydroxide ions are formed from the reaction with water. So adding a small amount of **ammonia** solution gives the **same** results as **sodium hydroxide**.

In some cases, if you add an **excess** of ammonia solution, a **further reaction** happens.
With excess $OH^-$ the $H_2O$ ligands get **displaced** and with excess $NH_3$, **both** the $H_2O$ and $OH^-$ ligands are **displaced** by $NH_3$ ligands. This produces a **soluble metal ion complex**.
The table shows you all the examples you need to know about.

| Metal aqua-ion | With $OH^-_{(aq)}$ or $NH_{3(aq)}$ | With excess $OH^-_{(aq)}$ | With excess $NH_{3(aq)}$ |
|---|---|---|---|
| $[Cu(H_2O)_6]^{2+}$ blue solution | $Cu(H_2O)_4(OH)_2$ blue precipitate | no change | $[Cu(NH_3)_4(H_2O)_2]^{2+}$ deep blue solution |
| $[Fe(H_2O)_6]^{2+}$ green solution | $Fe(H_2O)_4(OH)_2$ green precipitate | no change | no change |
| $[Fe(H_2O)_6]^{3+}$ yellow solution | $Fe(H_2O)_3(OH)_3$ brown precipitate | no change | no change |
| $[Cr(H_2O)_6]^{3+}$ violet solution | $Cr(H_2O)_3(OH)_3$ green precipitate | $[Cr(OH)_6]^{3-}$ green solution | $[Cr(NH_3)_6]^{3+}$ purple solution |
| $[Mn(H_2O)_6]^{2+}$ very pale pink solution | $Mn(H_2O)_4(OH)_2$ brown precipitate | no change | no change |
| $[Ni(H_2O)_6]^{2+}$ green solution | $Ni(H_2O)_4(OH)_2$ green precipitate | no change | $[Ni(NH_3)_6]^{2+}$ blue solution |
| $[Zn(H_2O)_6]^{2+}$ colourless solution | $Zn(H_2O)_3(OH)_3$ white precipitate | $[Zn(OH)_4]^{2-}$ colourless solution | $[Zn(NH_3)_4]^{2+}$ colourless solution |

## Practice Questions

Q1 Give an example of a ligand substitution reaction that involves a change of coordination number.
Q2 What do you see when ammonia solution is slowly added to a copper(II) sulfate solution until it's in excess?
Q3 Why does adding excess ammonia give different results from adding sodium hydroxide to copper(II) sulfate solution?

### Exam Questions

1 Solution A is aqueous copper(II) sulfate and is pale blue in colour.
When concentrated hydrochloric acid is added, solution B forms. B is yellow in colour.
When excess concentrated aqueous ammonia is added to A, solution C forms. C is deep blue in colour.
  a) Identify the formulae of the complexes in solutions A, B and C.    [3 marks]
  b) Write the full equation to show the conversion of solution A to solution B.    [1 mark]
  c) Draw and name the shapes of the complex ions in solutions A, B and C.    [6 marks]

2 A green aqueous solution of a transition metal compound gives the following reactions:

| Solution added | First addition | In excess |
|---|---|---|
| Sodium hydroxide | Green precipitate forms | No further change |
| Ammonia solution | Green precipitate forms | Precipitate dissolves to give a blue solution |

  a) Identify the transition metal in these experiments.    [1 mark]
  b) Give the formula of the ion in the original green solution responsible for the colour.    [1 mark]
  c) Explain the formation of the precipitates in these experiments.    [5 marks]
  d) Explain why the precipitate dissolves in excess ammonia and give the formula of the ion that forms.    [3 marks]
  e) Explain the change in colour when excess ammonia is added.    [1 mark]

## When is a precipitate a solution – when the question's on ligand reactions...

*I fancy pasta for tea tonight. OK, so it's only gonna be a tin of tomatoes with some mixed herbs that have been on the shelf since I moved in, but we can't all be master chefs. Anyway, whilst I go and cook you make sure you can remember all those examples of ligand complexes. It might not be fun, but knowing your complex colours can pick you up some easy marks.*

# Copper and Chromium

Transition metals can form a range of different compounds because they can have lots of different oxidation states. The two examples you need to know about are copper and chromium.

## Copper Ions *Usually Show Oxidation States of +1 or +2*

1) $Cu^{2+}$ ions are **stable** in aqueous solution. They're **reduced** to Cu metal by more **electropositive metals**, like zinc or nickel. E.g. $Cu^{2+} + Zn \rightarrow Cu + Zn^{2+}$. This type of reaction is known as a **displacement** reaction.

2) **Solid** copper(I) compounds are **stable**, but **aqueous** $Cu^+$ ions are **unstable** and **disproportionate** in aqueous solution — see below.

3) Copper(I) ions can form some stable **complexes** if there are **suitable ligands** e.g. $[CuCl_2]^-$ forms if there are excess $Cl^-$ ions. The ligands **stabilise** the copper(I) and prevent it from disproportionating.

4) Copper(I) complexes **aren't coloured** because they have a full **3d subshell** ($3d^{10}$) — see page 87.

5) But **solid copper(I) compounds** can be coloured, e.g. copper(I) oxide ($Cu_2O$) is red.

## Copper(I) Ions *Disproportionate in Aqueous Solution*

1) Copper(I) ions are **unstable** in aqueous solution and **disproportionate** to give copper and copper(II) ions.

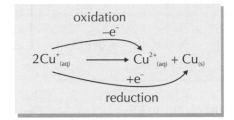

*Disproportionate means the copper(I) is both oxidised and reduced at the same time.*

2) You can predict this disproportionation reaction from the standard electrode potentials (see p76).

From the anticlockwise rule (see p76) the half-equations (and their cell potentials) are:

$$Cu^+ \rightarrow Cu^{2+} + e^- \qquad E^\circ = +0.52 \text{ volts}$$
$$Cu^+ + e^- \rightarrow Cu \qquad E^\circ = +0.15 \text{ volts}$$

Which combine to give the overall reaction:

$$2Cu^+ \rightarrow Cu^{2+} + Cu$$

So the whole cell potential $E^\circ_{cell} = +0.52 - (+0.15) = +\textbf{0.37 volts}$ — the reaction is **likely** to happen.

## Chromium Ions *Usually Exist in the +2, +3 or +6 Oxidation States*

Chromium is used to make **stainless steel**. It's also added to steel to make it **harder**.

It exists in compounds in many oxidation states. The +3 state is the most stable, followed by the +6 and then +2.

Chromium forms **two ions** with oxygen in the +6 oxidation state — **chromate(VI) ions**, $CrO_4^{2-}$, and **dichromate(VI) ions**, $Cr_2O_7^{2-}$.

Both these ions are **good oxidising agents** because they can easily be reduced to $Cr^{3+}$.

When $Cr^{3+}$ **ions** are surrounded by 6 water ligands they're **violet**. But the water ligands are usually **substituted** with impurities in the water e.g. $Cl^-$.

This makes the solution look green.

| Oxidation state | Formula of ion | Colour of ion in water |
|---|---|---|
| +6 | $Cr_2O_7^{2-}_{(aq)}$ | Orange |
| +6 | $CrO_4^{2-}_{(aq)}$ | Yellow |
| +3 | $Cr^{3+}_{(aq)}$ | Green (Violet) |
| +2 | $Cr^{2+}_{(aq)}$ | Blue |

There's more on the oxidation states of chromium on the next page.

# Copper and Chromium

## Chromium Ions can be Oxidised and Reduced

Chromium has lots of different oxidation states and can take part in lots of redox reactions.

1) Dichromate(VI) ions can be **reduced** using a reducing agent such as **zinc and dilute acid**.

Oxidation states: +6        0    +2     +3

$$Cr_2O_7^{2-}{}_{(aq)} + 14H^+{}_{(aq)} + 3Zn_{(s)} \rightarrow 3Zn^{2+}{}_{(aq)} + 2Cr^{3+}{}_{(aq)} + 7H_2O_{(l)}$$
    orange                            green

2) Zinc will **reduce** $Cr^{3+}$ further to $Cr^{2+}$ —

$$2Cr^{3+}{}_{(aq)} + Zn_{(s)} \rightarrow Zn^{2+}{}_{(aq)} + 2Cr^{2+}{}_{(aq)}$$
   green                    blue

But unless you use an inert atmosphere, you're wasting your time — $Cr^{2+}$ is so **unstable** that it oxidises straight back to $Cr^{3+}$ in air.

3) You can oxidise $Cr^{3+}$ to chromate(VI) ions with **hydrogen peroxide** in an **alkaline** solution.

Oxidation states:    +3                     +6

$$2Cr^{3+}{}_{(aq)} + 10OH^-{}_{(aq)} + 3H_2O_{2(aq)} \rightarrow 2CrO_4^{2-}{}_{(aq)} + 8H_2O_{(l)}$$
    green                         yellow

Here's a summary of all the chromium reactions you need to know:

$$Cr_2O_7^{2-}{}_{(aq)} \underset{OH^-{}_{(aq)}}{\overset{H^+{}_{(aq)}}{\rightleftharpoons}} CrO_4^{2-}{}_{(aq)}$$

REDUCTION $H^+{}_{(aq)}/Zn_{(s)}$

OXIDATION $OH^-{}_{(aq)}/H_2O_{2(aq)}$

$$Cr^{3+}{}_{(aq)}$$

REDUCTION $Zn_{(s)}$ (inert atmosphere)

OXIDATION air

$$Cr^{2+}{}_{(aq)}$$

4) Dichromate(VI) ions can also be **converted** to chromate(VI) ions if a **strong alkali** is added or the **reverse reaction** happens in an **acidic solution**.

$$2CrO_4^{2-} + 2H^+ \rightarrow Cr_2O_7^{2-} + H_2O$$
$$Cr_2O_7^{2-} + 2OH^- \rightarrow 2CrO_4^{2-} + H_2O$$

## Chromium(II) Ethanoate Oxidises Easily — Making it Tricky to Produce

Chromium(II) ethanoate, $Cr_2(CH_3COO)_4(H_2O)_2$, is a chromium(II) complex. To make it, you start off with chromium(III) chloride solution. The reaction happens in **two parts**.

1) **Green** chromium(III) chloride is **reduced** with zinc in acid solution to give a **blue** solution of $Cr^{2+}$ ions (like you saw above).

$$2Cr^{3+} + Zn \rightarrow 2Cr^{2+} + Zn^{2+}$$

2) **Sodium ethanoate** is mixed with this solution and a **red precipitate** of **chromium(II) ethanoate** forms.

$$2Cr^{2+} + 4CH_3COO^- + 2H_2O \rightarrow [Cr_2(CH_3COO)_4(H_2O)_2]$$

3) Unfortunately it's not that simple as the complex is **very easily oxidised**. You have to do the whole experiment in an **inert atmosphere** (such as nitrogen) to keep the air out (which is very fiddly). Not only that, but you have to remove the oxygen from all the liquids in your experiment before using them (e.g. by bubbling nitrogen though them).

### Experiment — Making Chromium(II) Ethanoate

1) Slowly add **hydrochloric acid** to a flask containing chromium(III) chloride solution and zinc mesh. The reduction of the $Cr^{3+}$ ions will produce **hydrogen**, which can escape through a rubber tube into a beaker of water.

2) As soon as you see the solution turn a **clear blue** colour, **pinch the rubber tube shut** so hydrogen can **no longer escape** from the flask.

3) The build up of **pressure** in the flask will force the $Cr^{2+}$ solution through the open glass tube and into a flask of **sodium ethanoate**.

4) As soon as the blue solution reacts with the sodium ethanoate, a **red precipitate** forms. Ta-da, you've made **chromium(II) ethanoate**.

5) **Filter** off the precipitate and **wash** it using **water**, then **ethanol**, then **ether** (while still keeping the chromium(II) ethanoate in an inert atmosphere to stop it getting oxidised).

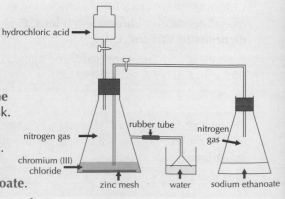

hydrochloric acid

rubber tube

nitrogen gas

nitrogen gas

chromium (III) chloride

zinc mesh        water      sodium ethanoate

# Copper and Chromium

## Chromium Hydroxide is Amphoteric

1) Amphoteric substances can react with both acids and alkalis.
Chromium hydroxide $[Cr(H_2O)_3(OH)_3]$ is an **amphoteric complex**.

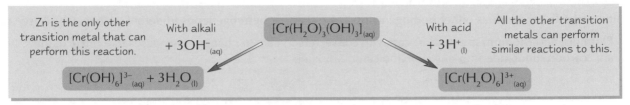

Zn is the only other transition metal that can perform this reaction.

With alkali
$+ 3OH^-_{(aq)}$

$[Cr(H_2O)_3(OH)_3]_{(aq)}$

With acid
$+ 3H^+_{(l)}$

All the other transition metals can perform similar reactions to this.

$[Cr(OH)_6]^{3-}_{(aq)} + 3H_2O_{(l)}$

$[Cr(H_2O)_6]^{3+}_{(aq)}$

2) It's important to note that these are **reactions** and **NOT** ligand exchanges.
The ligands are **chemically modified** by the acid (addition of an $H^+$ ion) or alkali (removal of an $H^+$ ion).

Chromium can still undergo **ligand exchange** when it's mixed with excess ammonia.

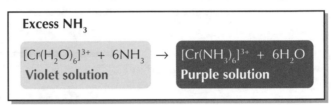

**Excess NH$_3$**

$[Cr(H_2O)_6]^{3+} + 6NH_3 \rightarrow$   $[Cr(NH_3)_6]^{3+} + 6H_2O$
**Violet solution**                       **Purple solution**

## Practice Questions

Q1 Why are solutions of copper(I) complex ions colourless?

Q2 What happens to copper(I) ions when they are dissolved in water?

Q3 How many 3d electrons does chromium have when in the +3 oxidation state?

Q4 What colours are the +3 and +2 chromium aqua-ions?

**Exam Questions**

1   In Anglesey there is an old Roman copper mine.  In the mine are pools of bright blue water.
Local people used to extract copper from these pools using scrap iron dipped into the pools.
   a)   Which complex ion is responsible for the blue colour of the pools?                    [1 mark]
   b)   What kind of reaction takes place between the iron and the copper ions?               [1 mark]
   c)   Write an ionic equation for the reaction.                                             [1 mark]

2   Potassium dichromate(VI) is a powerful oxidising agent in acid solution.
   a)   What is the formula of potassium dichromate(VI)?                                      [1 mark]
   b)   When potassium dichromate(VI) is acidified and mixed with zinc powder in air a colour change is seen
       i)   Describe the colour change.                                                       [1 mark]
       ii)  Give the changes in oxidation state for Cr and Zn and write an ionic equation for the reaction.   [3 marks]
       iii) If the reaction is carried out in an inert atmosphere, a different result will occur.
            State how the result will differ and explain why.                                [3 marks]

3   Chromium(II) ethanoate is a complex that can be made from chromium(III) chloride.
   a)   The first step is to change the oxidation state of the chromium.
       i)   Name this process.                                                                [1 mark]
       ii)  Explain how this is carried out.                                                  [1 mark]
   b)   This process needs to be carried out in an oxygen-free environment.
       i)   Why is this necessary?                                                            [1 mark]
       ii)  Outline the steps needed to ensure this.                                          [2 marks]
   c)   Explain how the reaction is carried out to give a sample of chromium(II) ethanoate.   [4 marks]
   d)   The chromium(II) solution is mixed with sodium ethanoate solution to form a red precipitate.
       What is the formula of the complex?                                                    [1 mark]

## My girlfriend is usually in the +6 or +8 aggravation states...

*Oxidation states are confusing. Fact. Unfortunately there's no way round them. The key thing to remember is OIL RIG — oxidation is loss and reduction is gain of electrons. Armed with this you should be able to work out if something is getting oxidised or reduced and what its oxidation state is. If you're still a bit fuzzy on the details see page 72 for more info.*

# Uses of Transition Metals & Their Compounds

*Transition metals have loads of uses — here are the ones you need to know about.*

## Transition Metals can Catalyse Reactions

Transition metals make really good catalysts because they can use their s and d orbitals to form bonds with reactants and because they can change oxidation state easily.

Transition metals can work as either **homogeneous** (same state) or **heterogeneous** (different state) catalysts (see page 17).

**Platinum** and **rhodium** are used in **catalytic converters** in cars to change nasty gases like **nitric oxide** and **carbon monoxide** into nitrogen and carbon dioxide.

$$2NO_{(g)} + 2CO_{(g)} \longrightarrow N_{2(g)} + 2CO_{2(g)}$$

Here's how it works —

1) **Reactant molecules** arrive at the **surface** and **bond** with the solid catalyst. This is called **adsorption**.

2) The bonds between the **reactant's** atoms are **weakened** and they **break up**. This forms **radicals**. These radicals then **get together** and make **new molecules**.

This example shows you how a catalytic converter changes nitric oxide and carbon monoxide to nitrogen and carbon dioxide.

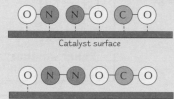

Catalyst surface

Catalyst surface

*\ The adsorption must be strong enough to weaken reactant bonds, but not too strong or it won't let go of the atoms.*

In catalytic converters, the catalyst is usually in the form of a **mesh** or a **fine powder** to increase the **surface area**. Alternatively it might be spread over an **inert support**.

**The Contact process** is a method of creating large quantities of sulfuric acid. **Vanadium** is used as a **catalyst** in one of the early stages of the process. Vanadium(V) oxide reacts with sulfur dioxide and is **reduced** to vanadium(IV).

$$V_2O_{5(s)} + SO_{2(g)} \rightarrow V_2O_{4(s)} + SO_{3(g)}$$

The vanadium(IV) oxide is then **oxidised** back to vanadium(V) by oxygen.

$$2V_2O_{4(s)} + O_{2(g)} \rightarrow 2V_2O_{5(s)}$$

The overall reaction for the process is:

$$2SO_{2(g)} + O_{2(g)} \rightarrow 2SO_{3(g)}$$

## Catalyst Development can Make Chemistry Greener

1) The **development** of new catalysts is an important area of chemical research — catalysts can help make chemical processes more environmentally friendly.

2) A catalyst can often allow a reaction to take place at **lower temperature** or **pressure**. This saves energy and can reduce costs too.

3) Catalysed reactions often have a higher **atom economy** (see p36) than uncatalysed processes — this can **reduce** the amount of **raw materials** needed and decrease the amount of **waste products**.

### Example: making ethanoic acid from methanol and carbon monoxide

1) Originally, ethanoic acid was produced by oxidising **butane**. $2C_4H_{10} + 5O_2 \rightarrow 4CH_3COOH + 2H_2O$
   This process tended to produce a lot of by-products, so it had a **low atom economy**.

2) **Methanol** was first used to make ethanoic acid in the 1960s using a catalyst of **cobalt/iodine**. This was a great improvement, as methanol's a much **cheaper raw material** than butane. It can be produced from **biomass**, rather than crude oil, making it **more environmentally friendly** too. Not only that, but this process has a much **higher atom economy**. $CH_3OH + CO \rightarrow CH_3COOH$

3) By 1966 a **rhodium/iodine catalyst** had been developed which meant the temperature and pressure required for the reaction could be **reduced** to 150 °C and 30 atmospheres. This saved a huge amount of **energy**, which meant **lower production costs** and **less pollution** produced.

4) In the 1980s, a newly developed **iridium/iodine** catalyst made the reaction even faster and more efficient.

# Uses of Transition Metals & Their Compounds

## Transition Metals Have **Many** Uses

1) In **construction** — they are generally strong and unreactive, e.g. iron, nickel, copper.

2) In **jewellery** — they tend to be malleable and inert and they often look shiny, e.g. gold, silver and platinum.

3) In **paint pigments** and **coloured glass** — e.g. iron(II) oxide in green bottles for wine and beer, and cobalt(II) oxide in blue stained glass.

4) In **chemotherapy** — e.g. cisplatin:

- **Cisplatin** is a complex of platinum(II) with two chloride ions and two ammonia molecules in a square planar shape.

- The two Cl⁻ ions have to be **next to each other** — if they were at opposite corners this would be a different isomer (transplatin) with different biological properties.

- Cisplatin is **active against a variety of cancers**, including lung and bladder cancer because it **prevents cancer cells from dividing** by crosslinking the DNA. This prevents the DNA from being able to replicate so the cell dies.

- The downside is that cisplatin also prevents normal cells from reproducing, including blood, which can **suppress the immune system** and increase the risk of infection. Cisplatin may also cause **damage to the kidneys**.

5) In **polychromic sunglasses** — which **darken** when exposed to the **UV radiation** in sunlight.

- Polychromic lenses are usually embedded with a **silver halide** (e.g. silver choride), which **decomposes** in UV radiation to form **silver atoms**.

- These silver atoms cause the lenses to **darken**, causing a **tinting effect**.

- The process is **reversed** when the lenses are no longer exposed to the UV radiation — the silver chloride reforms and the lenses go back to being untinted.

- So when you go indoors where there is a much lower level of UV radiation, your glasses will go back to being untinted.

*Kyle's fashion tip: Polychromic sunglasses add a touch of cool to any outfit.*

## Practice Questions

Q1 Which two transition metals are used in catalytic converters?

Q2 What oxidation states does vanadium have in the Contact process.

Q3 Explain how a rhodium/iodine catalyst helped make ethanoic acid production 'greener'.

Q4 What is the transition metal used in polychromic sunglasses?

### Exam Questions

1  Cisplatin is an anti-cancer drug.
   a)  Draw the structure of cisplatin. [1 mark]
   b)  Explain how cisplatin works to destroy cancer cells. [2 marks]

2  Transition metals have a variety of uses in today's society.
   a)  Transition metals make very good catalysts.
       i) Give two properties of transition metals that allow them to catalyse a reaction. [2 marks]
       ii) What do the terms homogeneous catalyst and heterogeneous catalyst mean? [2 marks]
   b)  Transition metals play a vital role in the chemical industry as catalysts.
       i) Give two examples of transition metal catalysts and for each example name a
          reaction or process it catalyses. [2 marks]
       ii) Describe two ways that catalysts are able to make a reaction more environmentally friendly. [2 marks]
   c)  Give two other uses of transition metals. Include an example for each use. [2 marks]

## Bagpuss, Sylvester, Tom — the top three on my catalyst...

*Hopefully you'll have realised from these pages that transition metals are really quite useful. I'm surprised there aren't statues built in their honour. Make sure you know all the uses for your exam — then why not celebrate with a cheese triangle of triumph (or any victory foodstuff of your choice) — you've made it to the end of the section.*

# Aromatic Compounds

*In the old days something just had to be whiffy to qualify as an aromatic compound.*
*These days, they're a bit more fussy about the definition...*

## Aromatic Compounds are Derived from Benzene

**Arenes** or **aromatic compounds** contain a **benzene ring**.
Benzene has the formula $C_6H_6$ — there are two ways of representing it:

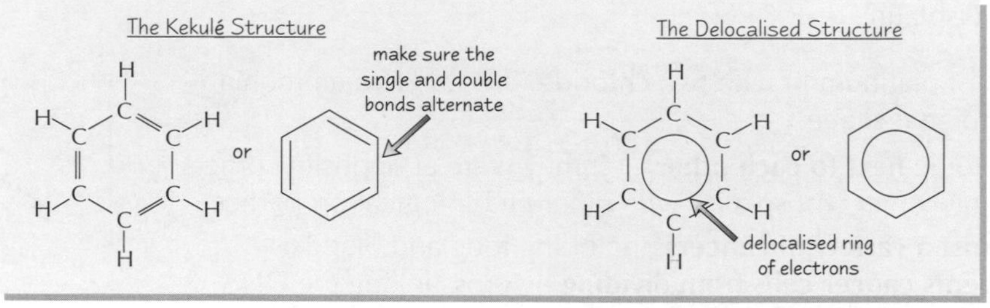

The Kekulé Structure                              The Delocalised Structure

make sure the single and double bonds alternate

or

delocalised ring of electrons

or

Arenes are named in two ways. There's no easy rule — you just have to learn these examples:

Some are named as substituted benzene rings...

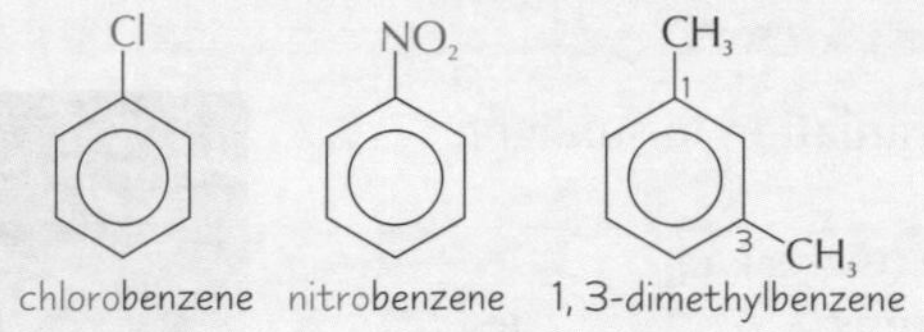

chlorobenzene    nitrobenzene    1, 3-dimethylbenzene

...while others are named as compounds with a phenyl group ($C_6H_5$) attached.

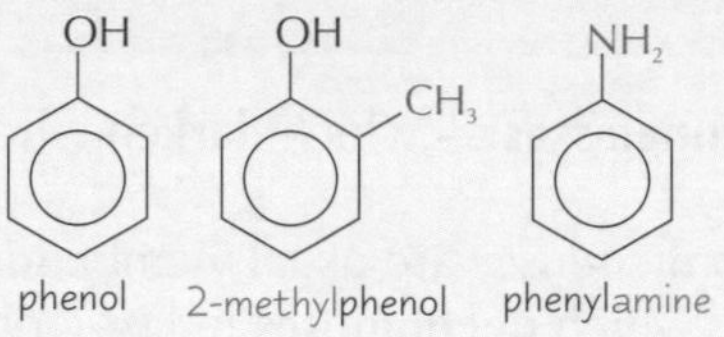

phenol    2-methylphenol    phenylamine

## The Kekulé Model of Benzene Came First

1) The Kekulé structure was proposed by Friedrich August Kekulé in 1865. It consists of a **ring** of carbon atoms with **alternating single** and **double** bonds, which constantly **flip** between the two carbons.

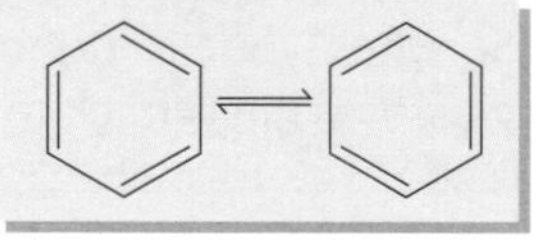

2) If the Kekulé model was correct, you'd expect there to always be three bonds with the length of a **C–C bond** (154 pm) and three bonds with the length of a **C=C bond** (134 pm).

3) But **X-ray diffraction studies** have shown that all of the carbon-carbon bonds in benzene are the **same length** (139 pm) — i.e. they are **between** the length of a single bond and a double bond.

   **Infrared studies** have also shown that **none** of the carbon-carbon bonds in benzene are normal double or single bonds because they absorb energy at a **different frequency**.

4) So the Kekulé structure **can't** be completely right. But it's still sometimes used today, because it's useful for drawing **reaction** mechanisms.

## The Delocalised Model Replaced Kekulé's Model

1) The **delocalised model** says that the **p-orbitals** of all six carbon atoms **overlap** to create $\pi$-**bonds**.

2) This creates two **ring-shaped** clouds of electrons — one above and one below the plane of the six carbon atoms.

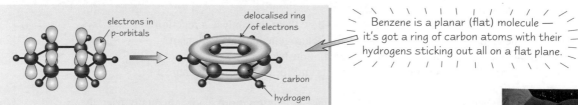

electrons in p-orbitals

delocalised ring of electrons

carbon

hydrogen

Benzene is a planar (flat) molecule — it's got a ring of carbon atoms with their hydrogens sticking out all on a flat plane.

3) All the bonds in the ring are the **same length** because all the bonds are the **same**. So this model fits the **X-ray diffraction** and **infrared data**.

4) The electrons in the rings are said to be **delocalised** because they don't belong to a specific carbon atom. They are represented as a circle inside the carbon ring rather than as double or single bonds.

Gary woke up after the stag party to find himself in a very delocalised orbit.

# Aromatic Compounds

## Delocalisation of Electrons Gives the Molecule Stability

1) Cyclohexene has **one** double bond. When it's hydrogenated, the enthalpy change is **–120 kJ mol⁻¹**. If benzene had three double bonds (as in the Kekulé structure), you'd expect it to have an enthalpy of hydrogenation of –360 kJ mol⁻¹.

2) But the **experimental** enthalpy of hydrogenation of benzene is **–208 kJ mol⁻¹** — far less exothermic than expected.

3) Energy is **put in** to break bonds and **released** when bonds are made. So **more energy** must have been put in to break the bonds in benzene than would be needed to break the bonds in the Kekulé structure.

4) This difference indicates that benzene is **more stable** than the Kekulé structure would be. This is all down to the **delocalised ring of electrons**.

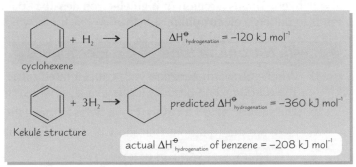

## Benzene Burns with a Smoky Flame

Benzene is a **hydrocarbon**, so it burns in oxygen to give carbon dioxide and water:

$$2C_6H_6 + 15O_2 \rightarrow 12CO_2 + 6H_2O$$

If you burn benzene in **air**, you get a very **smoky flame** — there's too little oxygen to burn the benzene completely. A lot of the carbon atoms stay as carbon and form particles of **soot** in the hot gas — making the flame **smoke**.

## Practice Questions

Q1 Draw the Kekulé and delocalised models of benzene.

Q2 Explain how infrared absorption data provides evidence for the delocalised model of benzene.

Q3 Explain what is meant by the term 'delocalised electrons'.

Q4 Why does benzene burn in the air with a smoky flame?

### Exam Questions

1 In 1865, the German chemist Friedrich August Kekulé suggested a structure for benzene.

   a) What is the formula of benzene? [1 mark]

   b) Draw the Kekulé structure of benzene. [1 mark]

   The current model of the benzene molecule contains a delocalised electron ring.

   c) Explain how X-ray diffraction studies provide evidence for the delocalised model rather than Kekulé's model. [3 marks]

2 The Kekulé structure of benzene contains three carbon-carbon double bonds. Cyclohexene, $C_6H_{10}$, contains only one carbon-carbon double bond.

   Both benzene and cyclohexene produce cyclohexane when they are hydrogenated. The enthalpy of hydrogenation of benzene is –208 kJ mol⁻¹. The enthalpy of hydrogenation of cyclohexene is –120 kJ mol⁻¹.

   a) Explain how these results indicate that the Kekulé structure of benzene is incorrect. [3 marks]

   b) Explain how these results suggest that the actual structure of benzene is more stable than the Kekulé structure would be. [2 marks]

## Everyone needs a bit of stability in their life...

*The structure of benzene is really weird — even top scientists struggled to find out what its molecular structure looked like. If you're asked anything about why benzene reacts the way it does, it's bound to be something to do with the ring of delocalised electrons. And don't forget that there's a hydrogen at every corner of the benzene ring — one for each carbon.*

# Reactions of Aromatic Compounds

*Benzene is an alkene but it often doesn't behave like one — whenever this is the case, you can pretty much guarantee that our kooky friend Mr Delocalised Electron Ring is up to his old tricks again...*

## Arenes Undergo **Electrophilic Substitution** Reactions...

The benzene ring is a region of **high electron density**, so it attracts **electrophiles**. As the benzene ring's so stable, it tends to undergo **electrophilic substitution** reactions, which preserve the delocalised ring.

### ...with **Nitronium Ions** as the Electrophile

1)  When you warm **benzene** with **concentrated nitric** and **sulfuric acids**, you get **nitrobenzene**. The nitrobenzene product forms as a layer which floats on top of the acid.

2)  The sulfuric acid's a **catalyst** — it helps to make the nitronium ion, $NO_2^+$, which is the **electrophile**.

3)  Here are the equations that show how the electrophile's formed:

$$HNO_3 + H_2SO_4 \rightarrow H_2NO_3^+ + HSO_4^-$$
$$H_2NO_3^+ \rightarrow NO_2^+ + H_2O$$

4)  And here's the reaction mechanism:

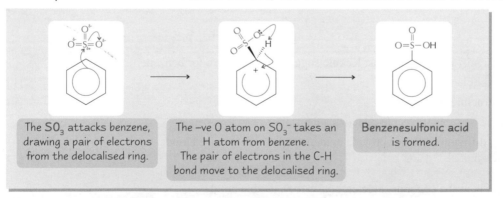

The nitronium ion attacks the benzene ring.

An unstable intermediate forms.

The H+ ion is lost.

+ H⁺ → This H+ ion reacts with $HSO_4^-$ to reform the catalyst, $H_2SO_4$.

5)  If you only want one $NO_2$ group added (**mononitration**), you need to keep the temperature **below 55 °C**. Above this temperature you'll get lots of substitutions.

### ...and with **Sulfur Trioxide Molecules** as the Electrophile

1)  If you want to make **benzenesulfonic acid** (and you never know, one day you might...), you'll need to warm benzene to 40 °C with **fuming sulfuric acid** for about half an hour.

2)  Fuming sulfuric acid is basically **sulfur trioxide**, $SO_3$, dissolved in **sulfuric acid**.

3)  The electrophile in this reaction is **sulfur trioxide**, and the mechanism is similar to the nitration one:

The $SO_3$ attacks benzene, drawing a pair of electrons from the delocalised ring.

The –ve O atom on $SO_3^-$ takes an H atom from benzene. The pair of electrons in the C-H bond move to the delocalised ring.

Benzenesulfonic acid is formed.

Escaping from prison is a breeze with the patented CGP electro-file.

## Halogen Carriers Help to Make Good Electrophiles

An electrophile must have a pretty strong **positive charge** to be able to attack the stable benzene ring. Most compounds **aren't polarised enough** — but some can be made into **stronger electrophiles** using a catalyst called a **halogen carrier**.

Halogen carriers accept a **lone pair of electrons** from the halogen in the electrophile. As the lone pair of electrons is pulled away, the **polarisation** in the electrophile **increases** and sometimes a **carbocation** even forms. This makes the electrophile heaps stronger.

$$\overset{\delta+}{R}-\overset{\delta-}{Cl}: \text{----}\rightarrow AlCl_3 \longrightarrow R^+ \ AlCl_4^-$$
halogenoalkane   halogen carrier   carbocation

Halogen carriers include **aluminium halides**, **iron halides** and **iron**.

# Reactions of Aromatic Compounds

## Friedel-Crafts Alkylation Reactions Produce Alkylbenzenes

Friedel and Crafts discovered that a **halogenoalkane** will react with benzene in the presence of a **halogen carrier** to produce an **alkylbenzene**. The halogen carrier used is usually **aluminium chloride**, $AlCl_3$.

It's another **electrophilic substitution** reaction — the electrophile is the **carbocation** ($R^+$) made when the halogenoalkane reacts with the halogen carrier.

First you need to form the electrophile:

$$RCl + AlCl_3 \rightarrow R^+ + AlCl_4^-$$

Then it can attack the benzene ring:

The carbocation ($R^+$) attacks the benzene ring.

An H atom is removed by $AlCl_4^-$.

alkylbenzene

the alkyl group has been substituted for the hydrogen.

the halogen carrier is regenerated

$+ HCl + AlCl_3$

*Alkylbenzenes are **more reactive** than benzene, so it's difficult to stop the reaction at just one substitution — you usually get **polyalkylation**.*

$AlCl_3$ is very sensitive to **hydrolysis**, so the reaction is done in **dry** conditions — the reactants are **refluxed** in **dry ether**.

## Friedel-Crafts Acylation Reactions Produce Phenylketones

**Acyl chlorides** (see page 59) are **polar** molecules — so they can easily lose their chlorine atoms to form **carbocations**. They react with benzene by **electrophilic substitution** in the presence of a **halogen carrier** — producing **phenylketones**.

Handily, it's very similar to the Friedel-Crafts alkylation reaction. You form the electrophile from the acyl chloride and the halogen carrier:

$$RCOCl + AlCl_3 \rightarrow RCO^+ + AlCl_4^-$$

Then it attacks the benzene ring:

The carbocation ($RCO^+$) attacks the benzene ring.

An H atom is removed by $AlCl_4^-$.

phenylketone

the acyl group has been substituted for the hydrogen.

the halogen carrier is regenerated

$+ HCl + AlCl_3$

The reaction mixture is heated under reflux with a **dry ether**.

*Phenylketones are **less reactive** than benzene — so you'll only get one substitution.*

## Practice Questions

Q1 Describe the role of a halogen carrier in electrophilic substitution reactions.

Q2 Draw the mechanism for the reaction of benzene with chloromethane, $CH_3Cl$, in the presence of an $AlCl_3$ catalyst.

**Exam Question**

1 Two electrophilic substitution reactions of benzene are summarised in this diagram:

a) i) Name the product A, and the reagents B and C, and give the conditions D. [4 marks]

ii) Outline a mechanism for this reaction. [3 marks]

iii) Write two equations to show the formation of the electrophile. [2 marks]

b) i) Name the product F, and the reagent E. [2 marks]

ii) What is the electrophile in this reaction? [1 mark]

c) Explain why benzene and other arenes will undergo electrophilic substitution reactions. [2 marks]

## *Why does every sentence I write contain the word 'delocalised'...*

*Arenes love their delocalised (there I go again...) ring — it makes them stable, and they don't want to give it up for anything. You can get them to take part in electrophilic substitution reactions though, because they can do those and still keep it intact.*

# More Reactions of Aromatic Compounds

*You're not quite done with delocalised electron rings yet. Prepare yourself for a few more reactions...*

## Arenes Will React With **Halogens** Using a **Halogen Carrier**

1) If you shake a cycloalkene, like **cyclohexene**, with **bromine water**, bromine adds across the double bond to give a dibromoalkane. This is an **electrophilic addition** reaction — it decolorises the bromine water, and is used as a test for **alkenes**.

*The mechanism for this reaction is the same as for any alkene reacting with $Br_2$ — if you can't remember it, take a peek at your AS notes.*

2) But benzene **won't** decolorise bromine water — it takes too much energy to break up the delocalised electron ring.

3) As you saw on the last page, benzene will undergo **electrophilic substitution** reactions with strong electrophiles.

4) **Bromine**, $Br_2$, isn't a strong enough electrophile to react with benzene on its own. But if you add a **halogen carrier**, like $FeBr_3$, it strongly **polarises** the $Br_2$ molecule, creating a strong electrophile that can attack the benzene ring.

5) First of all you need to form the **electrophile**: $Br_2 + FeBr_3 \rightarrow Br^+ + FeBr_4^-$

6) Then it attacks the benzene ring:

*The electrophile ($Br^+$) attacks the benzene ring.* *An H atom is removed by $FeBr_4^-$.* *a bromine atom has been substituted for the hydrogen.* *bromobenzene* *+ HBr + FeBr₃* *the catalyst is reformed.*

7) You end up with bromobenzene — a Br atom has been **substituted** for one of the H atoms.

## Benzene Will Undergo Some **Addition Reactions**

If you want to add groups to benzene, you have to use very **harsh conditions** in order to break that **stable** delocalised electron system.

For example, benzene will react with **hydrogen** in the presence of a **finely divided nickel catalyst** at **150 °C** and **10 atm** to form **cyclohexane**.

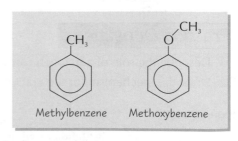

## You Can Use **Methylbenzene** or **Methoxybenzene** Instead of Benzene

1) If you're doing any of the reactions on pages 98 to 100 in the lab, you'll probably use **methylbenzene** or **methoxybenzene** as the reactant **instead** of benzene.

2) Because of its delocalised electron ring, benzene is a really **stable** molecule. So its reactions are usually **very slow**.

3) The **CH₃** and **OCH₃** groups in methylbenzene and methoxybenzene donate electrons to the **delocalised ring**, increasing its electron density, and making it more reactive. So they both react **faster** than benzene.

*Methylbenzene    Methoxybenzene*

4) Methylbenzene and methoxybenzene are both much **less toxic** than benzene too, so they're **safer** to use.

5) You'll end up with slightly **different products** — but the basic **reactions** will work just the same.

## Phenols Are Benzene Rings with **–OH** Groups Attached

**Phenol** is a benzene ring with an OH group substituted for one of the H atoms. It has the formula $C_6H_5OH$. Other phenols can have various groups attached to the benzene ring.

*phenol    2-methylphenol    4-chlorophenol    4-nitrophenol*

*Number the carbons starting from the one with the –OH group.*

# More Reactions of Aromatic Compounds

## Phenol Reacts with Bromine Water

1) If you shake **phenol** with orange **bromine water**, they will **react**, and the bromine water will be **decolorised**.

2) Benzene **doesn't** react with bromine water (as you saw on page 100), so phenol's reaction must be to do with the **OH group**.

3) One of the **electron pairs** in a p-orbital of the oxygen atom **overlaps** with the **delocalised ring** of electrons in the benzene ring.

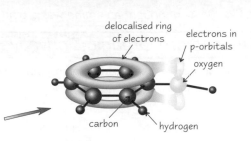
delocalised ring of electrons
electrons in p-orbitals
oxygen
carbon
hydrogen

4) This increases the **electron density** of the ring, especially at positions 2, 4 and 6, making it more likely to be attacked by the bromine molecule in these positions. (You don't need to know why the electron density increases more at these positions than the others — this is just so you know why the Br atoms end up where they do)

5) The hydrogen atoms at 2, 4 and 6 are substituted by bromine atoms — it's an **electrophilic substitution** reaction. The product is **2,4,6-tribromophenol** — it's insoluble in water and **precipitates** out of the mixture as a **white solid**. It smells of antiseptic.

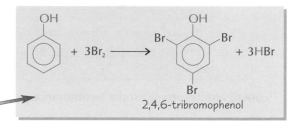
2,4,6-tribromophenol

## Phenol Can be Nitrated Using Dilute Nitric Acid

1) Phenol will react with **dilute nitric acid** to give two **isomers** of **nitrophenol**, and water.

2) Nitrating phenol is much **easier** than nitrating benzene — that requires **concentrated** nitric and sulfuric acids.

3) The difference is due to the **activating** effect of the **OH group** again — and that's also why you're most likely to get NO₂ groups at positions 2 and 4 on the carbon ring.

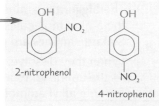
2-nitrophenol
4-nitrophenol

## Practice Questions

Q1 Describe the conditions needed to get benzene to react with hydrogen to make cyclohexane.

Q2 Draw the structures of methylbenzene and methoxybenzene.

Q3 Write a balanced equation for the reaction between phenol ($C_6H_5OH$) and bromine ($Br_2$).

Q4 Draw the two isomers formed when phenol reacts with dilute nitric acid.

### Exam Questions

1 Benzene will react with bromine, $Br_2$, in the presence of iron(III) bromide, $FeBr_3$. This reaction that takes place is an electrophilic substitution reaction.

   a) Write an equation for the formation of the electrophile. [1 mark]

   b) Draw out the mechanism for the reaction. [4 marks]

   c) Name the aromatic product formed. [1 mark]

2 Bromine water can be used to distinguish between benzene and phenol.

   a) Describe what you would observe when benzene is shaken with bromine water. [1 mark]

   b) Describe what you would observe when phenol is shaken with bromine water. [3 marks]

   c) Name the aromatic compound formed when phenol reacts with bromine water. [1 mark]

   d) Explain why phenol reacts differently from benzene with bromine water. [2 marks]

   e) What type of reaction occurs between phenol and bromine? [1 mark]

## Phenol Destination 4 — more chemicals, more equations, more horror...

*And that about wraps it up for reactions of benzene (and, of course, reactions of benzene with other stuff stuck on it). So when you're quite sure you've learned the benzene and bromine mechanism, and the cheeky extra couple of benzene bits, plus the fiddly phenol stuff, find your favourite hat, throw it in the air, give a loud cheer, and move on to amines...*

# Amines

*If, like me, you thought an amine was a type of Japanese cartoon, it's not — it's a nitrogen containing functional group.*

## Amines are Organic Derivatives of Ammonia

If one or more of the **hydrogens** in **ammonia** ($NH_3$) is replaced with an **organic group**, you get an **amine**.

| | | | | |
|---|---|---|---|---|
| methylamine | dimethylamine | trimethylamine | tetramethylamine ion (quaternary ammonium ion) | phenylamine |
| (primary amine) | (secondary amine) | (tertiary amine) | | (primary amine) |

aliphatic amines       aromatic amine

**Small amines** smell similar to **ammonia**, with a **slightly 'fishy'** twist. **Larger amines** smell very 'fishy'.

## Small Amines Dissolve in Water to form an Alkaline Solution

1) **Small amines** are **soluble in water** — this is because the amine group can form **hydrogen bonds** with the water molecules.

2) The **bigger** the amine is, the **greater** the **London forces** between the amine molecules will be, and the less soluble it is. So **large amines** are **much less soluble** in water than small ones.

3) When they dissolve, amines form **alkaline** solutions — the amine takes a hydrogen ion from water, forming **alkyl ammonium ions** and **hydroxide ions**.

$$CH_3CH_2NH_{2(aq)} + H_2O_{(l)} \rightleftharpoons CH_3CH_2NH_3{}^+{}_{(aq)} + OH^-{}_{(aq)}$$

## Amines React with Acids to Form Salts

1) Amines act as **bases** because they can **accept protons** — there's a **lone pair of electrons** on the **nitrogen** atom that can form a **dative covalent bond** with an $H^+$ ion.

2) Because they are bases, amines are **neutralised** by **acids** to make **ammonium salts**. For example, **ethylamine** reacts with **hydrochloric** acid to form ethylammonium chloride:

$$CH_3CH_2NH_2 + HCl \rightarrow CH_3CH_2NH_3{}^+Cl^-$$

## Amines will Form a Complex Ion With Copper(II) Ions

1) In **copper(II) sulphate** solution, the $Cu^{2+}$ ions form $[Cu(H_2O)_6]^{2+}$ complexes with water. This solution's **blue**.

2) If you add a **small** amount of **methylamine solution** to copper(II) sulphate solution you get a **pale blue precipitate** — the amine acts as a **Brønsted-Lowry base** (proton acceptor) and takes two $H^+$ ions from the complex. This leaves copper hydroxide , $[Cu(H_2O)_4(OH)_2]$, which is insoluble.

3) Add more methylamine solution, and the **precipitate dissolves** to form a beautiful **deep blue solution**. Some of the ligands are replaced by methylamine molecules, which donate their lone pairs to form dative covalent bonds with the $Cu^{2+}$ ion. This forms soluble $[Cu(CH_3NH_2)_4(H_2O)_2]^{2+}$ complex ions.

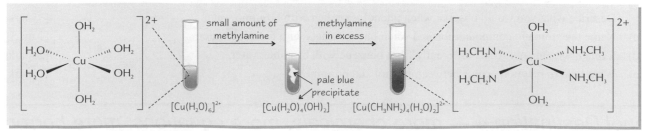

4) The **same** set of reactions will happen with **other** amine molecules. For **larger** amines, the final product may **change** because the amine molecules just **can't** fit around the copper ion.

# Amines

## Amines can be *Acylated* to form *N-substituted Amides*

When amines react with acyl chlorides, an **H atom** on the amine is swapped for the **acyl group**, RCO, to produce an **N-substituted amide** (see page 104) and **HCl**. The HCl reacts with another molecule of the amine to produce a **salt**.

1) In the case of **butylamine** ($C_4H_9NH_2$), the reactions are:

**Stage 1:**

H₃C—C(=O)—Cl + H—N—H(C₄H₉) → HCl + H₃C—C(=O)—N—H(H₉C₄)

Ethanoyl chloride    Butylamine    N-butylethanamide

**Stage 2:**

H—N—H(C₄H₉) + HCl → H—N⁺—H Cl⁻(H, C₄H₉)

Butylamine    Butylammonium chloride

The combined equation for this reaction is: $CH_3COCl + 2C_4H_9NH_2 \rightarrow CH_3CONHC_4H_9 + [C_4H_9NH]^+Cl^-$

To carry out this reaction, ethanoyl chloride is added to a **concentrated aqueous solution** of the amine. A violent reaction occurs, which produces a **solid, white mixture** of the products.

*This is just like the 'halogenoalkane and ammonia' reaction you met at AS level.*

A similar reaction will happen between a **primary amine** and a **halogenoalkane**.

For example:    $CH_3\overset{\delta+}{C}H_2\overset{\delta-}{Cl} + \overset{..}{N}H_2C_4H_9 \rightarrow CH_3CH_2NHC_4H_9 + HCl$

Chloroethane    Butylamine    Ethylbutylamine

The lone pair of electrons on the nitrogen attack the $\delta+$ carbon atom on the halogenoalkane, displacing the chlorine and making the salt $[CH_3CH_2NH_2C_4H_9]^+Cl^-$. The chlorine then removes a hydrogen from the nitrogen to produce a **secondary amine** — $CH_3CH_2NHC_4H_9$. This type of reaction can repeat again to produce a **tertiary amine**.

2) **Phenylamine** ($C_6H_5NH_2$) also reacts with ethanoyl chloride in the same way:

**Stage 1:**

H₃C—C(=O)—Cl + (benzene ring)NH₂ → HCl + H₃C—C(=O)—NH—(benzene ring)

Ethanoyl chloride    Phenylamine    N-phenylethanamide

**Stage 2:**

(benzene ring)NH₂ + HCl → (benzene ring)NH₃⁺ Cl⁻

Phenylammonim chloride

Although the **solid products** of this reaction should be white, they are usually **stained brown** with unreacted phenylamine.

**Paracetamol** can be made by a similar reaction starting from **p-aminophenol**:

The 'p' in p-aminophenol stands for 'para'. It means that the two functional groups are directly **opposite** each other on the benzene ring.

H₃C—C(=O)—Cl + (benzene ring with OH and NH₂) → HCl + (benzene ring with OH and NH—C(=O)—CH₃)

p-aminophenol    Paracetamol

## Practice Questions

Q1  Explain why small amines dissolve in water but large ones don't.

Q2  Give the formula and colour of the complex ion formed when an excess of methylamine solution is mixed with copper(II) sulfate solution.

### Exam Question

1  Butylamine solution will react with ethanoyl chloride, $CH_3COCl$, to form N-butylethanamide, $CH_3CONH(C_4H_9)$.

a)  Give the molecular formula of butylamine.                                    [1 mark]

b)  Butylamine solution is alkaline. Explain why this is.                          [2 marks]

c)  Write balanced equations for the two stages of the reaction between butylamine and ethanoyl chloride.    [2 marks]

## You've got to learn it — amine it might come up in your exam...

*Rotting fish smells so bad because the flesh releases amine molecules as it decomposes. But is it the fish that smells of amines or the amines that smell of fish? That's just one of those 'chicken or egg' things that no-one can answer...*

# Amides and Aromatic Amines

*Prepare yourself for the extremely colourful world of aromatic amines. And the.. erm.. completely colourless world of amides. Well, you can't have everything I suppose.*

## Amides *are Carboxylic Acid Derivatives*

**Amides** contain the functional group $-CONH_2$.

The **carbonyl group** pulls electrons away from the rest of the group, so amides behave differently from amines.

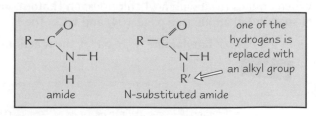

Here are a few molecules that have amide functional groups:

Ethanamide | Butanamide | This is urea — it's an amide too.

## Ammonia *and* Amines *can be* Acylated *to form* Amides

Acylation is when an **acyl group** is substituted for an **H atom**. You can acylate **ammonia** or an **amine** to make an **amide**.

If you react an acyl chloride with **ammonia**, you'll get an **amide.**
(You need to be careful with this one — it's a pretty violent reaction.)

ethanoyl chloride + $NH_3$ → ethanamide + HCl

If you react the acyl chloride with an **amine** instead, you'll get an **N-substituted amide**.
(This is the same reaction that you saw on page 103.)

ethanoyl chloride + $CH_3NH_2$ → N-methylethanamide + HCl

With both of these reactions, the **HCl** that's formed can go on to react with **more** of the ammonia or amine. So you'll usually end up with an **amide** and an **ammonium salt**.

## Aromatic *Amines are made by* Reducing *a* Nitro Compound

Aromatic amines are produced by **reducing** a nitro compound e.g. **nitrobenzene**. There are **two steps** to the method:

1) First you **reduce** the nitro compound, by heating it with **tin** and **concentrated hydrochloric acid** under **reflux** — this makes an **ammonium salt**. If you use **nitrobenzene**, this salt will be $C_6H_5NH_3^+Cl^-$.

2) Then add some **sodium hydroxide** solution. The hydroxide ions remove an $H^+$ from the salt, giving an aromatic amine. If you started with nitrobenzene, then you'll end up with **phenylamine**.

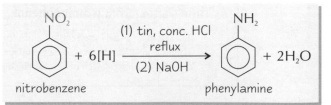

nitrobenzene $+ 6[H]$ $\xrightarrow[\text{(2) NaOH}]{\text{(1) tin, conc. HCl}\atop\text{reflux}}$ phenylamine $+ 2H_2O$

## Aromatic Amines *are Used to Make* Azo Dyes

1) Azo dyes are man-made dyes that contain the **azo group**, $-N=N-$. They're made by reacting aromatic amines with phenols.

2) In most azo dyes, the azo group links **two aromatic groups**.

3) Having two aromatic groups creates a very **stable molecule** — the azo group becomes part of the **delocalised electron system**.

4) Different **colours** of azo dye are made by combining different phenols and amines. The **colours** are the result of **light absorption** by the delocalised electron system.

(They're mostly shades of red, orange and yellow, but you can get green and blue ones too.)

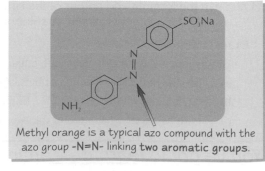

Methyl orange is a typical azo compound with the azo group -N=N- linking **two aromatic groups**.

# Amides and Aromatic Amines

## Azo Dyes can be made in a Coupling Reaction

The first step in creating an azo dye is to make a **diazonium salt** — diazonium compounds contain the group $-\overset{+}{N}\equiv N$.
The **azo dye** is then made by **coupling** the diazonium salt with an **aromatic** compound that is susceptible to **electrophilic attack** — like a **phenol**.

Here's the method for creating a yellow-orange azo dye:

### React Phenylamine with Nitrous Acid to make a Diazonium Salt

1) **Nitrous acid ($HNO_2$)** is **unstable**, so it has to be made *in situ* from sodium nitrite and hydrochloric acid.

$$NaNO_2 + HCl \rightarrow HNO_2 + NaCl$$

*'in situ' means in the reaction*

2) **Nitrous acid** reacts with **phenylamine** and **hydrochloric acid** to form **benzenediazonium chloride**. The temperature **must** be around **5 °C** to prevent a phenol forming instead.

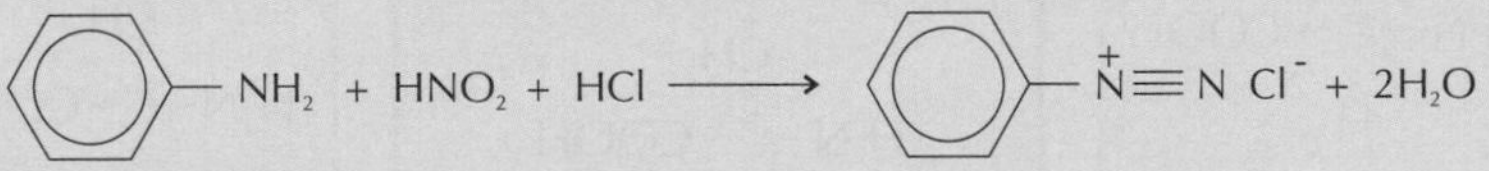

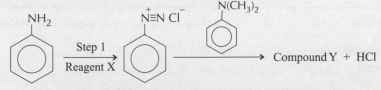

3) The diazonium salts aren't very stable and **decompose quickly** — so they have to be **immediately** used in the next step of the reaction.

### Make the Azo Dye by Coupling the Diazonium Salt with a Phenol

1) First, the **phenol** has to be dissolved in **sodium hydroxide** solution to make **sodium phenoxide** solution.
2) It's then stood in **ice**, and chilled **benzenediazonium chloride** is added.
3) Here's the overall equation for the reaction:

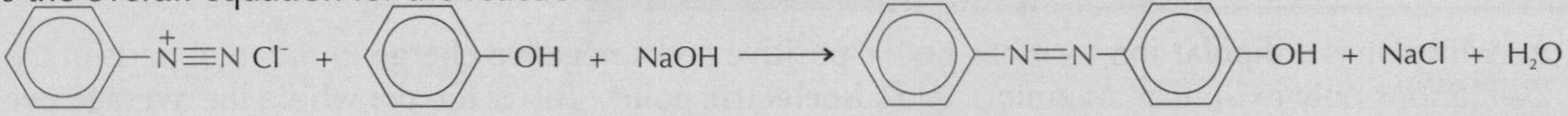

yellow-orange azo compound

4) The azo dye **precipitates** out of the solution immediately.
5) Phenol is a **coupling agent**. The lone pairs on its oxygen increase the **electron density** of the benzene ring (see page 101). This gives the diazonium ion (a **weak electrophile**) something to attack.

Aromatic azo compounds are **stable** because the azo functional group –N=N– becomes part of the **delocalised electron system**. Because they're stable, they make great dyes — the molecules don't fall apart, so the colours **don't fade**.

## Practice Questions

Q1 Write an equation for the reaction between propanoyl chloride, $CH_2CH_2COCl$, and ammonia.
Q2 Write an equation for the reaction between propanoyl chloride, $CH_2CH_2COCl$, and methylamine.
Q3 Describe how you could prepare phenylamine, starting from nitrobenzene.

### Exam Question

1 Consider this synthesis pathway:

a) i) Reagent X, used in Step 1, is made from $HCl_{(aq)}$ and one other reagent.
   Name the other reagent and write an equation to show the generation of reagent X *in situ*. [2 marks]
   ii) Give the conditions for Step 1. [1 mark]

b) Compound Y is a yellow solid.
   i) Draw a possible structure for Compound Y. [1 mark]
   ii) Suggest a use for Compound Y. [1 mark]

## Do you expect me to talk? No, Mr Diazonium Salt, I expect you to dye...

*I realise that there are loads of reactions to learn on these two pages, and you might be feeling a little overwhelmed at the prospect of learning them all, but er... don't be. Just break it down into sections and keep going over it until you're happy — or at least until you've stopped cursing me, the exam board, nitrogen, and the good name of dyes everywhere.*

# Amino Acids

*What do you get if you cross an amine with a carboxylic acid? Give up yet? I'll give you a clue — it's in the page title...*

## Amino Acids have an **Amino Group** and a **Carboxyl** Group

An amino acid has a **basic amino group** ($NH_2$) and an **acidic carboxyl group** (COOH). This makes them **amphoteric** — they've got both acidic and basic properties.

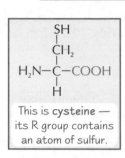
variable group
amino group    carboxyl group

*α*–**amino acids** have both the amino group and the carboxyl group attached to the **same carbon atom** — this is called the '*α* carbon'. So the general formula of an *α*–amino acid is **RCH(NH₂)COOH**.

Here are a few examples:

| | | | |
|---|---|---|---|
| H₂N—C—COOH (with H above and H below) | H₂N—C—COOH (with CH₃ above and H below) | H₂N—C—COOH (with benzene ring, CH₂ above and H below) | H₂N—C—COOH (with SH, CH₂ above and H below) |
| This is **glycine** — it's the simplest possible α–amino acid. | This is the amino acid **alanine**. | This is **phenylalanine** — it has a benzene ring in its R group. | This is **cysteine** — its R group contains an atom of sulfur. |

Amino acids are the monomers that are used to make **proteins** (see page 111).

## Amino Acids Can Exist As **Zwitterions**

A zwitterion is a **dipolar ion** — it has both a **positive** and a **negative charge** in different parts of the molecule. Zwitterions only exist near an amino acid's **isoelectric point**. This is the **pH** where the **average overall charge** on the amino acid is zero. It's different for different amino acids — it depends on their R-group.

| In conditions more **acidic** than the isoelectric point, the –NH₂ group is likely to be **protonated**. | At the isoelectric point, both the carboxyl group and the amino group are likely to be ionised — forming a **zwitterion**. | In conditions more **basic** than the isoelectric point, the –COOH group is likely to **lose** its proton. |
|---|---|---|
| low pH | zwitterion | high pH |

## Paper Chromatography is used to **Identify Unknown** Amino Acids

You can easily identify amino acids in a **mixture** using a simple **paper chromatography** experiment. Here's how:

1) Draw a **pencil line** near the bottom of a piece of chromatography paper and put a **spot** of the amino acid mixture on the line.

2) Dip the bottom of the paper (not the spot) into a **solvent**.

3) As the solvent spreads up the paper, the different amino acids in the mixture move with it, but at **different rates** — so they separate out.

4) When the solvent's **nearly** reached the top, take the paper out and **mark** the distance that the solvent has moved (**solvent front**) in pencil.

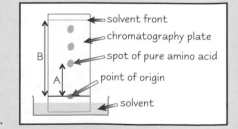
solvent front
chromatography plate
spot of pure amino acid
point of origin
solvent

5) Amino acids are **colourless**, so to locate the separated spots you stain them with **ninhydrin solution** (see p107).

6) You can work out the **R_f values** of the amino acids using this formula:

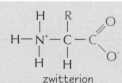
$$R_f \text{ of amino acid} = \frac{A}{B} = \frac{\text{distance travelled by spot}}{\text{distance travelled by solvent}}$$

7) Now you can use a **table of known amino acid R_f values** to identify the amino acids in the mixture.

# Amino Acids

## Amino Acids can be Detected using Ninhydrin

1) Solutions of **amino acids** are **colourless** — so when you've separated out a mixture of them using thin layer chromatography, you can't see the amino acid spots.

2) Handily, you can reveal just where the spots of the pure amino acids are by spraying the paper with a solution of **ninhydrin**.

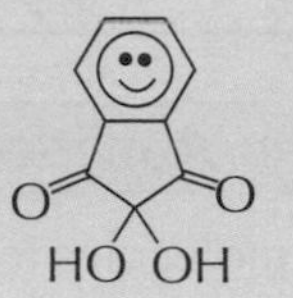

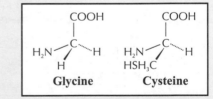

This is a scientifically accurate picture of ninhydrin — with a smiley face.

3) Ninhydrin reacts with **amino acids** to produce **ammonia**, aldehydes, carbon dioxide, and a substance called **hydrindantin**.

4) Hydrindantin reacts with the ammonia and more ninhydrin to give a **purple pigment**, called **Ruhemann's purple**. So the amino acid spots will turn purple.

## Amino Acids are Chiral Molecules

There are usually **four** different groups attached to the central carbon of an α-amino acid. This means that they are **chiral** molecules and have two **optical isomers** (see page 48).

If **plane-polarised**, **monochromatic light** is shone through an aqueous solution of an α–amino acid, the plane of the light gets **rotated** because of the **chiral carbon**.

The exception to this is **glycine** — it has two H atoms attached to the central carbon. This means that it **isn't chiral**, and it won't rotate the plane of plane polarised light.

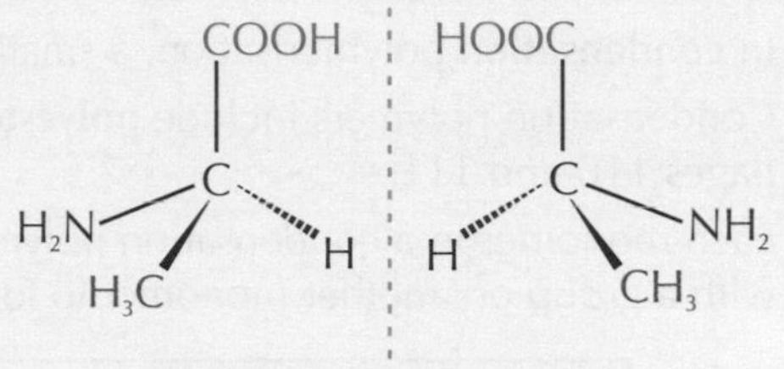

These are the two possible enantiomers of **alanine**.

## Practice Questions

Q1 Draw the general structure of an α-amino acid.

Q2 What is a zwitterion?

Q3 When separating amino acids using paper chromatography, what is ninhydrin used for?

Q4 Explain why most amino acids rotate the plane of plane-polarised monochromatic light.

### Exam Questions

1 Glycine and cysteine, shown on the right, are two naturally occurring amino acids.

    **Glycine**      **Cysteine**

  a) One way of distinguishing between glycine and cysteine is to observe their effect on plane-polarised monochromatic light. Explain why this method works.     [2 marks]

  b) Explain how paper chromatography could be used to separate and identify a mixture of amino acids.     [6 marks]

2 Amino acids are organic molecules that contain both a carboxyl group and an amino group.

  a) Give the general formula of an α-amino acid.     [1 mark]

  b) Explain what is meant by the 'isoelectric point' of an amino acid.     [1 mark]

  c) The α-amino acid serine has the formula $HOOCCH(NH_2)CH_2OH$.

    i) Draw the displayed formula of serine.     [1 mark]

    ii) Draw the structure that serine will take in a solution with a high pH.     [1 mark]

## Who killed the Zwittonians?

*Zwitterions are actually the last physical remains of a race of highly advanced beings known as Zwittonians from the galaxy I Zwiky 19. It is thought that they lived approximately 9.75 billion years ago before evolving beyond the need for physical bodies, exploding in a ball of energy and emitting zwitterion particles throughout the cosmos. Fascinating.... Also untrue.*

# Polymers

*Polymers are long molecules made by joining lots of little molecules together. They can be made using addition or condensation polymerisation, as you're about to see.*

## There are **Two Types** of Polymerisation — **Addition** and **Condensation**

### Alkenes *Join Up* to form *Addition Polymers*

1) **Polymers** are long chain molecules formed when lots of small molecules, called **monomers**, join together as if they're holding hands.

2) Alkenes will form polymers — the **double bonds** open up, and molecules join together to make long chains. The individual, small alkenes are the monomers.

3) This is called **addition polymerisation**.

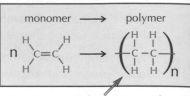

The bit in brackets is the 'repeating unit'. n is the number of repeating units.

### Condensation Polymers *are formed as* Water *is* Removed

1) In **condensation** polymerisation, a small molecule, usually **water**, is **lost** as the molecules link together.

2) Condensation polymers include **polyesters**, **polyamides** and **polypeptides** — there's lots more about these on pages 110 and 111.

3) Each monomer in a condensation polymer has at least **two functional groups**. Each functional group reacts with a group on another monomer to form a **link**, creating the polymer **chain**.

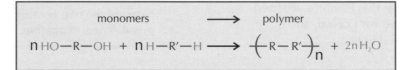

Remember, **R** just represents a chunk of an **organic molecule** — it could be pretty much anything.

## Addition Polymers *can be Formed from* Alkenes

As you saw above, you can make an **addition polymer** by joining together individual **alkene** molecules. Here are a few examples of addition polymers:

**Poly(phenylethene)** is formed from **phenylethene**...

the double bond opens up

'n' means there are lots of these units

phenylethene monomer    poly(phenylethene) polymer

...and this is what a section of the polymer chain would look like:

section of poly(phenylethene) polymer

You can write the name of a polymer with or without the brackets — e.g. poly(chloroethene) or polychloroethene.

**Poly(chloroethene)** is formed from **chloroethene**.

chloroethene monomer    poly(chloroethene) polymer

Poly(chloroethene) is also known as Poly(vinyl chloride) or PVC.

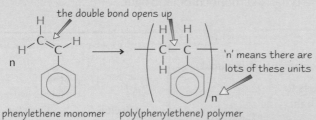

**Poly(propenamide)** is formed from **propenamide**.

propenamide monomer    poly(propenamide) polymer

In the exam, you might be given the monomer asked to draw repeating units like these for addition polymers.

# Polymers

## Example of an Addition Polymer: **Poly(ethenol)**

1) **Poly(ethenol)** is a **water soluble** addition polymer.
   It's made from ethenol monomers like this:  ⟶
   (Poly(ethenol) used to be called **polyvinyl alcohol**.)

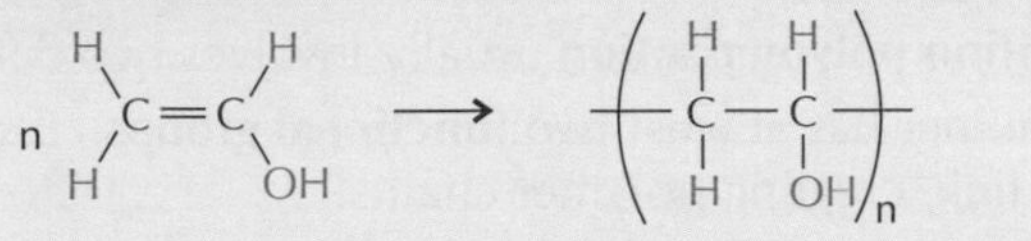

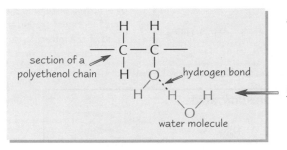
ethenol monomer          poly(ethenol) polymer

2) Poly(ethenol) is great for making the **water soluble laundry bags** that are used in **hospitals**.
   Soiled bed linen can be placed in one of these bags and the whole lot put in a washing machine
   **without** it being opened.  This reduces the risk of **spreading infection**.

3) The poly(ethenol) bag **breaks down** at 40 °C in the machine and releases its contents.

section of a
polyethenol chain          hydrogen bond

water molecule

4) The polymer is also used to **wrap liquid detergent**, as a clean
   and convenient way of handling it.  The whole package
   — called a **liquitab** — can be put in the washing machine,
   where the wrapping **dissolves**.

5) Poly(ethenol) is soluble because it can **hydrogen bond**
   with water through the **OH groups** along its chain.

## Practice Questions

Q1  What type of molecules are the monomers used in addition polymerisation?

Q2  Explain how condensation polymerisation works.

Q3  What would you call an addition polymer formed from tetrafluoroethene monomer molecules?

Q4  Poly(2-propenenitrile) is made from the monomer $CH_2CHCN$.  Draw the repeating unit of poly(2-propenenitrile).

Q5  Draw the monomer that's used to make poly(ethenol).

### Exam Questions

1  Poly(propene) is a strong and durable polymer that is used
   to make packaging and textiles.

   It is made from the monomer propene, shown on the right.

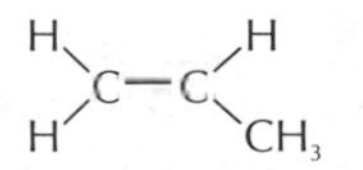

   **Propene**

   a)  Name the type of polymerisation reaction by which this polymer would be formed.    [1 mark]

   b)  Explain how the poly(propene) polymer is formed from the propene monomers.    [2 marks]

   c)  Draw the repeating unit of the poly(propene) polymer.    [1 mark]

2  Poly(propenamide) and poly(ethenol) are both water soluble polymers.

   a)  Draw the structure of the monomer that is used to make poly(propenamide).    [1 mark]

   b)  Draw the structure of the repeating unit of poly(ethenol).    [1 mark]

   c)  Explain why poly(ethenol) is water soluble.    [2 marks]

   d)  Give a use of poly(ethenol), and explain why it is used for the purpose you have suggested.    [2 marks]

## Wicked Witches are made of poly(ethenol)...

*...and Dorothy, being a chemistry whizz, figured this out and famously used it to her advantage.  A bucket of warm water,
and voila — witch soup.  Good witches, on the other hand, are made of poly(ethene), which can't form hydrogen bonds.
So water's an excellent way to distinguish between good and bad witches.  Just remember — only bad witches are soluble.*

# More Condensation Polymers

*You met condensation polymerisation briefly on page 108 — well now it's back with two pages all of its own...*

## Condensation Polymers Include **Polyesters**, **Polyamides** and **Polypeptides**

1) **Condensation polymerisation** usually involves two different types of monomers.

2) Each monomer has at least **two functional groups**. Each functional group reacts with a group on another monomer to form a link, creating polymer chains.

3) Each time a link is formed, a small molecule (often water) is lost — that's why it's called **condensation** polymerisation.

## Reactions Between **Dicarboxylic Acids** and **Diamines** Make **Polyamides**

The **carboxyl** groups of **dicarboxylic acids** react with the **amino** groups of **diamines** to form **amide links** (–CONH–). So the polymer that you make is called a **polyamide**.

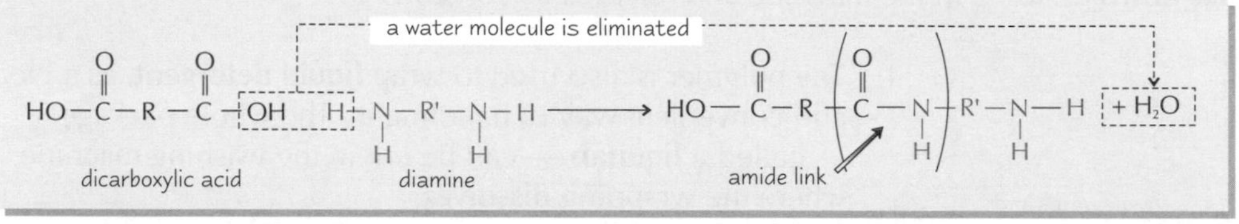

Dicarboxylic acids and diamines have functional groups at each end of the molecule, so long chains can form.

**Example**

**Nylon 6,6** — made from **1,6-diaminohexane** and **hexanedioic acid**.

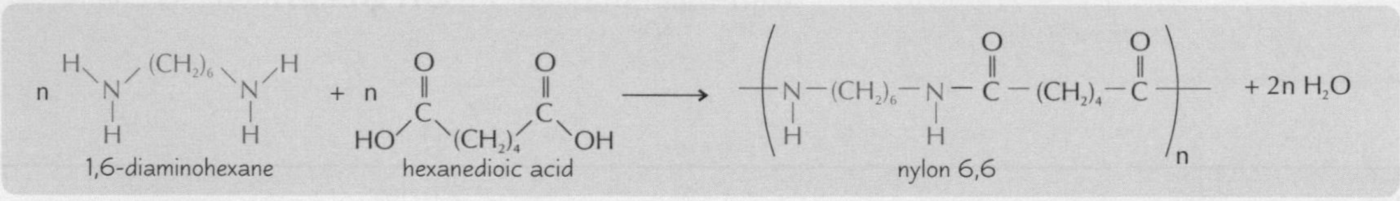

Nylon fibre is **strong, elastic** and **abrasion-resistant** — it's used to make ropes, carpets and clothes.

**Example**

**KEVLAR®** — made from **benzene-1,4-diamine** and **benzene-1,4-dicarboxylic acid**.

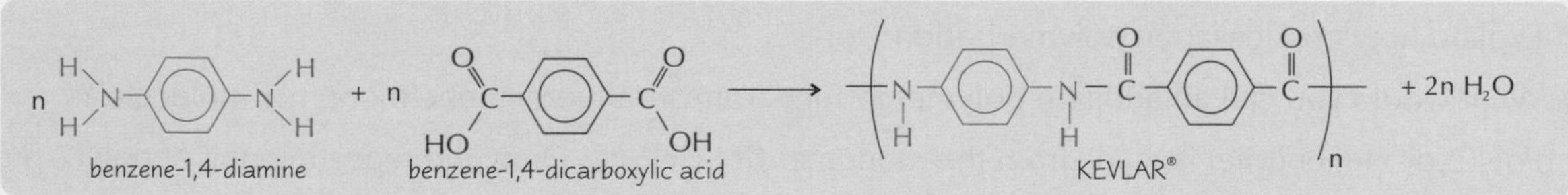

KEVLAR® is **strong** and **light** — five times stronger than steel. It's used to make bulletproof vests.

Polyamides are very useful because of their **physical properties**:

1) They have a **high tensile strength** — because of this, they're often used to make **rope**.

2) They can be used at **relatively high temperatures** and are **resistant to most chemicals** except **acids** (and a few alcohols). This makes polyamides great for use in **clothing** (unless you often spill acid all over yourself...).

## Reactions Between **Dicarboxylic Acids** and **Diols** Make **Polyesters**

The **carboxyl** groups of **dicarboxylic acids** can also react with the **hydroxyl** groups of **diols** to form **ester links** (–COO–).

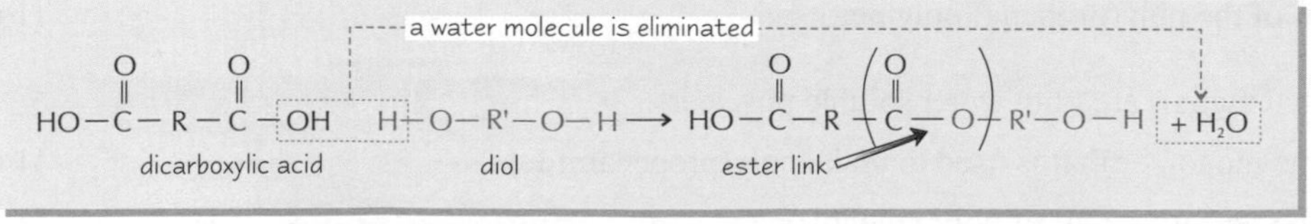

Like polyamides, polyesters are often used to make clothing.

Polymers joined by **ester links** are called **polyesters** — an example is **Terylene™**.

**Example**

**Terylene™**, or **PET** — made from **benzene-1,4-dicarboxylic acid** and **ethane-1,2-diol**.

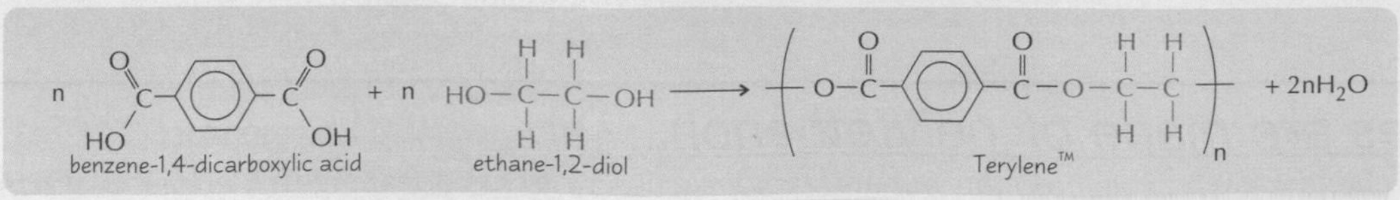

PET stands for **polyethylene terephthalate**.

Polyesters can be used to make clothing too — they're **strong** (but not as strong as nylon), **flexible** and **abrasion-resistant**.

# More Condensation Polymers

## Proteins are Condensation Polymers of Amino Acids

Proteins are made up of **lots** of amino acids (see page 106) joined together.
The chain is put together by **condensation** reactions. **Peptide links** are made between the amino acids.

Here's how two **amino acids** join together to make a **dipeptide**:

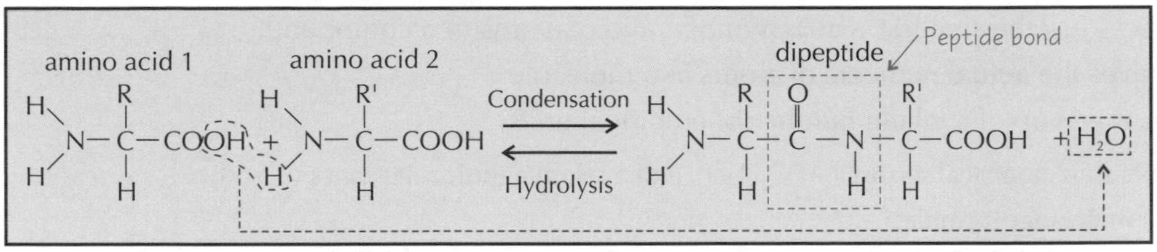

*Proteins are really **polyamides** — the monomers are joined by amide groups. In proteins these are called **peptide bonds** though.*

When lots of these reactions happen, you make a **long chain** — and that's a **protein**.

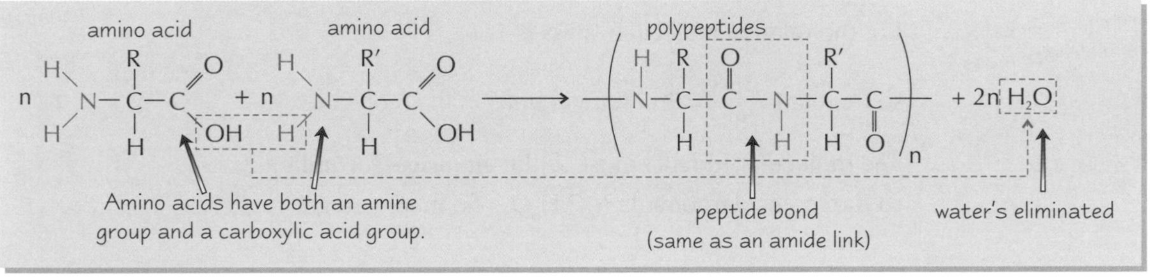

Amino acids have both an amine group and a carboxylic acid group.

peptide bond (same as an amide link)

water's eliminated

## Practice Questions

Q1 Why are polyamides and polyesters called 'condensation polymers'?.

Q2 Which two types of molecules react together to make a polyamide?

Q3 Draw the repeating unit of Terylene™ and circle the ester link.

Q4 Name a natural condensation polymer.

### Exam Questions

1 a) Nylon 6,6 is the most commonly produced form of nylon. A section of the polymer is shown below:

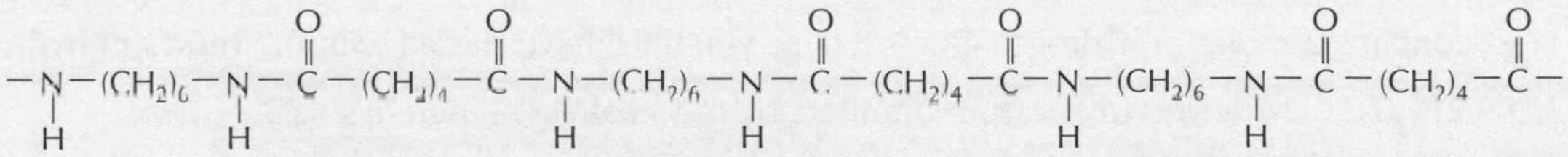

$$-N-(CH_2)_6-N-C-(CH_2)_4-C-N-(CH_2)_6-N-C-(CH_2)_4-C-N-(CH_2)_6-N-C-(CH_2)_4-C-$$

   i) Draw the structural formulas of the monomers from which nylon 6,6 is formed.
      It is not necessary to draw the carbon chains out in full. [2 marks]
   ii) Name the type of linkage found between the monomers in this polymer. [1 mark]

   b) A polyester is formed by the reaction between the monomers hexanedioic acid and 1,6-hexanediol.
   i) Draw the repeating unit for the polyester. [1 mark]
   ii) Explain why this is an example of condensation polymerisation. [1 mark]

2 When two amino acids react together, a dipeptide is formed.
   a) Explain the meaning of the term dipeptide. [2 marks]
   b) The amino acids serine and glycine are shown on the right.
      Draw the structures of the two dipeptides that could be
      formed when serine and glycine react together. [2 marks]

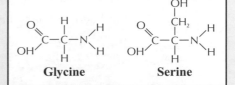

**Glycine**            **Serine**

## Never miss your friends again — form a polymer...

*It's a job for Q designing all these polymers — bulletproof vests, nylon parachutes — just think, you could be the next mad inventor, working for the biggest secret agency in the world. And you'd have a really fast car, which would obviously turn into a flashy speedboat with the press of a button... and retractable wings so you could fly... just think of the possibilities.*

# Empirical and Molecular Formulas

*It's the last section — hurray!!! But it starts with some maths — boooo. But you've seen it before at AS — hurray!!!*
*I can't keep doing this — boooo. Oh go on then, one more — hurray!!! And don't forget to brush your teeth — ????*

## Empirical *and* Molecular *Formulas are* Ratios

You have to know what's what with empirical and molecular formulas, so here goes...

1) The **empirical formula** gives just the smallest whole number ratio of atoms in a compound.

2) The **molecular formula** gives the **actual** numbers of atoms in a molecule.

3) The molecular formula is made up of a **whole number** of empirical units.

> **Example:** A molecule has an empirical formula of $C_4H_3O_2$, and a relative molecular mass of 166.
> Work out its molecular formula.
>
> First find the **empirical mass** — $(4 \times 12) + (3 \times 1) + (2 \times 16)$
> $= 48 + 3 + 32 = 83\ g$
>
> But the **relative molecular mass** is 166,
>
> so there are $\dfrac{166}{83} = 2$ empirical units in the molecule.
>
> The molecular formula must be the **empirical formula × 2**,
> so the molecular formula = $C_8H_6O_4$. So there you go.

*Compare the empirical and relative molecular mass.*

*Empirical mass is just like the relative formula mass... (if that helps at all...).*

## Empirical *Formulas are Calculated from* Experiments

You need to be able to work out empirical formulas from **experimental results** too.

> **Example:** When a hydrocarbon is burnt in excess oxygen, 4.4 g of carbon dioxide and 1.8 g of water are made.
> What is the empirical formula of the hydrocarbon?
>
> No. of moles of $CO_2 = \dfrac{mass}{M} = \dfrac{4.4}{12 + (16 \times 2)} = \dfrac{4.4}{44} = 0.1$ moles
>
> 1 mole of $CO_2$ contains 1 mole of carbon atoms, so you must have started with **0.1 moles of carbon atoms**.
>
> No. of moles of $H_2O = \dfrac{1.8}{(2 \times 1) + 16} = \dfrac{1.8}{18} = 0.1$ moles
>
> 1 mole of $H_2O$ contains 2 moles of hydrogen atoms (H), so you must have started with **0.2 moles of hydrogen atoms**.
>
> Ratio C : H = 0.1 : 0.2 . Now you divide both numbers by the **smallest** — here it's 0.1.
> So, the ratio C : H = 1 : 2. So the empirical formula must be $CH_2$.

*First work out how many moles of the products you have.*

*This works because the only place the carbon in the carbon dioxide and the hydrogen in the water could have come from is the hydrocarbon.*

As if that's not enough, you also need to know how to work out
empirical formulas from the **percentages** of the different elements.

> **Example:** A compound is found to have percentage composition 56.5% potassium,
> 8.7% carbon and 34.8% oxygen by mass. Calculate its empirical formula.
>
> In **100 g** of compound there are:
>
> $\dfrac{56.5}{39} = 1.449$ moles of K     $\dfrac{8.7}{12} = 0.725$ moles of C     $\dfrac{34.8}{16} = 2.175$ moles of O
>
> Divide each number of moles by the **smallest number** — in this case it's 0.725.
>
> K: $\dfrac{1.449}{0.725} = 2.0$     C: $\dfrac{0.725}{0.725} = 1.0$     O: $\dfrac{2.175}{0.725} = 3.0$
>
> The ratio of K : C : O = 2 : 1 : 3. So you know the empirical formula's got to be $K_2CO_3$.

*Use* $n = \dfrac{mass}{M}$

*If you assume you've got 100 g of the compound, you can turn the % straight into mass, and then work out the number of moles as normal.*

# Empirical and Molecular Formulas

## Molecular Formulas are Calculated from Experimental Data Too

Once you know the empirical formula, you just need a bit more info and you can work out the **molecular formula** too.

### Example:

When 4.6 g of an alcohol, with relative molecular mass 46, is burnt in excess oxygen, it produces 8.8 g of carbon dioxide and 5.4 g of water.

*Alcohols contain C, H and O.*

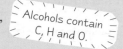

Calculate the empirical formula for the alcohol and then its molecular formula.

*The carbon in the $CO_2$ and the hydrogen in the $H_2O$ must have come from the alcohol — work out the number of moles of each of these.*

No. of moles of $CO_2 = \dfrac{\text{mass}}{M} = \dfrac{8.8}{44} = 0.2$ moles

1 mole of $CO_2$ contains 1 mole of C. So, 0.2 moles of $CO_2$ contains **0.2 moles of C**.

No. of moles $H_2O = \dfrac{\text{mass}}{M} = \dfrac{5.4}{18} = 0.3$ moles

1 mole of $H_2O$ contains 2 moles of H. So, 0.3 moles of $H_2O$ contain **0.6 moles of H**.

Mass of C = no. of moles × M = 0.2 × 12 = 2.4 g
Mass of H = no. of moles × M = 0.6 × 1 = 0.6 g
Mass of O = 4.6 − (2.4 + 0.6) = 1.6 g

Number of moles O = $\dfrac{\text{mass}}{M} = \dfrac{1.6}{16} = 0.1$ moles

*Now work out the mass of carbon and hydrogen in the alcohol. The rest of the mass of the alcohol must be oxygen — so work out that too. Once you know the mass of O, you can work out how many moles there is of it.*

Molar Ratio = C : H : O = 0.2 : 0.6 : 0.1 = 2 : 6 : 1

**Empirical formula = $C_2H_6O$**

*When you know the number of moles of each element, you've got the molar ratio. Divide each number by the smallest.*

Mass of empirical formula = (12 × 2) + (1 × 6) + 16 = 46 g

In this example, the mass of the empirical formula equals the relative molecular mass, so the empirical and molecular formulas are the same.

*Compare the empirical and molecular mass.*

**Molecular formula = $C_2H_6O$**

*You also need to know how to work out the molecular, empirical and structural formulas from the spectrographic techniques (see pages 62-69).*

## Practice Questions

Q1 What's the difference between empirical and molecular formulas?
Q2 What's the empirical formula of ethene?
Q3 What's the molecular formula of a molecule with empirical formula $CH_2$ and a molecular mass of 112?

### Exam Questions

1   An aldehyde contains only carbon, hydrogen and oxygen.
    When it is burnt in excess oxygen 0.1 g of the compound gives 0.228 g of carbon dioxide and 0.093 g of water.
    a)   Calculate the empirical formula of this compound.                         [4 marks]
    b)   What percentage of the compound by mass is hydrogen?                       [2 marks]
    c)   If the molecular mass is 58, what is the molecular formula?                [1 mark]
    d)   Draw the structure of the molecule.                                        [1 mark]

2   A common explosive contains 37% carbon, 2.2% hydrogen, 18.5% nitrogen and 42.3% oxygen, by mass.
    It has a molecular mass of 227 and can be made from benzene.
    a)   Calculate the empirical formula of the compound and hence its molecular formula.   [4 marks]
    b)   Suggest a possible structure of the molecule.                             [1 mark]

## These pages contain the formulas for A2 Chemistry success...

*I really wanted to make some geeky Star Wars™ reference about how the empirical formula is some sort of special milk that's given to baby Storm Troopers, but I couldn't quite get it right. Oh well, I guess I'm just going to have to fill this space with something else.... so here I go............. filling the space.......... with......... something else............ close enough.*

# Practical Techniques

*You can't call yourself a chemist unless you know these practical techniques. Unless your name's Boots.*

## Refluxing *Makes Sure You* **Don't Lose** *Any* **Volatile Organic Substances**

Organic reactions are slow and the substances are usually flammable and volatile (they've got low boiling points). If you stick them in a beaker and heat them with a Bunsen they'll evaporate or catch fire before they have time to react.

You can reflux a reaction to get round this problem.

The mixture's heated in a flask fitted with a vertical 'Liebig' condenser — this condenses the vapours and recycles them back into the flask, giving them time to react.

The heating is usually electrical — hot plates, heating mantles, or electrically controlled water baths are normally used. This avoids naked flames that might ignite the compounds.

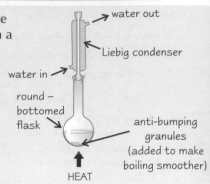

water out
Liebig condenser
water in
round–bottomed flask
anti-bumping granules (added to make boiling smoother)
HEAT

## There are **Lots of Ways** to **Purify** a Sample

### Washing

The product of a reaction can be contaminated with unreacted reagents or unwanted side products. You can remove some of these by washing the product.
E.g. aqueous sodium hydrogencarbonate solution can be used to remove acid from an organic product. Any excess acid is reacted with the sodium hydrogencarbonate to give $CO_2$ gas, and the organic product (assuming it's insoluble in the aqueous layer) can be easily removed using a separating funnel.

### Solvent Extraction

You can separate a product from a mixture by dissolving it in a solvent. This only works if only the product dissolves. Shake the mixture with fresh solvent several times to make sure you extract as much product as possible from the mixture.

### Drying

A lot of organic reactions either use water or produce water. To dry a liquid product you can add anhydrous calcium chloride granules. Calcium chloride removes water from the mixture by forming solid crystals, which can be filtered off.

### Recrystallisation

Recrystallisation will let you remove a small amount of an impurity in a solid.
1) Add very hot solvent to the impure solid until it just dissolves — it's really important not to add too much.
2) This should give a saturated solution of impure product.
3) Let the solution cool down slowly. Crystals of the product will form as it cools.
4) It's important that the product is very soluble at high temperatures and nearly insoluble at low temperatures.
5) The impurities stay in solution. They're present in much smaller amounts than the product, so they'd take much longer to crystallise out.
6) Remove the crystals by filtration, wash with ice-cold solvent and leave to dry.
   You're left with crystals of the product that are much purer than the original solid.

## Melting *and* Boiling *Points are Good Indicators of* Purity

Most pure substances have a specific melting and boiling point. If they're impure, the melting point's lowered and the boiling point is raised. If they're very impure, melting and boiling will occur across a wide range of temperatures.

To accurately measure the melting point:
Put a small amount of the solid in a capillary tube and place in a beaker of oil with a very sensitive thermometer. Slowly heat, with constant stirring, until the solid just melts and read the temperature on the thermometer.

To measure the boiling point:
Measure the temperature that the liquid is collected at during distillation.

# Practical Techniques

## Fractional Distillation *Separates Two or More Liquids*

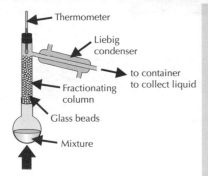

Thermometer

Liebig condenser

to container to collect liquid

Fractionating column

Glass beads

Mixture

Fractional distillation separates liquids with **different boiling points**.

The mixture's **heated** in the apparatus shown and the liquid in the flask boils. As the vapour goes up the **fractionating column**, it gets **cooler**. If the temperature falls below its boiling point, the molecules **condense** and run back down through the glass beads. As the temperature increases, each liquid will reach the top of the column at a different time, in order of their boiling points. The liquid with the lowest boiling point will be distilled first.

Sometimes the high temperatures used during distillation can cause a product to **decompose**. To help stop this happening **steam** can be passed into the mixture — this **lowers** the **boiling point** of the product so it can evaporate at a temperature that doesn't cause it to decompose.

## Lots of Techniques *are Used to Prepare a Compound*

Here are a couple of preparations you need to know about.

**Example: Cholesteryl benzoate** is used in liquid crystal displays, hair colours and cosmetics. It's an ester of cholesterol (alcohol) and benzoic acid, but is prepared from benzoyl chloride.

1) Start by dissolving the cholesterol in the solvent pyridine (toxic).
2) Then add the benzoyl chloride (a lachrymator — makes you cry like tear gas).
3) Heat in a steam bath for 10 minutes, then cool and add methanol.
4) Filter off the crystals of the ester that form and wash them with methanol.
5) Recrystallise the ester using ethyl ethanoate as the solvent.

*The preparation is done in a fume cupboard because of the harmful reagents.*

**Example: Methyl 3-nitrobenzoate** is prepared by nitrating methyl benzoate.

1) Dissolve methyl benzoate in concentrated sulfuric acid that has been cooled in an ice bath.
2) Then add a 50:50 mixture of concentrated sulfuric and nitric acids dropwise, with constant stirring. You need to keep the temperature below 10 °C with ice.
3) Stir the mixture for 15 minutes, then pour it over crushed ice in a beaker. When the ice has melted, filter off the crystals of product that have formed.
4) Wash the crystals with water and then recrystallise them using ethanol.

*The experiment needs to be carried out below 10 °C to keep the yield high.*

## Practice Questions

Q1 Why is refluxing needed in many organic reactions?

Q2 Why is the melting point helpful in deciding the purity of a substance?

Q3 Draw the apparatus needed for fractional distillation.

Q4 Why is electrical heating often used in organic chemistry?

**Exam Question**

1   Two samples of stearic acid melt at 69 °C and 64 °C respectively.  Stearic acid dissolves in hot propanone but not in water.

　　a)　　Explain which sample is purer. [2 marks]

　　b)　　How could the impure sample be purified? [5 marks]

　　c)　　How could the sample from b) be tested for purity? [1 mark]

## There's just a **fraction** *too much information on these pages for me...* boom boom

*And that, my friends, is what chemistry is all about — playing with funny looking pieces of glass and making crystals in pretty colours whilst wearing a white coat, goggles and stood in a fume cupboard. Ok, not actually stood in the fume cupboard, that would just be silly. You'd keep hitting your head and you can't do chemistry with a bumped head.*

# Organic Functional Groups

*I spy with my little eye a functional group starting with A...*

## Functional Groups are the Most Important Parts of a Molecule

Functional groups are the parts of a molecule that are responsible for the way the molecule reacts. These are the main ones you need to know (which are all covered earlier in the book)...

| Group | Found in | Prefix / Suffix | Example |
|---|---|---|---|
| $-C\overset{O}{\underset{OH}{}}$ | carboxylic acids | carboxy– –oic acid | ethanoic acid |
| $-C\overset{O}{\underset{Cl}{}}$ | acyl chlorides | –oyl chloride | ethanoyl chloride |
| $-C-O-C-$ (O, O) | acid anhydrides | –oic anhydride | ethanoic anhydride |
| $-C-O-$ (O) | esters, polyesters | –oate | ethyl methanoate |
| $-C\overset{O}{\underset{H}{}}$ | aldehydes | –al | propanal |
| $C=O$ | ketones | –one | propanone |

| Group | Found in | Prefix / Suffix | Example |
|---|---|---|---|
| $-OH$ | alcohols, phenols | hydroxy– –ol | propanol |
| $-NH_2$ | primary amines | amino– –amine | methylamine |
| $NH$ | secondary amines | –amine | dimethylamine |
| $N-$ | tertiary amines | –amine | trimethylamine |
| $-NO_2$ | nitro benzenes | nitro- | nitrobenzene |
|  (benzene ring) | aromatic compounds | phenyl– –benzene | phenylamine |
| $C=C$ | alkenes | -ene | butene |

The functional groups in a molecule give you clues about its **properties** and the **reactions** it might take part in. For example, a **–COOH group** will (usually) make a molecule **acidic** and mean it will react with alcohols to make esters.

## Use the Functional Groups for Classifying and Naming Compounds

Organic molecules can get pretty complicated, often with many functional groups. You need to be able to **pick out** the functional groups on an unknown molecule, **name them** and **name the molecule** in a systematic way.

1)  The **main functional group** is used as the **suffix** and the other functional groups are added as **prefixes**.

2)  The table above shows the order of importance of the functional groups, with COOH being the most important, down to phenyl which is the least. (Note — alkenes are treated differently, with 'ene' always appearing in the suffix.)

3)  If you need to include more than one functional group prefix, then list them in **alphabetical order**.

**Example:**  Look at compound A, shown on the right.

   a)  What class of chemicals does compound A belong to?

   b)  Give the systematic name of compound A.

**A**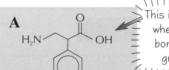

*This is a skeletal formula where only the carbon bonds and functional groups are shown.*

   a)  It's got a COOH group and an NH₂ group, so it must be an **amino acid** (see p.106)

   b)  COOH is the main functional group, so number the carbon atoms from this side. There's a **3-carbon** chain, so it's a **propanoic acid**. The **phenyl** group is on the **2nd** carbon atom. The **amino** group is on the **3rd** carbon atom.

   So the full name would be...
   **3-amino-2-phenylpropanoic acid.**

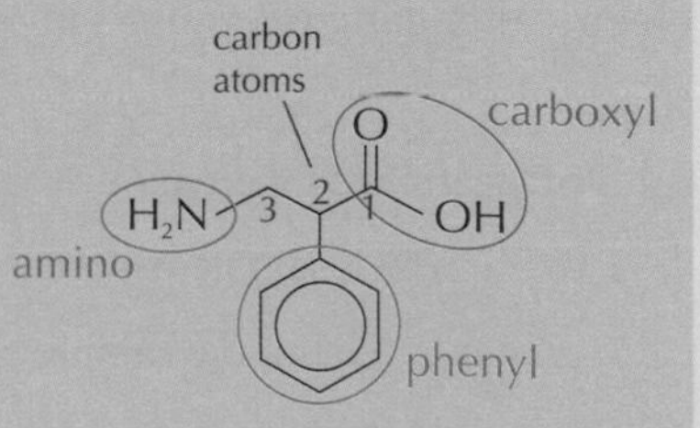

# Organic Functional Groups

**Example:** Look at compounds B and C, shown on the right.
For each compound:

a) circle and name the functional groups.

b) work out the molecular and empirical formulas.

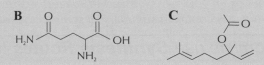

a) **B**
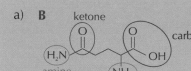

**C**
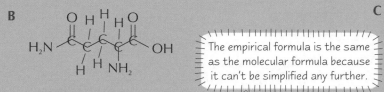

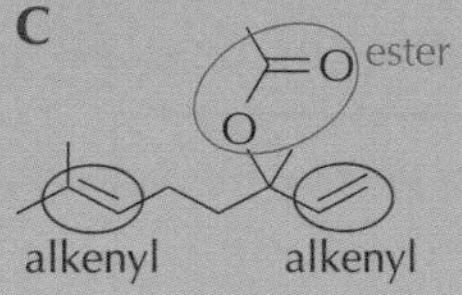

b) To work out the molecular and empirical formulas from a skeletal formula, you need to work out how many C and H atoms there are. H atoms are the trickiest to find — remember, each C atom will have 4 bonds.

**B**

molecular formula = $C_5H_{10}N_2O_3$

empirical formula = $C_5H_{10}N_2O_3$

*The empirical formula is the same as the molecular formula because it can't be simplified any further.*

**C**

molecular formula = $C_{12}H_{20}O_2$

empirical formula = $C_6H_{10}O$

## Practice Questions

**Q1** Name these functional groups and say what types of molecule they're found in:
a) –COCl,   b) –COOCO–,   c) –COO–.

**Q2** Draw the functional group of each of these families of compound:
a) carboxylic acid,   b) aromatic compounds,   c) secondary amines.

### Exam Questions

1  a) Name the functional groups in molecules A–C.    [3 marks]
   b) Which molecule(s) are aromatic?    [1 mark]
   c) Which molecule(s) can be oxidised to an aldehyde?    [1 mark]
   d) Which molecule(s) will have a pH less than 7?    [1 mark]

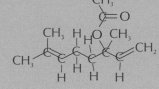

**A** $CH_3CH_2CH_2OH$    **B** $CH_3—C=CH—CH_3$ with OH

**C** OH

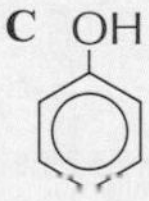

2  This diagram shows the structure of urea, a compound excreted in urine as a product of protein metabolism.

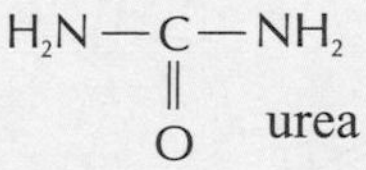

$H_2N—C—NH_2$ with O double bond, urea

   a) Name the functional groups in this molecule.    [2 marks]
   b) Urea reacts with methanal, HCHO, to form a polymer resin.
      It contains the same bonds as those that link amino acids in proteins.
      i) Draw the functional group in methanal.    [1 mark]
      ii) Why is urea suitable for making into a polymer?    [2 marks]

3  Methyl salicylate is a compound produced by various plants that is used in deep heating liniments applied to sore muscles and joints. It is also used as a flavouring in some confectionery.

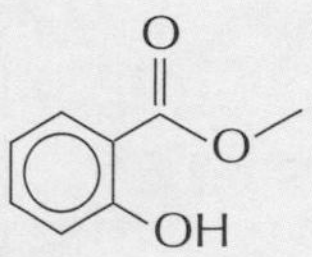

methyl salicylate

   a) Identify the functional groups in this molecule.    [3 marks]
   b) From its name and structure what group of compounds does it belong to?    [1 mark]
   c) Deduce its molecular formula.    [1 mark]
   d) It is produced from salicylic acid and methanol. Draw the structure of salicylic acid.    [1 mark]

## I used to be in a band — we played 2,4,6-tritechno hiphopnoic acid jazz...

*As well as recognising functional groups, this page gives you practice of a few other useful skills you'll need for your exam, e.g. interpreting different types of formula. If you're rusty on the difference between structural, molecular and displayed formulas, have a look back at your AS book — it's fundamental stuff that could trip you up in the exam if you don't know it.*

# Organic Synthesis

*In your exam you may be asked to suggest a pathway for the synthesis of a particular molecule. These pages contain a summary of some of the reactions you should know.*

## Chemists use **Synthesis Routes** to Get from One Compound to Another

Chemists have got to be able to make one compound from another. It's vital for things like **designing medicines**. It's also good for making imitations of **useful natural substances** when the real things are hard to extract.

If you're asked how to make one compound from another in the exam, make sure you include:

1) Any **special procedures**, such as refluxing (see page 114).
2) The **conditions** needed, e.g. high temperature or pressure, or the presence of a catalyst.
3) Any **safety** precautions, e.g. do it in a fume cupboard.

*If you're having difficulty working out a synthesis try taking the product apart and work backwards towards the reactants.*

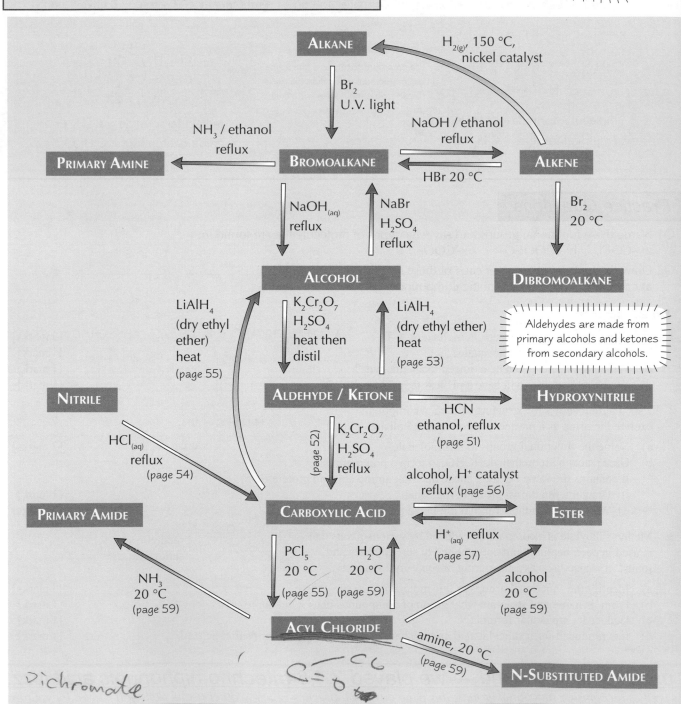

Aldehydes are made from primary alcohols and ketones from secondary alcohols.

# Organic Synthesis

## There are Synthesis Routes for **Aromatic Compounds** Too

There are quite a lot of these to remember too — if you can't remember any of the reactions, look back to the relevant pages and take a quick peek over them.

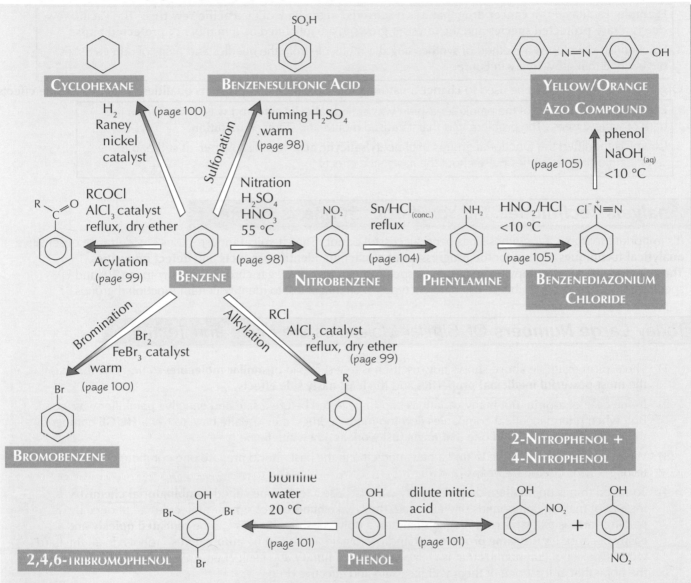

## Chemists Have to Carefully **Plan** a **Synthetic Route**

Organic chemists often have to work out how to **make** a **target molecule** from existing reagents and it's quite likely to be a **multi-stage** process. When they plan the synthesis of a molecule there are some things they need to keep in mind:

1) **Stereoisomers.** Making the correct stereoisomer is a really important consideration in the pharmaceutical industry because different **stereoisomers** might have **different properties**.
   E.g. thalidomide is a drug with a chiral centre that was prescribed in the 1960s — one enantiomer helped morning sickness but the other caused serious birth defects.

   Understanding the **mechanism** of a reaction lets chemists plan which stereoisomer will be produced (see page 49). E.g. $S_N2$ **nucleophilic substitution** can produce a **single isomer** product if a single isomer is used as the starting molecule — although the molecule will get inverted.

2) **Safety.** Many organic chemicals, and the reagents used in synthesis, are **dangerous**, so whenever an organic synthesis is planned **safety measures** have to be considered. For small scale preparations, reactions can be performed in **fume hoods** to remove toxic gases and **electric mantles** can be used to heat solutions so there are no naked flames near flammable reagents.

# Organic Synthesis

## Organic Synthesis is Important for Research and Making Useful Products

A lot of drugs were originally produced from **natural substances** in plants. But often it isn't viable to use the plant to make large quantities. So, a lot of research goes into developing them from more available reagents.

> **Example:** Paclitaxel is a **cancer drug** that was discovered in the bark of the **Pacific Yew tree**. The Pacific Yew tree is a **rare protected species** and the forests it grows in are inhabited by a number of **protected birds**.
>
> So chemists developed a method of synthesising the molecule from the needles and twigs of other species of yew tree that grow freely in Europe.

Organic synthesis can also be used to **change** a natural product, either to **improve its qualities** or **reduce its side effects**.

> **Example:** The first form of the painkiller aspirin was called **salicylic acid** and was derived from the bark of willow trees. The problem was that it caused mouth and stomach **irritation**.
>
> Chemists modified the functional groups until **acetylsalicylic acid** was discovered. It still had the same painkilling properties but without the nasty side effects.

## Analysis Techniques Tell You if Your Synthesis Worked

It's important to know if a synthesis has been successful or not. The chemical industry uses a wide **range** of sensitive **analytical techniques** to monitor the **progression of a reaction**, **identify products** and **detect impurities**. These include IR spectroscopy (page 68), mass spectrometry (page 62), gas chromatography (page 70) and UV spectrometry. It is also possible to use different types of chemical test to identify certain functional groups.

## Today Large Numbers Of Similar Molecules are Made and Tested

1) The aspirin example above shows how useful it is to test a load of **similar molecules** to find one that has the **most powerful medicinal properties** and the **least nasty side effects**.

2) In the case of aspirin, not many variations had to be tested before a safe and effective painkiller was found. But, when pharmaceutical companies develop modern drugs, they usually have to test a **HUGE** number of molecules before they find one that might just work as a new medicine.

3) When chemists were trying to find a new medicine in the past, they'd prepare one compound at a time for testing — this could take years.

4) To speed things up, modern drug-discovery chemists use a technique called **combinatorial chemistry**. Instead of making compounds one at a time, they make **hundreds** of similar molecules all at once by passing various reactants over reagents held on a polymer support. This can be **repeated quickly** and **easily** because it's the **same process** over and over again and it can be **automated** so robots do all the hard work. The set of compounds that is created is called a **library** and each chemical in the library is tested in the hope that at least one of them will be a safe and effective drug.

## Practice Questions

Q1 How do you convert an ester to a carboxylic acid?
Q2 How do you make an aldehyde from a primary alcohol?
Q3 What do you produce if you reflux a primary amide with an acid?

**Exam Questions**

1 Ethyl methanoate is one of the compounds responsible for the smell of raspberries.
Outline, with reaction conditions, how it could be synthesised in the laboratory from methanol. [7 marks]

2 How would you synthesise propanol starting with propane? State the reaction conditions and reagents needed for each step and any particular safety considerations. [8 marks]

## I saw a farmer turn a tractor into a field once — now that's impressive...

There's loads of information here. Tons and tons of it. But you've covered pretty much all of it before, so it shouldn't be too hard to make sure it's firmly embedded in your head. If it's not, you know what to do — go back over it again. Then cover the diagrams up, and try to draw them out from memory. Keep going until you can do it perfectly.

# Practical and Investigative Skills

*You're going to have to do some practical work too — and once you've done it, you have to make sense of your results...*

## Make it a **Fair Test** — Control your **Variables**

You probably know this all off by heart but it's easy to get mixed up sometimes. So here's a quick recap:

> **Variable** — A variable is a **quantity** that has the **potential to change**, e.g. mass. There are two types of variable commonly referred to in experiments:
> - **Independent variable** — the thing that you **change** in an experiment.
> - **Dependent variable** — the thing that you **measure** in an experiment.

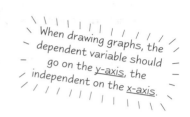

*When drawing graphs, the dependent variable should go on the y-axis, the independent on the x-axis.*

So, if you're investigating the effect of **temperature** on rate of reaction using the apparatus on the right, the variables will be:

| Independent variable | Temperature |
|---|---|
| **Dependent variable** | Amount of gas produced — you can measure this by collecting it in a gas syringe |
| **Other variables** — you MUST keep these the same | Concentration and volume of solutions, mass of solids, pressure, the presence of a catalyst and the surface area of any solid reactants |

## Know Your Different Sorts of **Data**

Experiments always involve some sort of measurement to provide **data**.
There are different types of data — and you need to know what they are.

> **Discrete** — you get discrete data by **counting**. E.g. the number of bubbles produced in a reaction would be discrete. You can't have 1.25 bubbles. That'd be daft. Shoe size is another good example of a discrete variable.

> **Continuous** — a continuous variable can have **any value** on a scale. For example, the volume of gas produced or the mass of products from a reaction. You can never measure the exact value of a continuous variable.

> **Categoric** — a categoric variable has values that can be sorted into **categories**. For example, the colours of solutions might be blue, red and green. Or types of material might be wood, steel, glass.

> **Ordered (ordinal)** — Ordered data is similar to categoric, but the categories can be **put in order**. For example, if you classify reactions as 'slow', 'fairly fast' and 'very fast' you'd have ordered data.

## Organise Your Results in a **Table** — And Watch Out For **Anomalous** Ones

Before you start your experiment, make a **table** to write your results in.
You'll need to repeat each test at least three times to check your results are reliable.

This is the sort of table you might end up with when you investigate the effect of **temperature** on **reaction rate**.
(You'd then have to do the same for **different temperatures**.)

| Temperature | Time (s) | Volume of gas evolved (cm³) Run 1 | Volume of gas evolved (cm³) Run 2 | Volume of gas evolved (cm³) Run 3 | Average volume of gas evolved (cm³) |
|---|---|---|---|---|---|
| | 10 | 8 | 7 | 8 | **7.7** |
| **20 °C** | 20 | 17 | 19 | 20 | **18.7** |
| | 30 | 28 | (20) | 30 | **29** |

Find the average of each set of repeated values.

You need to add them all up and divide by how many there are.

E.g.: (8 + 7 + 8) ÷ 3 = 7.7 cm³

Watch out for **anomalous results**. These are ones that don't fit in with the other values and are likely to be wrong. They're likely to be due to random errors — here the syringe plunger may have got stuck.
Ignore anomalous results when you calculate the average.

# Practical and Investigative Skills

## Graphs: *Line, Bar or Scatter* — Use the *Best Type*

You'll usually be expected to make a **graph** of your results.  Not only are graphs **pretty**, they make your data **easier to understand** — so long as you choose the right type.

Line graphs are best when you have **two sets of continuous data**.  For example:

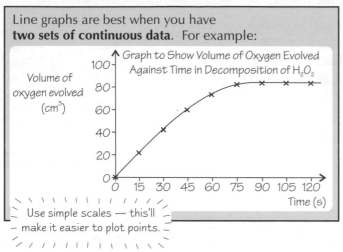

Graph to Show Volume of Oxygen Evolved Against Time in Decomposition of $H_2O_2$

Volume of oxygen evolved ($cm^3$)

Time (s)

Use simple scales — this'll make it easier to plot points.

You should use a bar chart when one of your data sets is **categoric or ordered data**.  For example:

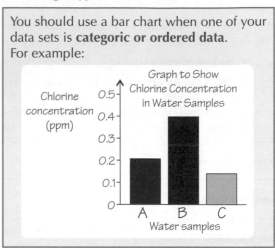

Graph to Show Chlorine Concentration in Water Samples

Chlorine concentration (ppm)

Water samples

**Scatter plots** are great for showing how two sets of data are related (or **correlated**).

Don't try to join all the points — draw a **line of best fit** to show the **trend**.

Scatter Graph to Show Relationship Between Relative Molecular Masses and Melting Points of Straight-Chain Alcohols

Melting point (K)

Relative Molecular Mass

### *Scatter Graphs Show the Relationships Between Variables*

Correlation describes the **relationship** between two variables — the independent one and the dependent one.

Data can show:

1) **Positive correlation** — as one variable **increases** the other **increases**.  The graph on the left shows positive correlation.

2) **Negative correlation** — as one variable **increases** the other **decreases**.

3) **No correlation** — there is **no relationship** between the two variables.

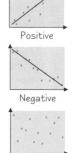

Positive

Negative

None

**Whatever type of graph you make, you'll ONLY get full marks if you:**

- Choose a sensible scale — don't do a tiny graph in the corner of the paper.
- Label both axes — including units.
- Plot your points accurately — using a sharp pencil.

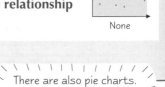

There are also pie charts.  These are normally used to display categoric data.

## Correlation *Doesn't Necessarily* Mean *Cause* — *Don't Jump to Conclusions*

1) Ideally, only **two** quantities would **ever** change in any experiment — everything else would remain **constant**.

2) But in experiments or studies outside the lab, you **can't** usually control all the variables. So even if two variables are correlated, the change in one may **not** be causing the change in the other. Both changes might be caused be a **third variable**.

Watch out for bias too — for instance, a bottled water company might point these studies out to people without mentioning any of the doubts.

**Example**

For example:  Some studies have found a correlation between **drinking chlorinated tap water** and the risk of developing certain cancers.  So some people argue that this means water shouldn't have chlorine added.

**BUT** it's hard to control all the variables (e.g. lifestyle factors) between people who do drink tap water and people who don't.

Or, the cancer risk could be affected by something else in tap water — or by whatever the non-tap water drinkers drink instead...

# Practical and Investigative Skills

## Don't Get **Carried Away** When Drawing Conclusions

The **data** should always **support** the conclusion. This may sound obvious but it's easy to **jump** to conclusions. Conclusions have to be **specific** — not make sweeping generalisations.

> ### Example
>
> The rate of an enzyme-controlled reaction was measured at **10 °C, 20 °C, 30 °C, 40 °C, 50 °C and 60 °C**. All other variables were kept constant, and the results are shown in this graph.
>
> A science magazine **concluded** from this data that enzyme X works best at **40 °C**. The data **doesn't** support this.
>
> The enzyme **could** work best at 42 °C or 47 °C but you can't tell from the data because **increases** of **10 °C** at a time were used. The rate of reaction at in-between temperatures **wasn't** measured.
>
> All you know is that it's faster at **40 °C** than at any of the other temperatures tested.
>
>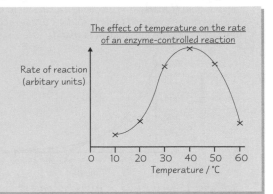
> The effect of temperature on the rate of an enzyme-controlled reaction
>
> ### Example
>
> > The experiment above **ONLY** gives information about this particular enzyme-controlled reaction. You can't conclude that **all** enzyme-controlled reactions happen faster at a particular temperature — only this one. And you can't say for sure that doing the experiment at, say, a different constant pressure, wouldn't give a different optimum temperature.

## You Need to Look **Critically** at Your Results

There are a few bits of lingo that you need to understand. They'll be useful when you're evaluating how convincing your results are.

1) **Valid results** — Valid results answer the original question. For example, if you haven't **controlled all the variables** your results won't be valid, because you won't be testing just the thing you wanted to.

2) **Accurate** — Accurate results are those that are **really close** to the **true** answer.

3) **Precise results** — These are results taken using **sensitive instruments** that measure in **small increments**, e.g. pH measured with a meter (pH 7.692) will be **more precise** than pH measured with paper (pH 7).

   > It's possible for results to be precise **but not accurate**, e.g. a balance that weighs to 1/1000 th of a gram will give precise results but if it's not **calibrated** properly the results won't be accurate.

   You may have to calculate the percentage error of a measurement.
   E.g. if a balance is calibrated to within 0.1 g, and you measure a mass as 4 g, then the percentage error is: $(0.1 \div 4) \times 100 = 2.5\%$.
   Using a larger quantity reduces the percentage error. E.g. a mass of 40 g has a percentage error of: $(0.1 \div 40) \times 100 = 0.25\%$.

4) **Reliable results** — **Reliable** means the results can be **consistently reproduced** in independent experiments. And if the results are reproducible they're more likely to be **true**. If the data isn't reliable for whatever reason you **can't draw** a valid **conclusion**.

   For experiments, the **more repeats** you do, the **more reliable** the data. If you get the **same result** twice, it could be the correct answer. But if you get the same result **20 times**, it'd be much more reliable. And it'd be even more reliable if everyone in the class got about the same results using different apparatus.

## Work **Safely** and **Ethically** — Don't Blow Up the Lab or Harm Small Animals

In any experiment you'll be expected to show that you've thought about the **risks and hazards**. It's generally a good thing to wear a lab coat and goggles, but you may need to take additional safety measures, depending on the experiment. For example, anything involving nasty gases will need to be done in a fume cupboard.

You need to make sure you're working **ethically** too. This is most important if there are other people or animals involved. You have to put their welfare first.

# Answers

## Unit 4: Section 1 — Rates of Reaction
### Page 5 — Reaction Rates

1 a) There is an increase in number of ions *[1 mark]* so follow the reaction by measuring electrical conductivity *[1 mark]* OR There is an increase in $H^+$ concentration *[1 mark]* so follow using a pH meter *[1 mark]*.

b) To find the rate of reaction plot a graph of propanone concentration against time *[1 mark]*. The gradient of a tangent to the line is equal to the rate of the reaction *[1 mark]* so draw a tangent at a particular time and calculate the gradient *[1 mark]*.

2 a)

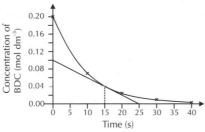

Rate after 15 s = 0.1 ÷ 25 = 0.004 mol dm⁻³ s⁻¹

Rate after 15 s = $0.1 \div 25 = 0.004$ mol dm$^{-3}$ s$^{-1}$

*[6 marks in total — 1 mark for concentration of BDC plotted on y-axis and time on x-axis, 1 mark for points plotted accurately, 1 mark for smooth best-fit curve, 1 mark for tangent drawn at 15 s, 1 mark for rate within range 0.004 ±0.001, 1 mark for correct units]*

b) The volume of nitrogen *[1 mark]*, using a gas syringe *[1 mark]* OR the pH *[1 mark]* using a pH meter *[1 mark]*.

### Page 7 — Orders of Reaction

1 a)

| Time (s) | 0 | 250 | 500 | 750 | 1000 |
|---|---|---|---|---|---|
| $[H_2O_2]$ mol dm⁻¹ | 2.0 | 1.0 | 0.5 | 0.25 | 0.125 |

*[2 marks — 1 for 2 correct answers or 2 for 4 correct answers]*

b)

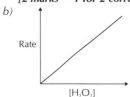

*[1 mark for correctly labelled axes, 1 mark for line starting at origin, 1 mark for straight line]*

2 a)

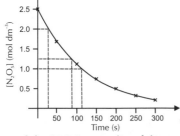

*[1 mark for $[N_2O_5]$ on y-axis and time on x-axis, 1 mark for points plotted accurately, 1 mark for smooth best-fit curve]*.

b) i) Horizontal line from 1.25 on y-axis to curve and vertical line from curve to x-axis *[1 mark]*. Time value = 85 s *[1 mark, allow 85 ±2]*

ii) Vertical lines from curve at 2.0 mol dm⁻³ and 1.0 mol dm⁻³ *[1 mark]*. Time value difference = 113 (±2) − 28 (±2) = 85 s *[1 mark, allow 85 ±4]*

c) The order of reaction is 1 *[1 mark]* because the half-life of ≈ 85 s is independent of concentration *[1 mark]*.

### Page 9 — Rate Equations

1 a) Rate = $k[NO_{(g)}]^2 [H_{2(g)}]$ *[2 marks for correct equation, otherwise 1 mark if equation is correct apart from orders]*
Sum of individual orders = 2 + 1 = 3rd order overall *[1 mark]*.

b) i) $0.00267 = k \times (0.004)^2 \times 0.002$ *[1 mark]*
$k = 0.00267 \div ((0.004)^2 \times 0.002)$
$k = 83437.5$ *[1 mark]* dm⁶ mol⁻² s⁻¹.

Units: $k$ = mol dm⁻³ s⁻¹/[(mol dm⁻³)² × (mol dm⁻³)]
= dm⁶ mol⁻² s⁻¹ *[1 mark]*.

ii) The rate constant would decrease *[1 mark]*.
If the temperature decreases, the rate decreases too.
A lower rate means a lower rate constant.

2 a) If [A] is doubled then the rate also doubles *[1 mark]*, when [B] is doubled the rate will quadruple *[1 mark]* so overall the rate will increase by a factor of 2 × 4 = 8 *[1 mark]*.

b) If [A] is halved the rate will also halve *[1 mark]*, when [B] doubles, the rate quadruples *[1 mark]* so overall the rate increases by a factor of ½ × 4 = 2 *[1 mark]*.

### Page 11 — Deducing Orders and Rate Equations

1 a) Comparing experiments 1 and 2: when [D] is doubled and [E] is kept constant the initial rate quadruples *[1 mark]*. So the reaction is 2nd order with respect to [D] *[1 mark]*.
Comparing experiments 1 and 3: when [E] doubles and [D] is kept constant the initial rate doubles *[1 mark]*. So the reaction is 1st order with respect to [E] *[1 mark]*.
Always explain your reasoning carefully — state which concentrations are constant and which are changing.

b) rate = $k[D]^2[E]$ *[1 mark]*

2 a) Comparing experiments 1 and 3: when [X] is doubled and [Y] is kept constant the initial rate also doubles *[1 mark]* so the order is 1 *[1 mark]*.

b) Comparing experiments 1 and 2: when [Y] is tripled and [X] is kept constant the initial rate increases by a factor of 9 (= 3²) *[1 mark]* so the order is 2 *[1 mark]*.

c) rate = $k[X][Y]^2$ *[1 mark]*

### Page 13 — Rates and Reaction Mechanisms

1 a) rate = $k[H_2][ICl]$ *[1 mark]*

b) i) If the molecule is in the rate equation, it must be in the rate-determining step *[1 mark]*. The orders of the reaction tell you how many molecules of each reactant are in the rate-determining step *[1 mark]*. So the rate-determining step contains one molecule of $H_2$ and one molecule of ICl *[1 mark]*.

ii) Incorrect *[1 mark]*. $H_2$ and ICl are both in the rate equation, so they must both be in the rate-determining step *[1 mark]* OR the order of the reaction with respect to ICl is 1, so there must be only one molecule of ICl in the rate-determining step *[1 mark]*.

2 a) Order with respect to HBr = 1 and $O_2$ = 1 *[1 mark]*

b) HBr and $O_2$ must both be in the rate-determining step *[1 mark]*. They must be in a 1:1 molar ratio *[1 mark]*.

c) 1 HBr + $O_2$ → $HBrO_2$ (Rate-determining step)
2 $HBrO_2$ + HBr → 2HBrO
3 2HBrO + 2HBr → $2H_2O$ + $2Br_2$
*[1 mark for correct order of reactions, 1 mark for correctly identifying the rate-determining step]*

### Page 15 — Halogenoalkanes & Reaction Mechanisms

1 D *[1 mark]*
1-chloropropane is a primary halogenoalkane, which means it will react using an $S_N2$ mechanism. So both 1-chloropropane and sodium hydroxide must be in the rate equation, as the rate will depend on the concentration of both them.

2 A *[1 mark]*
The rate determining step for an $S_N1$ mechanism is the dissociation of the halogenoalkane to form a carbocation.

3 a) 1-iodobutane is a primary iodoalkane *[1 mark]*

b) Rate = $k[CH_3CH_2CH_2CH_2I][OH^-]$ *[1 mark]*

c) Mechanism is $S_N2$ *[2 marks for $S_N2$ otherwise 1 mark for $S_N$ or nucleophilic substitution]*

d)

$$CH_3CH_2CH_2 \quad \left[ CH_3CH_2CH_2 \ H \right] \quad CH_3CH_2CH_2$$

*[4 marks for complete mechanism otherwise 1 mark for each curly arrow, 1 mark for correct transition molecule]*

# Answers

## Page 18 — Activation Energy and Catalysts

1   C **[1 mark]**
It's incorrect because a catalyst provides an alternative reaction route of lower activation energy.

2 a) Activation energy is the minimum amount of energy **[1 mark]** particles need to react **[1 mark]**.

  b)

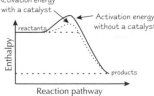

**[1 mark for graph with activation energy with and without catalyst]**
The catalyst provides an alternative route with a lower activation energy for a reaction **[1 mark]**. At the lower activation energy there are more particles with enough energy to react **[1 mark]**.

  c) i)

| T | $k$ | 1/T | ln $k$ |
|---|---|---|---|
| 305 | 0.181 | 0.00328 | -1.709 |
| 313 | 0.468 | **0.00319** | **-0.759** |
| 323 | 1.34 | **0.00310** | **0.293** |
| 333 | 3.29 | 0.00300 | 1.191 |
| 344 | 10.1 | **0.00291** | **2.313** |
| 353 | 22.7 | 0.00283 | 3.122 |

**[1 mark for all 3 1/T values, 1 mark for all 3 ln k values]**

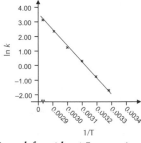

**[1 mark for at least 5 accurate points, 1 mark for line of best fit]**
ii) Any correct determination of gradient **[1 mark]**
Value = $-10\ 750 \pm 250$ **[1 mark]**
iii) $-E_a/R = -10\ 750$ **[1 mark]**. $E_a = 10\ 750 \times 8.31$ **[1 mark]**
= 89 333 J mol$^{-1}$ OR 89.3 kJ mol$^{-1}$ **[1 mark]**

## Unit 4: Section 2 — Entropy
## Page 20 — Entropy

1 a) Entropy is a measure of the number of ways that particles can be arranged **[1 mark]**, as well as the number of ways that energy can be shared out between particles **[1 mark]**.

  b) i) Entropy will increase **[1 mark]** because 2 moles of solid is converted into 2 moles of solid and 1 mole of gas — so there are more particles, and gas particles have more entropy than those in solids **[1 mark]**.

    ii) Entropy will increase **[1 mark]** because 1 mole of solid and 1 mole of gas are converted into 2 moles of gas, and gas particles have more entropy than those in solids **[1 mark]**.

    iii) Entropy will decrease **[1 mark]** because 4 moles of gas are converted into 2 moles of gas, and there is less entropy when there are fewer particles **[1 mark]**.

    iv) Entropy will decrease **[1 mark]** because 1½ moles of gas are converted into 1 mole of liquid, and there is less entropy when there are fewer particles, and liquid particles have less entropy than gas particles **[1 mark]**.

2   Reaction is not likely to be spontaneous **[1 mark]** because there is a decrease in entropy **[1 mark]**.

## Page 23 — Entropy Change

1 a) You would expect an increase in the entropy of the system **[1 mark]** because a solid is combining with a substance in solution to produce another solution, a liquid and a gas — this leads to an increase in

disorder **[1 mark]**. There is also an increase in the number of molecules which will also lead to an increase in disorder **[1 mark]**.

  b) The reaction is endothermic, so the entropy change of the surroundings will be negative **[1 mark]**. This means that the entropy change of the system must sufficiently positive to counteract this change **[1 mark]**. The total entropy change will be positive and the reaction will be spontaneous **[1 mark]**.

2 a) You would expect a decrease in the entropy of the system **[1 mark]** because a solid is combining with a gas to produce only a solid — that's a decrease in disorder **[1 mark]**.

  b) $\Delta S_{system} = S_{products} - S_{reactants}$ **[1 mark]**
= $(2 \times 26.9) - ((2 \times 32.7) + 205) = 53.8 - 270.4$ **[1 mark]**
= $-216.6$ J K$^{-1}$ mol$^{-1}$ **[1 mark, include units]**

  c) $\Delta S_{surroundings} = -\Delta H/T = -(-1\ 204\ 000 \div 298)$ **[1 mark]**
= $+4040.3$ J K$^{-1}$ mol$^{-1}$ **[1 mark]**
$\Delta S_{total} = \Delta S_{system} + \Delta S_{surroundings} = (-216.6) + 4040.3$ **[1 mark]**
= $+3823.7$ J K$^{-1}$ mol$^{-1}$ **[1 mark]**

## Page 25 — Dissolving

1 a) Enthalpy change of solution is the enthalpy change when 1 mole of solute **[1 mark]** is dissolved in sufficient solvent that no further enthalpy change occurs on further dilution **[1 mark]**.

  b) $Ag^+_{(g)} + I^-_{(g)} \rightarrow AgI_{(s)}$ **[1 mark for correct symbols and 1 mark for state symbols]**.

  c) $\Delta S_{surroundings} = -\Delta H/T = -112300 \div 298$ **[1 mark]**
= $-376.8$ J K$^{-1}$ mol$^{-1}$ **[1 mark]**.
$\Delta S_{total} = \Delta S_{system} + \Delta S_{surroundings} = 69.1 - 376.8$
= $-307.7$ J K$^{-1}$ mol$^{-1}$ **[1 mark]**.
This value is negative so silver iodide is insoluble in water **[1 mark]**.

2 a)

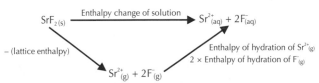

**[1 mark for each of the 4 enthalpy changes labelled, 1 mark for a complete, correct cycle.]**
Don't forget — you have to double the enthalpy of hydration for F$^-$ because there are two in SrF$_2$.

  b) $-(-2492) + (-1480) + (2 \times -506)$ **[1 mark]** = 0 kJ mol$^{-1}$ **[1 mark]**

## Unit 4: Section 3 — Equilibria
## Page 27 — Dynamic Equilibria

1   C **[1 mark]**
The equilibrium concentrations will be the same whenever the initial concentrations of each element in the reaction are the same.
A contains $1 \times 2 = 2$ mol dm$^{-3}$ of N and $1.5 \times 2 = 3$ mol dm$^{-3}$ of H.
B contains $0.5 \times 2 + 1 \times 1 = 2$ mol dm$^{-3}$ of N and $1 \times 3 = 3$ mol dm$^{-3}$ of H.
C contains $2 \times 1 = 2$ mol dm$^{-3}$ of N and $2 \times 3 = 6$ mol dm$^{-3}$ of H.
D contains $0.75 \times 2 + 0.5 \times 1 = 2$ mol dm$^{-3}$ of N and
$0.75 \times 2 + 0.5 \times 3 = 3$ mol dm$^{-3}$ of H.
Experiment C has a greater concentration of H than the other experiments, so it will have different equilibrium concentrations.

2 a) A dynamic equilibrium is one in which both forward and reverse reactions are still proceeding **[1 mark]** at the same rate **[1 mark]**.

  b) i) The value of the equilibrium constant would be unchanged **[1 mark]** because the temperature remains constant **[1 mark]**.
    ii) The value of the equilibrium constant would change **[1 mark]** because the temperature has changed **[1 mark]**.
Not enough information is given for you to say whether the value increases or decreases.

    iii) $K_c = \dfrac{[PCl_3][Cl_2]}{[PCl_5]}$ **[1 mark]**

We know that for the reverse reaction at this temperature:

$K_c = \dfrac{[PCl_5]}{[PCl_3][Cl_2]} = 125$

So for this reaction, $K_c = 1 / 125 = 0.08$ **[1 mark]**.

# Answers

## Page 29 — Equilibrium Constants

1    C 6.0 mol dm⁻³ **[1 mark]**

$$K_c = \frac{[HCl]^2}{[H_2][Cl_2]}$$

$[HCl]^2 = 60 \times [H_2] \times [Cl_2]$
$[HCl]^2 = 60 \times 2 \times 0.3 = 36$
$[HCl] = \sqrt{36} = 6.0$ mol dm⁻³.

2 a)  i) mass/$M_r$ = 42.5/46 = 0.92 **[1 mark]**
       ii) moles of $O_2$ = mass/$M_r$ = 14.1/32 = 0.44 **[1 mark]**
           moles of NO = 2 × moles of $O_2$ = 0.88 **[1 mark]**
           moles of $NO_2$ = 0.92 − 0.88 = 0.04 **[1 mark]**
  b) Concentration of $O_2$ = 0.44 ÷ 22.8 = 0.019 mol dm⁻³
     Concentration of NO = 0.88 ÷ 22.8 = 0.039 mol dm⁻³
     Concentration of $NO_2$ = 0.04 ÷ 22.8 = 1.75 × 10⁻³ mol dm⁻³ **[1 mark]**

$$K_c = \frac{[NO]^2[O_2]}{[NO_2]^2} \text{ [1 mark]}$$

$$\Rightarrow K_c = \frac{(0.039)^2 \times (0.019)}{(1.75 \times 10^{-3})^2} \text{ [1 mark]} = 9.4 \text{ [1 mark] mol dm}^{-3} \text{ [1 mark]}$$

(Units = (mol dm⁻³)² × (mol dm⁻³) /(mol dm⁻³)² = mol dm⁻³)

## Page 31 — Gas Equilibria

1 a)  $$K_p = \frac{p(SO_2)p(Cl_2)}{p(SO_2Cl_2)} \text{ [1 mark]}$$

  b) $Cl_2$ and $SO_2$ are produced in equal amounts **[1 mark]**.
     $p(Cl_2) = p(SO_2) = 60.2$ kPa **[1 mark]**
     Total pressure = $p(SO_2Cl_2) + p(Cl_2) + p(SO_2)$ **[1 mark]**
     $p(SO_2Cl_2) = 141 − 60.2 − 60.2 = 20.6$ kPa **[1 mark]**

  c) $$K_p = \frac{(60.2)(60.2)}{(20.6)} \text{ [1 mark]} = 176 \text{ [1 mark] kPa [1 mark]}$$

     (Units = (kPa × kPa)/ kPa = kPa)

2 a) $p(O_2) = \frac{1}{2} \times 36$ **[1 mark]** = 18 kPa **[1 mark]**
  b) $p(NO_2)$ = total pressure − p(NO) − $p(O_2)$
     = 99 − 36 − 18 **[1 mark]** = 45 kPa **[1 mark]**

  c) $$K_p = \frac{p(NO_2)^2}{p(NO)^2 p(O_2)} \text{ [1 mark]} = \frac{(45)^2}{(36)^2(18)} \text{ [1 mark]}$$

     = 0.087 **[1 mark]** kPa⁻¹ **[1 mark]**

     (Units = kPa²/(kPa² × kPa) = kPa⁻¹)

## Page 33 —Equilibrium Constants and Entropy

1    B $\Delta S_{surroundings}$ will increase **[1 mark]**.
2 a) $\Delta S_{total}$ = 175.8 − (57200 ÷ 333) **[1 mark]** = 4.03 JK⁻¹mol⁻¹ **[1 mark]**
  b) $\ln K = \Delta S_{total} \div R$ **[1 mark]** = 4.03 ÷ 8.31 = 0.484
     $K = e^{0.484} = 1.62$ **[1 mark]**
  c) $\Delta S_{total}$ = 175.8 − (57200 ÷ 433) **[1 mark]** = 43.7 JK⁻¹mol⁻¹ **[1 mark]**
     and $\ln K$ = 43.7 ÷ 8.31 **[1 mark]** so K = 192.2 **[1 mark]**
  d) At 60 °C the equilibrium is approximately balanced between product and reactant **[1 mark]**. The increase in temperature has lead to the reaction being almost complete — the position of equilibrium has moved well over to the right **[1 mark]**.

## Page 35 — Le Chatelier's Principle

1) a) If the temperature of the system is increased, the position of equilibrium moves to the left **[1 mark]**. This decreases the equilibrium concentration of $CH_3OH_{(g)}$ **[1 mark]**.
  b) If the pressure of the system is decreased, the position of equilibrium moves to the left **[1 mark]**. This decreases the equilibrium concentration of $CH_3OH_{(g)}$ **[1 mark]**.
  c) A catalyst has no effect on the position of equilibrium **[1 mark]** so there is no change to the equilibrium concentration of $CH_3OH_{(g)}$ **[1 mark]**.
2 a) $T_2$ is lower than $T_1$ **[1 mark]**.
     A decrease in temperature shifts the position of equilibrium in the exothermic direction, producing more product **[1 mark]**. More product means $K_p$ increases **[1 mark]**.
  b) The yield of $SO_3$ increases **[1 mark]**. (A decrease in volume means an increase in pressure. This shifts the equilibrium to the right.) $K_p$ is unchanged **[1 mark]**.

## Page 37 — Equilibria in Industrial Processes

1 a) Lower temperatures would favour/ increase the yield of the forward reaction, which is exothermic **[1 mark]**. The reaction would be too slow at lower temperatures **[1 mark]**, so the temperature is a compromise between maximum yield and a faster reaction **[1 mark]**.
  b) Catalysts have no affect on product yield **[1 mark]**.
  c) Any unreacted $SO_2$ and $O_2$ could be recycled back into the reaction vessel **[1 mark]**.
  d) **Any two from the following, up to a maximum of 4 marks:**
     • Whether the reaction will go **[1 mark]**.
       The entropy changes involved must be greater than −100 JK⁻¹mol⁻¹ **[1 mark]**
     • How fast the reaction will go **[1 mark]**.
       If a substance reacts too slowly, a catalyst may need to be added or the temperature or pressure of the reaction system may need to be increased **[1 mark]**.
     • The potential to increase the atom economy of the reaction **[1 mark]**.
       The greater the atom economy, the less the waste — this is better for the environment and will reduce costs **[1 mark]**.
     • Whether there are ways of reducing energy consumption **[1 mark]**. This better for the environment and will reduce costs **[1 mark]**.
     • What safety procedures need to be in place **[1 mark]**.
       If high temperatures and pressures are used, safety measures will have to be in place to protect workers and the environment **[1 mark]** OR if the products / waste products are toxic / highly flammable, safety measures will have to be in place to protect workers and the environment **[1 mark]**.

## Unit 4: Section 4 — Acid-Base Equilibria
## Page 39 — Acids and Bases

1 a) $HCN \rightleftharpoons H^+ + CN^-$  OR  $HCN + H_2O \rightleftharpoons H_3O^+ + CN^-$ **[1 mark]**
  b) Strongly to the left **[1 mark]** as it is a weak acid so it is only partially ionised **[1 mark]**.
  c) $CN^-$ **[1 mark]**
2 a) A substance in which the hydrogen ion concentration is equal to the hydroxide ion concentration **[1 mark]**
  b) $H_2O \rightleftharpoons H^+ + OH^-$  OR  $2H_2O \rightleftharpoons H_3O^+ + OH^-$ **[1 mark]**

  c) $$K_c = \frac{[H^+][OH^-]}{[H_2O]} \text{ [1 mark]}$$

  d) Rearranging gives $K_c \times [H_2O] = [H^+][OH^-]$
     But $[H_2O]$ is effectively constant **[1 mark]**, so $K_c \times [H_2O]$ is a constant — call this $K_w$. Then $K_w = [H^+][OH^-]$ **[1 mark]**
  e) At 298 K, $K_w = 1 \times 10^{-14}$ mol² dm⁻⁶ $= [H^+][OH^-]$ **[1 mark]**
     But $[H^+] = [OH^-]$ since water is neutral,
     so $[H^+]^2 = 1 \times 10^{-14}$, $[H^+] = 1 \times 10^{-7}$ mol dm⁻³ **[1 mark]**

## Page 42 — pH Calculations

1 a) $$K_a = \frac{[H^+][A^-]}{[HA]} \text{ or } K_a = \frac{[H^+]^2}{[HA]} \text{ [1 mark]}$$

  b) Assume that [HA] at equilibrium is 0.280 because very few HA will dissociate **[1 mark]**.

     $$K_a = \frac{[H^+]^2}{[HA]}$$

     $[H^+] = \sqrt{(5.60 \times 10^{-4}) \times 0.280} = 0.0125$ mol dm⁻³ **[1 mark]**
     $pH = -\log_{10}[H^+] = -\log_{10}(0.0125) = 1.90$ **[1 mark]**

2    Assume that [HA] at equilibrium is 0.150 because very few HA will dissociate **[1 mark]**.
     $[H^+] = 10^{-2.65} = 2.24 \times 10^{-3}$ mol dm⁻³ **[1 mark]**

     $$K_a = \frac{[H^+]^2}{[HX]} \text{ [1 mark]} = \frac{[2.24 \times 10^{-3}]^2}{[0.15]}$$

     $= 3.34 \times 10^{-5}$ **[1 mark]** mol dm⁻³ **[1 mark]**

3 a) Assume that [HA] at equilibrium is 0.1 because very few HA will dissociate **[1 mark]**. $[H^+] = 10^{-2.6} = 2.51 \times 10^{-3}$ mol dm⁻³ **[1 mark]**

     $$K_a = \frac{[H^+]^2}{[C_6H_5COOH]} \text{ [1 mark]} = \frac{[2.51 \times 10^{-3}]^2}{[0.1]}$$

     $= 6.31 \times 10^{-5}$ **[1 mark]** mol dm⁻³ **[1 mark]**

# Answers

b) $[H^+] = \sqrt{K_a[C_6H_5COOH]}$ **[1 mark]**

$= \sqrt{(6.31 \times 10^{-5}) \times 0.01} = 7.9 \times 10^{-4}$ mol dm$^{-3}$ **[1 mark]**

c) $pH = -\log_{10}[H^+] = -\log(7.9 \times 10^{-4}) = 3.1$ **[1 mark]**

d) $[H^+] = \sqrt{6.31 \times 10^{-5} \times 1} = 7.9 \times 10^{-3}$ mol dm$^{-3}$ **[1 mark]**

so $pH = -\log(7.9 \times 10^{-3}) = 2.1$ **[1 mark]**

e) As the solution is diluted by a factor of 10 the pH increases by 0.5 **[1 mark]**

## Page 44 — Titration Curves and Indicators

1 a) 9 (accept values in the range 8 – 10) **[1 mark]**

b) 15 ml **[1 mark]**

c) Phenolphthalein **[1 mark]** because pH 9 is within its range **[1 mark]**

d)

volume of NH₃ added **[1 mark]**

e) You would use a pH meter as the change in pH is gradual, so is difficult to see with an indicator **[1 mark]**.

2 a) i) 8 (accept values in the range 7 – 9) **[1 mark]**

ii) 1.2 (accept values in the range 1.0 – 1.4) **[1 mark]**

b) $K_a = \dfrac{[H^+][HCOO^-]}{[HCOOH]}$ **[1 mark]**

c) It is reduced to half its original value, 0.05 mol dm$^{-3}$ **[1 mark]**

d) At the half equivalence point $pK_a = pH = 1.2$ **[1 mark]**
so $K_a = 10^{-1.2} = 6.3 \times 10^{-2}$ mol dm$^{-3}$ **[1 mark]** [Allow marks for correct method with value from 2a)ii) if answer does not equal 1.2]

## Page 46 — Buffers

1 a) $K_a = \dfrac{[C_6H_5COO^-][H^+]}{[C_6H_5COOH]}$ **[1 mark]**

$\Rightarrow [H^+] = 6.4 \times 10^{-5} \times \dfrac{0.40}{0.20} = 1.28 \times 10^{-4}$ mol dm$^{-3}$ **[1 mark]**

$pH = -\log_{10}(1.28 \times 10^{-4}) = 3.9$ **[1 mark]**

b) The buffer solution contains benzoic acid and benzoate ions in equilibrium: $C_6H_5COOH \rightleftharpoons H^+ + C_6H_5COO^-$ **[1 mark]**
Adding $H_2SO_4$ increases the concentration of $H^+$ **[1 mark]**.
The equilibrium shifts left to reduce concentration of $H^+$, so the pH will only change very slightly **[1 mark]**.

2 a) $CH_3(CH_2)_2COOH \rightleftharpoons H^+ + CH_3(CH_2)_2COO^-$ **[1 mark]**

b) $[CH_3(CH_2)_2COOH] = [CH_3(CH_2)_2COO^-]$,
so $[CH_3(CH_2)_2COOH] \div [CH_3(CH_2)_2COO^-] = 1$ **[1 mark]**
and $K_a = [H^+]$.
$pH = -\log_{10}(1.5 \times 10^{-5})$ **[1 mark]** $= 4.8$ **[1 mark]**
If the concentrations of the weak acid and the salt of the weak acid are equal, they cancel from the $K_a$ expression and the buffer $pH = pK_a$.

## Unit 4: Section 5 — Further Organic Chemistry
## Page 49 — Isomerism

1 a) The property of having stereoisomers, which are molecules with the same molecular formula and with their atoms arranged in the same way **[1 mark]**, but with a different orientation of the bonds in space **[1 mark]**.

b) For example:

**[1 mark for each correct structure, 1 mark for correct Z/E labels.]**

c) i) For example:

**[1 mark for each correctly drawn structure — they don't have to be orientated in the same way as in the diagram above, as long as the molecules are mirror images of each other.]**

ii) An asymmetric carbon/a chiral carbon/a carbon with four different groups attached **[1 mark]**.

iii) Shine (monochromatic) plane-polarised light through a solution of the molecule **[1 mark]**. The enantiomers will rotate the light in opposite directions **[1 mark]**.

2 a)

**[1 mark for structure, 1 mark for identifying the chiral centre]**
It doesn't really matter how you mark the chiral centre, as long as you've made it clear which carbon you've marked.

b) Since the butan-2-ol solution is a racemic mixture, it must contain equal amounts of both enantiomers **[1 mark]**. The two enantiomers will exactly cancel out each other's light-rotating effect **[1 mark]**.

c) The reaction has proceeded via an $S_N1$ mechanism **[1 mark]**. You know this because the original solution contained a single optical isomer, but the product is a racemic mixture **[1 mark]**.

## Page 51 — Aldehydes and Ketones

1 a)

Aldehyde – propanal          Ketone – propanone
**[1 mark for aldehyde, 1 mark for ketone]**

b) Nucleophilic addition **[1 mark]**

c)

**[2 marks total, 1 mark for each correct structure]**

d)

**[1 mark for correct structures, 1 mark for correct curly arrows]**

e) The reaction between $CN^-$ and the aldehyde will produce a racemic mixture **[1 mark]**. The aldehyde is planar and can be attacked by the $CN^-$ from either side **[1 mark]** and the product has a chiral centre, whereas the product with the ketone doesn't **[1 mark]**.

2 a)

**[4 marks in total, 1 mark for each correct structure, 1 mark for correctly circled molecule]**

b) Hexanal is not able to form hydrogen bonds with other hexanal molecules **[1 mark]**. Hexan-1-ol does form hydrogen bonds using its OH group **[1 mark]**.

## Page 53 — More on Aldehydes and Ketones

1 a) A is propanal **[1 mark]**.

The molecule is an aldehyde because the reaction between compound A and Fehling's solution produced a brick red precipitate. Ketones don't react with Fehling's solution.

b)

**[1 mark]**

c) Use LiAlH₄ **[1 mark]** in dry diethyl ether **[1 mark]**.

d) No reaction would happen **[1 mark]**. This is a test for a methyl group next to a carbonyl group which this molecule does not have **[1 mark]**.

# Answers

2 a)

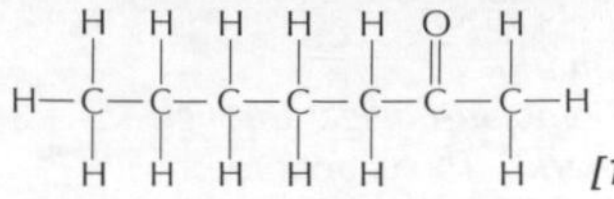

**[1 mark]**

Brady's reagent tells you that it is a carbonyl **[1 mark]**.
Tollens' reagent tells you that it is not an aldehyde **[1 mark]**.
The iodine result tells you that it has a methyl carbonyl group **[1 mark]**.

b) You can measure the melting point of the precipitate formed with Brady's reagent **[1 mark]**. Each carbonyl compound gives a precipitate with a specific melting point which can be looked up in tables **[1 mark]**.

c)

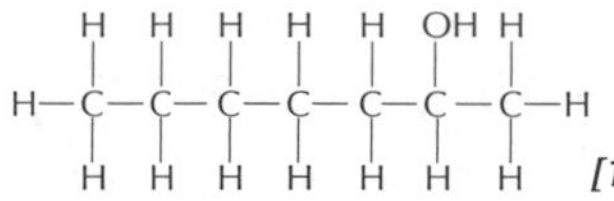

**[1 mark]**

## Page 56 — Carboxylic Acids

1 a) Propanoic acid partially dissociates in water to release $H^+$ ions **[1 mark]**. Propanol doesn't do this **[1 mark]**.

b) Add a carbonate/hydrogencarbonate **[1 mark]**. Propanol will show no reaction **[1 mark]**. Propanoic acid will produce bubbles of carbon dioxide **[1 mark]**.

c) i)

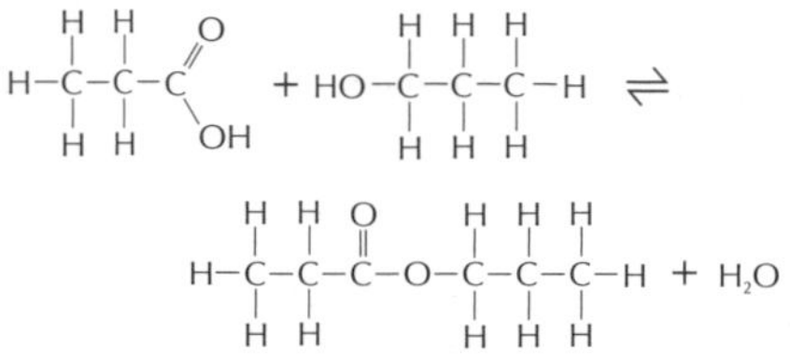

**[1 mark for correct equation, 1 mark for reversible arrow]**

ii) Propyl propanoate **[1 mark]**.

2 a) Mango juice may have been too dark in colour to see the indicator colour change **[1 mark]**.

b) 17.5 ml of 0.5 mol dm⁻³ sodium hydroxide contains
$(17.5 \div 1000) \times 0.5 = 0.00875$ moles **[1 mark]**.
From the equation,
3 moles of sodium hydroxide react with 1 mole of citric acid.
$0.00875 \div 3 = 0.00292$ moles of acid were used **[1 mark]**.
25 ml of diluted juice contains 0.00292 moles of citric acid,
so 100 ml contains $4 \times 0.00292 = 0.0117$ moles **[1 mark]**.
25 ml of undiluted juice has 0.0117 moles of citric acid **[1 mark]**.
Concentration of acid in undiluted juice
$= (1000 \div 25) \times 0.0117 = 0.467$ mol dm⁻³ **[1 mark]**.

3 a)

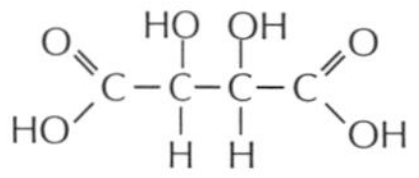

**[1 mark]**

b)

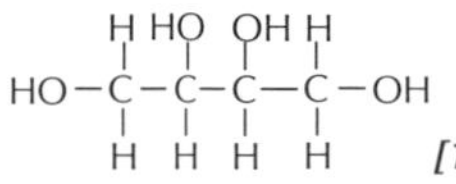

**[1 mark]**

$LiAlH_4$ **[1 mark]**, in dry diethyl ether **[1 mark]**.

c) Potassium hydroxide/potassium carbonate/potassium hydrogencarbonate **[1 mark]**
You might never have heard of 2,3-dihydroxybutanedioic acid before, but that's OK. You just have to apply what you know about carboxylic acids to it. Potassium bitartrate ends in -ate, so it's a salt.

## Page 59 — Esters / Acyl Chlorides

1 a) 2-methylpropyl ethanoate **[1 mark]**

b) Ethanoic acid **[1 mark]**

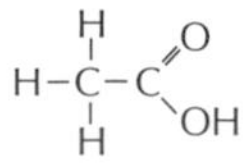

**[1 mark]**

2-methylpropan-1-ol **[1 mark]**

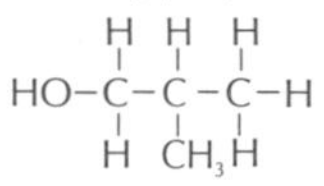

**[1 mark]**

This is acid hydrolysis **[1 mark]**.

c) With sodium hydroxide, sodium ethanoate is produced, but in the reaction in part b), ethanoic acid is produced **[1 mark]**.

2 a) Transesterification **[1 mark]**

b) The oil/ester is heated with methanol or ethanol **[1 mark]**. Methanol or ethanol is exchanged for glycerol in the ester **[1 mark]**.

c) It is a sustainable/renewable resource **[1 mark]** unlike conventional diesel which is a finite resource as it is made from crude oil **[1 mark]**.

## Unit 4: Section 6
## — Spectroscopy and Chromatography
## Page 61 — UV and Microwave Radiation

1 C alkanes **[1 mark]**
Alkanes aren't polar so they can't be heated by microwaves.

2 Water molecules are polar **[1 mark]**. They try to align themselves with the electric field created by the microwaves **[1 mark]**. As they do so they collide with other molecules, generating heat **[1 mark]**.

3 a) Ultraviolet/UV radiation **[1 mark]**

b) It breaks the bond between the atoms **[1 mark]**, so that two free radicals are formed **[1 mark]**.

c) Initiation
$Cl_2 \rightarrow Cl\bullet + Cl\bullet$ **[1 mark]**
Propagation
$Cl\bullet + H_2 \rightarrow HCl + H\bullet$ **[1 mark]**
$H\bullet + Cl_2 \rightarrow HCl + Cl\bullet$ **[1 mark]**
Termination
$Cl\bullet + Cl\bullet \rightarrow Cl_2$ **[1 mark]**
$H\bullet + H\bullet \rightarrow H_2$ **[1 mark]**
$H\bullet + Cl\bullet \rightarrow HCl$ **[1 mark]**

## Page 63 — Mass Spectrometry

1 D 58 **[1 mark]**

2 a) 88 **[1 mark]**

b) A has a mass of 43, so it's probably $CH_3CH_2CH_2^+$ **[1 mark]**.
B has a mass of 45, so it's probably $COOH^+$ **[1 mark]**.
C has a mass of 73, so it's probably $CH_2CH_2COOH^+$ **[1 mark]**.

c) Since the molecule is a carboxylic acid that contains the three fragments that you found in part (b), it must have this structure:

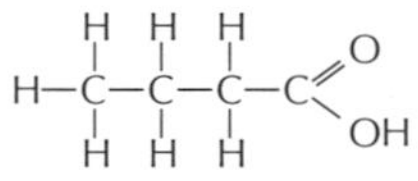

**[1 mark]**

This is butanoic acid **[1 mark]**.

## Page 65 — NMR Spectroscopy

1 a) Three **[1 mark]**.
They'll be three peaks because the molecule has three proton environments — it's $CH_3CH_2COOH$.

b) Substance B must be an aldehyde **[1 mark]**.
Aldehydes are the only molecules that give peaks between $\delta = 9$ and $\delta = 10$.

2 a) 1.3 ppm, 2.5 ppm and 3.8 ppm **[1 mark for all three correct. Allow values of 1.1 to 1.5, 2.3 to 2.7 and 3.6 to 4]**.

b) Structure: $CH_3CH_2OH$ OR

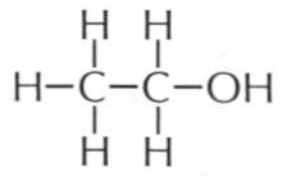

**[1 mark]**

The single hydrogen causing the peak at $\delta = 2.5$ ppm must be in the OH group of the alcohol **[1 mark]**. The two hydrogens at a shift of 3.8 ppm likely to be part of a $CH_2OH$ group **[1 mark]**. The three other hydrogens at a shift of 1.3 ppm must be in a $CH_3$ group **[1 mark]**.

## Page 67 — More about NMR

1 a) They are in a halogenoalkane H–C–halogen group
OR they are in a $CH_2Cl$ group **[1 mark]**.
You've got to read the question carefully here — it tells you that the molecule's a chloroalkane. So the group at 3.6 ppm must be the halogenoalkane functional group.

b) They are in an alkane H–C–C group
OR they are in a $CH_3$ group **[1 mark]**.

c) $CH_3CH_2Cl$ **[1 mark]**

d) The peak at $\delta = 3.6$ ppm is split into a quartet by the 3 protons on the adjacent carbon **[1 mark]**. Similarly, the peak at $\delta = 1.3$ is split into a triplet by the 2 adjacent protons **[1 mark]**.

# Answers

2 a)

$$H-\overset{\overset{\displaystyle H}{|}}{\underset{\underset{\displaystyle H}{|}}{C}}-\overset{\overset{\displaystyle H}{|}}{\underset{\underset{\displaystyle H}{|}}{C}}-\overset{\overset{\displaystyle H}{|}}{\underset{\underset{\displaystyle H}{|}}{C}}-OH \qquad H-\overset{\overset{\displaystyle H}{|}}{\underset{\underset{\displaystyle H}{|}}{C}}-\overset{\overset{\displaystyle OH}{|}}{\underset{\underset{\displaystyle H}{|}}{C}}-\overset{\overset{\displaystyle H}{|}}{\underset{\underset{\displaystyle H}{|}}{C}}-H \qquad H-\overset{\overset{\displaystyle H}{|}}{\underset{\underset{\displaystyle H}{|}}{C}}-O-\overset{\overset{\displaystyle H}{|}}{\underset{\underset{\displaystyle H}{|}}{C}}-\overset{\overset{\displaystyle H}{|}}{\underset{\underset{\displaystyle H}{|}}{C}}-H$$

*[1 mark for each correct displayed formula]*

b) *Compound Z is the ether isomer [1 mark for any statement indicating the correct isomer].*
*Explanation:*
*The NMR spectrum of compound Z does not have a peak that could correspond to a single proton in an OH group [1 mark]. Compound Z is not an alcohol [1 mark].*
*OR There are three peaks on the NMR spectrum of compound Z [1 mark]. Both alcohol isomers have four hydrogen environments, but the ether isomer has three [1 mark].*
*OR The peaks on the NMR spectrum of compound Z are in the ratio 3:2:3 [1 mark]. The only isomer with proton environments matching this ratio is the ether [1 mark].*
*OR The NMR spectrum of compound Z has a triplet peak, a single peak, and a quartet peak [1 mark]. The only isomer which could produce these splitting patterns is the ether [1 mark].*

## Page 69 — Infrared Spectroscopy

1    *D Methanoic acid [1 mark]*
*The spectrum has a broad absorption at around 3000, which corresponds to an OH group in an alcohol or a carboxylic acid. It also has a strong sharp absorption at 1700 — this corresponds to a C=O group, which is only present in methanoic acid.*

2 a) *A's due to an O–H group in a carboxylic acid [1 mark].*
*B's due to a C=O as in an aldehyde, ketone, carboxylic acid or ester [1 mark].*
*C's due to a C–O as in an ester or carboxylic acid [1 mark].*
*D's also due to a C–O as in an ester or acid [1 mark].*

b) *The spectrum suggests it's a carboxylic acid — it's got a COOH group [1 mark]. This group has a mass of 45, so the rest of the molecule has a mass of 29 (74 – 45), which is likely to be $C_2H_5$ [1 mark]. So the molecule could be $C_2H_5COOH$ — propanoic acid [1 mark].*

## Page 71 — Chromatography

1    *C The stationary phase is a liquid. [1 mark]*
2    *B The sample is heat sensitive. [1 mark]*
3 a) *The stationary phase consists of small solid particles packed in a tube [1 mark]. The sample is injected into a stream of high pressure liquid — this is the mobile phase [1 mark]. The detector monitors the output from the tube [1 mark].*

b) *The chromatogram shows a peak for each component of the mixture [1 mark]. UV light is passed through the liquid leaving the tube and the detector measures the absorbance [1 mark]. From these, the retention time can be seen and compared to databases to identify the substances [1 mark]. The areas under the peaks are in proportion to the relative amounts of each substance [1 mark].*

## Unit 5: Section 7 — Electrochemistry
## Page 73 — Redox Reactions

1    *C Cl has an oxidation state of –1 in NaCl and +1 in NaClO [1 mark]*
2 a) $2MnO_4^-{}_{(aq)} + 16H^+{}_{(aq)} + 10I^-{}_{(aq)} \rightarrow 2Mn^{2+}{}_{(aq)} + 8H_2O_{(l)} + 5I_{2(aq)}$
*[1 mark for correct reactants and products, 1 mark for correct balancing]*
*You have to balance the number of electrons before you can combine the half-equations. And always double-check that your equation definitely balances. It's easy to slip up and throw away marks.*

b) *Mn has been reduced [1 mark] from +7 to +2 [1 mark]. I has been oxidised [1 mark] from –1 to 0 [1 mark].*

c) *Reactive metals have a tendency to lose electrons, so are good reducing agents [1 mark]. I⁻ is already in its reduced form [1 mark].*

## Page 75 — Electrode Potentials

1    *A +0.31 V [1 mark]*
2 a) *+0.80 V – (–0.76 V) = 1.56 V [1 mark]*
b) $Zn_{(s)} + 2Ag^+{}_{(aq)} \rightarrow Zn^{2+}{}_{(aq)} + 2Ag_{(s)}$ *[1 mark]*
c) *The zinc half-cell. It has a more negative standard electrode potential/ it's less electronegative OR the zinc is oxidised and oxidation = loss of electrons [1 mark].*

## Page 77 — The Electrochemical Series

1 a) *The half-equations combine to give:*
$Zn + 2VO_2^+ + 4H^+ \rightarrow Zn^{2+} + 2VO^{2+} + 2H_2O$ *[1 mark].*
*so reaction from yellow ($VO_2^+$) to blue ($VO^{2+}$) is feasible [1 mark].*
b) *Cell potential = 1.00 – (–0.76) = +1.76 V [1 mark]*

2 a) *Using the anti-clockwise rule:*

*[1 mark]*

*The reverse reaction is favoured, so $MnO_2$ and HCl will not react [1 mark].*

b) *Increasing the concentration and temperature both change the electrode potentials [1 mark] resulting in a positive overall cell potential, allowing the reaction to take place [1 mark].*

## Page 79 — Redox Titrations

1 a) *The 7.5 cm³ of manganate solution contains:*
$(7.5 \times 0.018) \div 1000 = 1.35 \times 10^{-4}$ *moles of manganate ions [1 mark].*
*From the equation the number of moles of iron = 5 × the number of moles of manganate. So the number of moles of iron =*
$5 \times 1.35 \times 10^{-4} = 6.75 \times 10^{-4}$ *[1 mark].*
b) *In the tablet there will be 250 ÷ 25 = 10 times this amount =*
$6.75 \times 10^{-3}$ *moles [1 mark].*
c) *1 mole of iron has a mass of 56 g, so the tablet contains:*
$6.75 \times 10^{-3} \times 56 = 0.378$ *g of iron [1 mark].*
*The percentage of iron in the tablet = (0.378 ÷ 3.2) × 100 = 11.8% [1 mark].*

2 a) *A redox reaction [1 mark].*
b) *Number of moles = (concentration × volume) ÷ 1000*
*= (0.5 × 10) ÷ 1000 [1 mark] = 0.005 [1 mark]*
c) *Number of moles = (concentration × volume) ÷ 1000*
*= (0.1 × 20) ÷ 1000 [1 mark] = 0.002 [1 mark]*
d) *1 mole of $MnO_4^-$ ions needs 5 moles of electrons to be reduced. So to reduce 0.002 moles of $MnO_4^-$, you need*
*(0.002 × 5) = 0.01 moles of electrons [1 mark].*
*The 0.005 moles of tin ions must have lost 0.01 moles of electrons as they were oxidised OR all of these electrons must have come from the tin ions [1 mark].*
*Each tin ion changed its oxidation state by 0.01 ÷ 0.005 = 2 [1 mark]. The oxidation state of the oxidised tin ions is (+2) + 2 = +4 [1 mark].*

## Page 81 — More Redox Titrations

1 a) *The number of moles of thiosulfate used =*
*(19.33 × 0.15) ÷ 1000 = 0.0029 moles [1 mark].*
*From the iodine-thiosulfate equation, the number of moles of $I_2$ = half the number of moles of thiosulfate, so in this case the number of moles of $I_2$ = 0.00145 [1 mark].*
b) *From the equation, 2 copper ions produce 1 iodine molecule [1 mark], so the number of moles of copper ions = 2 × 0.00145 = 0.0029 [1 mark].*
c) *In 250 cm³ of the copper solution there are: (250 ÷ 25) × 0.0029 = 0.029 moles of copper [1 mark].*
*1 mole of copper has a mass of 63.5 g, so in the alloy there are: 0.029 × 63.5 = 1.84 g of copper [1 mark].*
*Percentage of copper in the alloy = (1.84 ÷ 4.20) × 100 = 43.8% [1 mark].*

## Page 83 — Uses of Fuel Cells

1 a) *The PEM only allows $H^+$ ions across it [1 mark], forcing the electrons around the circuit to get to the cathode. This creates an electrical current [1 mark].*
b) *Anode reaction: $H_2 \rightarrow 2H^+ + 2e^-$ [1 mark]*
*Cathode reaction: $2H^+ + \frac{1}{2}O_2 + 2e^- \rightarrow H_2O$ [1 mark]*
c) *They save money by not importing oil [1 mark]. They can produce the hydrogen fuel relatively cheaply by electrolysis, using either hydroelectric power or geothermal power to generate electricity [1 mark].*

# Answers

d) Any 3 from:
*They don't produce carbon dioxide.*
*The only waste product is water.*
*They're more efficient than internal combustion engines.*
*The fuel source is renewable.*
**[1 mark for each up to a maximum of 3 marks]**

e) *We currently have no infrastructure for producing, e.g. by electrolysis, or storing hydrogen fuel* **[1 mark]**.
*It would be very expensive to replace current vehicles with fuel cell vehicles* **[1 mark]**.

## Unit 5: Section 8 — Transition Metals
## Page 85 — Transition Metals — The Basics

1 a) $1s^2 2s^2 2p^6 3s^2 3p^6 3d^7 4s^2$ OR $[Ar]3d^7 4s^2$ **[1 mark]**
b) *The two 4s electrons* **[1 mark]**
c) *Any three from: coloured compounds, variable oxidation states, catalytic properties, forms complex ions* **[1 mark for each up to a maximum of three]**

2 a) *Iron:* $1s^2 2s^2 2p^6 3s^2 3p^6 3d^6 4s^2$ OR $[Ar]3d^6 4s^2$ **[1 mark]**
*Copper:* $1s^2 2s^2 2p^6 3s^2 3p^6 3d^{10} 4s^1$ OR $[Ar]3d^{10} 4s^1$ **[1 mark]**
b) *Copper has only one 4s electron* **[1 mark]** *because it is more stable with a full 3d subshell* **[1 mark]**.
c) *Iron loses the 4s electrons to form* $Fe^{2+}$ **[1 mark]**.
*It loses the 4s electrons AND the 3d electron from the orbital containing 2 electrons to form* $Fe^{3+}$ **[1 mark]**.
d) *There will be a colour difference* **[1 mark]**
e) $Fe^{2+}$ *ions are less stable than* $Fe^{3+}$ *ions because they have one 3d orbital that contains two electrons* **[1 mark]**, *and the repulsion between these paired electrons makes it relatively easy to remove one of them* **[1 mark]**.

## Page 88 — Complex Ions and Colour

1 a) *Hexadentate ligand means that it has 6 lone pairs of electrons,* **[1 mark]** *so can make 6 dative covalent bonds* **[1 mark]**.
b) $[Mn(EDTA)]^{2-}$ **[1 mark]**

2 a) i) *Dative covalent bonds/coordinate bonds* **[1 mark]**.
ii) *Both electrons in the bond are donated from the same atom* **[1 mark]**.
b) 6 **[1 mark]**
*Each ethanedioate ligand forms two bonds with the* $Fe^{3+}$ *ion — so that's 6 altogether.*
c) *Octahedral* **[1 mark]**
*Complex ions with a coordination number of 6 are usually octahedral.*

3 *Normally, all the 3d orbitals have the same energy level* **[1 mark]**.
*When ligands form dative covalent bonds with a metal ion they cause the 3d electron orbitals to split* **[1 mark]**. *The energy needed to make an electron jump from the lower 3d orbital to the higher 3d orbital is equal to a certain frequency of light* **[1 mark]**. *This frequency gets absorbed* **[1 mark]**. *All the other frequencies are transmitted and it is these frequencies that give the transition metal colour* **[1 mark]**.

## Page 90 — Complex Ions — Ligand Reactions

1 a) $A = [Cu(H_2O)_6]^{2+}$ **[1 mark]**, $B = [CuCl_4]^{2-}$ **[1 mark]**, $C = [Cu(NH_3)_4(H_2O)_2]^{2+}$ **[1 mark]**
b) $[Cu(H_2O)_6]^{2+}_{(aq)} + 4Cl^-_{(aq)} \rightleftharpoons [CuCl_4]^{2-}_{(aq)} + 6H_2O_{(l)}$ **[1 mark]**
c)
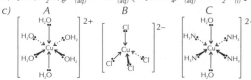
*A = octahedral, B = tetrahedral, C = octahedral.*
**[1 mark for each correct diagram, one mark for each shape name.]**

2 a) *Nickel* **[1 mark]**
b) $[Ni(H_2O)_6]^{2+}$ **[1 mark]**
c) *The nickel is normally surrounded by water ligands* **[1 mark]**. *When sodium hydroxide is added to the solution, the hydroxide ions displace some of the water ligands to form the neutral complex* $[Ni(H_2O)_4(OH)_2]$ **[1 mark]** *which is insoluble* **[1 mark]**.
*When ammonia is added to the solution it sets up an equilibrium which produces hydroxide ions* **[1 mark]**. *The formation of these hydroxide ions causes the same reaction as sodium hydroxide and creates the same insoluble, neutral complex* **[1 mark]**.

d) *Ammonia is substituted for the ligands* **[1 mark]** *to give the complex* $[Ni(NH_3)_6]^{2+}$ **[1 mark]** *which is soluble* **[1 mark]**.
e) *The change of ligand means that it absorbs different colour/frequency light.* **[1 mark]**

## Page 93 — Copper and Chromium

1 a) $[Cu(H_2O)_6]^{2+}$ **[1 mark]**
b) *Displacement reaction* **[1 mark]**
c) $Fe + Cu^{2+} \rightarrow Cu + Fe^{2+}$ **[1 mark]**

2 a) $K_2Cr_2O_7$ **[1 mark]**
b) i) *orange to green* **[1 mark]**
ii) *Cr is reduced from +6 to +3* **[1 mark]**
*Zn is oxidised from 0 to +2* **[1 mark]**
$Cr_2O_7^{2-} + 14H^+ + 3Zn \rightarrow 2Cr^{3+} + 7H_2O + 3Zn^{2+}$ **[1 mark]**
iii) *The solution turns blue* **[1 mark]** *because the* $Cr^{3+}$ *is reduced further to* $Cr^{2+}$ **[1 mark]**. *It is not oxidised back to* $Cr^{3+}$ *because it is in an inert atmosphere* **[1 mark]**.

3 a) i) *Reduction* **[1 mark]**
ii) *Chromium(III) chloride is reacted with zinc and acid* **[1 mark]**.
b) i) *To stop the* $Cr^{2+}$ *ion being oxidised* **[1 mark]**
ii) *The liquids are all degassed with nitrogen* **[1 mark]** *and the experiment is carried out in an inert atmosphere* **[1 mark]**.
c) *Hydrochloric acid is slowly added to the mixture in the flask until it is a clear blue colour. The hydrogen is allowed to escape through the tube into the water* **[1 mark]**.
*When the solution is blue, the side tube is pinched shut and the gas pressure forces the blue liquid into the solution of sodium ethanoate.* **[1 mark]**.
*A red precipitate of the chromium(II) ethanoate forms immediately* **[1 mark]**.
*The precipitate is filtered off and then washed with water, ethanol and ether, all in an inert atmosphere* **[1 mark]**.
d) $[Cr_2(CH_3COO)_4(H_2O)_2]$ **[1 mark]**

## Page 95 — Uses of Transition Metals & Their Compounds

1 a)
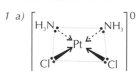
**[1 mark]**
b) *Cisplatin crosslinks the DNA which prevents it from being replicated* **[1 mark]**. *This prevents the cancer cells from dividing, so the cell dies* **[1 mark]**.

2 a) i) *Transition metals can use their s and d orbitals to form bonds with reactants* **[1 mark]** *and they have the ability to change oxidation state easily* **[1 mark]**.
ii) *A heterogeneous catalyst is in a different phase from the reactants* **[1 mark]**.
*A homogeneous catalyst is in the same phase as the reactants* **[1 mark]**.
b) i) *Possible answers include:*
*Iron in the Haber process*
*Vanadium(V) oxide in the Contact process*
*Platinum in catalytic converters*
**[1 mark for each, up to a maximum of 2 marks]**
ii) *Catalysts help make reactions more environmentally friendly by reducing the energy consumption* **[1 mark]** *and reducing raw/waste materials by improving atom economy* **[1 mark]**.
c) *Possible answers include:*
*Gold, silver, platinum, copper used in jewellery.*
*Iron used in construction.*
*Platinum used in cancer drugs.*
*Silver used in polychromic sunglasses.*
*Chromium, copper, iron, cobalt used in paint pigments and coloured bottles.*
**[1 mark for each, up to a maximum of 2 marks]**

# Answers

## Unit 5: Section 9 — Organic Compounds
### Page 97 — Aromatic Compounds

1 a) $C_6H_6$ *[1 mark]*

b) *[1 mark]*

You'd get the mark here for drawing any of the correct ways to represent the Kekulé structure properly — have a look back at page 96 if you're not sure what they are.

c) The Kekulé structure has alternating double and single bonds *[1 mark]*. If this model was correct, X-ray diffraction studies should show three bonds of C–C length, and three bonds of C=C length *[1 mark]*. But instead they show that all the carbon-carbon bonds are the same length *[1 mark]*.

2 a) The Kekulé structure contains three carbon-carbon double bonds *[1 mark]*. Its enthalpy of hydrogenation should be three times that of cyclohexene, or $(-120 \text{ kJ mol}^{-1}) \times 3 = -360 \text{ kJ mol}^{-1}$ *[1 mark]*. The actual enthalpy of hydrogenation of benzene is $-208 \text{ kJ mol}^{-1}$ — so the Kekulé structure is incorrect *[1 mark]*.

b) Benzene's enthalpy of hydrogenation is much less endothermic than the enthalpy of hydrogenation for the Kekulé structure would be *[1 mark]*. So more energy must be needed to break the carbon-carbon bonds in benzene than in the Kekulé structure *[1 mark]*. Energy is put in to break bonds (and released when they are formed). If you need more energy to break its bonds, then the benzene molecule must be more stable than the Kekulé structure.

### Page 99 — Reactions of Aromatic Compounds

1 a) i) A: nitrobenzene *[1 mark]*
B + C: concentrated nitric acid *[1 mark]* and concentrated sulfuric acid *[1 mark]*
D: warm, not more than 55 °C *[1 mark]*
ii) See page 98 for the mechanism. *[1 mark for each of the two curly arrows correct placed, and 1 mark for the correct intermediate shown.]*
iii) $HNO_3 + H_2SO_4 \rightarrow H_2NO_3^+ + HSO_4^-$ *[1 mark]*
$H_2NO_3^+ \rightarrow NO_2^+ + H_2O$ *[1 mark]*
b) i) F: benzenesulfonic acid *[1 mark]*
E: fuming sulfuric acid *[1 mark]*
ii) Sulfur trioxide/$SO_3$ *[1 mark]*
c) Benzene is very stable due to its delocalised electron ring *[1 mark]*. Substitution reactions preserve the delocalisation *[1 mark]*.

### Page 101 — More Reactions of Aromatic Compounds

1 a) $Br_2 + FeBr_3 \rightarrow Br^+ + FeBr_4^-$ *[1 mark]*
b) For correct mechanism, see page 100.
*[1 mark for each of the three curly arrows correctly placed, and 1 mark for the correct aromatic product formed].*
c) Bromobenzene *[1 mark]*
2 a) No reaction/nothing happens *[1 mark]*
b) Bromine water is decolorised *[1 mark]*.
White precipitate forms *[1 mark]*.
Smell of antiseptic *[1 mark]*.
c) 2,4,6-tribromophenol *[1 mark]*
d) Electrons from the oxygen (from the p-orbitals) overlap/become involved with the benzene ring's delocalised system *[1 mark]*, increasing the electron density of the ring *[1 mark]*.
e) Electrophilic substitution *[1 mark]*

### Page 103 — Amines

1 a) $C_4H_9NH_2$ OR $CH_3CH_2CH_2CH_2NH_2$ *[1 mark]*
b) The amine molecules remove protons/$H^+$/H ions from the water molecules *[1 mark]*. This gives alkyl ammonium ions and hydroxide ions, which make the solution alkaline *[1 mark]*.
c) $CH_3COCl + C_4H_9NH_2 \rightarrow CH_3CONH(C_4H_9) + HCl$ *[1 mark]*
$C_4H_9NH_2 + HCl \rightarrow C_4H_9NH_3^+ + Cl^-$ *[1 mark]*

### Page 105 — Amides and Aromatic Amines

1 a) i) Nitrous acid/$HNO_2$ *[1 mark]*
$NaNO_2 + HCl \rightarrow HNO_2 + NaCl$ *[1 mark]*
ii) Temperature about 5 °C *[1 mark]*

b) i) *[1 mark]*
ii) Dye *[1 mark]*
This is actually Butter Yellow, which was once used to colour margarine — until they found out it was carcinogenic and banned it. Eeek...

### Page 107 — Amino Acids

1 a) Cysteine is chiral but glycine isn't *[1 mark]*. So cysteine will rotate the plane of plane-polarised light, but glycine won't *[1 mark]*.
b) Draw a line near the bottom of a piece of chromatography paper, and put a spot of the amino acid mixture on it *[1 mark]*. Put the very bottom of the paper into a solvent, leave until the solvent has nearly reached the top of the paper and mark the distance the solvent has moved *[1 mark]*. Leave to dry and spray with ninhydrin (to reveal location of spots) *[1 mark]*. Measure how far the solvent front and the spots have travelled *[1 mark]*. Calculate the $R_f$ values of the amino acid spots *[1 mark]*. Compare to a table of known amino acid $R_f$ values *[1 mark]*.
2 a) $RCH(NH_2)COOH$ *[1 mark]*.
b) An amino acid's isoelectric point is the pH where its average overall charge is zero *[1 mark]*.
c) i) *[1 mark]*
ii) *[1 mark]*
It might seem a bit obvious to say this, but if you've drawn these out in more detail — like drawing the $NH_2$ group out with all its bonds shown — you'd get the mark.

### Page 109 — Polymers

1 a) Addition (polymerisation) *[1 mark]*
b) The double bond of the propene molecule open ups *[1 mark]* and the molecules join together to form a chain *[1 mark]*.
c) *[1 mark]*
2 a) *[1 mark]*
b) *[1 mark]*
c) Poly(ethenol) has OH groups along the polymer chain *[1 mark]*, which it can use to form hydrogen bonds with the water molecules *[1 mark]*.
d) Making water soluble laundry bags *[1 mark]* — soiled bed linen can be placed in the bags, and the bag put in the washing machine without opening (where it will dissolve during the wash), reducing the risk of spreading infection *[1 mark]*.
OR Making liquid detergent capsules/liquitabs *[1 mark]* — the whole package can be put straight into the washing machine/dishwasher, and the wrapping will dissolve in the wash *[1 mark]*.

### Page 111 — More Condensation Polymers

1 a) i)
*[1 mark each]*
ii) Amide link *[1 mark]*

# Answers

b) i)

OR

*[1 mark]*

ii) For each amide link that is formed, one water molecule is eliminated *[1 mark]*.

2 a) Two amino acids joined together *[1 mark]* by a peptide/amide/–CONH– link *[1 mark]*.

b)

*[1 mark]*

*[1 mark]*

The amino acids can join together in either order — that's why there are two dipeptides.

## Unit 5: Section 10 — Organic Synthesis
### Page 113 — Empirical and Molecular Formulas

1 a) 0.1 g of the aldehyde gives 0.228 g of $CO_2$.
0.228 ÷ 44 = 0.00518 moles of $CO_2$.
1 mole of $CO_2$ contains 1 mole of carbon.
So 0.1 g of the aldehyde must contain 0.00518 moles of C *[1 mark]*.
0.1 g of the aldehyde makes 0.093 g of $H_2O$.
0.093 ÷ 18 = 0.00517 moles of $H_2O$.
1 mole of $H_2O$ contains 2 moles of H.
So 0.1 g of the aldehyde must contain 2 × 0.00517
= 0.0103 moles of H *[1 mark]*.
0.00518 moles of C has a mass of 0.00518 × 12 = 0.0622 g
0.0103 moles of H has a mass of 0.0103 × 1 = 0.0103 g
0.0622 + 0.0103 = 0.0725g
So 0.1 g of the compound contains 1 − 0.0725 = 0.0275 g of O
*[1 mark]*.
0.0275 g of O = 0.0275 ÷ 16 = 0.00172 moles
So the mole ratio is C = 0.00518, H = 0.01034, O = 0.00172
Divide by the smallest (0.00172).
The ratio becomes C = 3, H = 6, O = 1.
So the empirical formula = $C_3H_6O$ *[1 mark]*.

b) Empirical formula has a mass of (3 × 12) + 6 + 16 = 58 *[1 mark]*.
So by mass, hydrogen is (6 ÷ 58) × 100 = 10.34% *[1 mark]*

c) Molecular formula is the same as the empirical formula as they have the same mass *[1 mark]*.

d)

*[1 mark]*

2 a) To get the mole ratio, divide each % by atomic mass:
C: 37 ÷ 12 = 3.083
H: 2.2 ÷ 1 = 2.2
N: 18.5 ÷ 14 = 1.321
O: 42.3 ÷ 16 = 2.644 *[1 mark]*
Then divide by the smallest (1.321):
C = 2.34, H = 1.67, N = 1, O = 2 *[1 mark]*
Multiply by 3 to get whole numbers:
C = 7, H = 5, N = 3 and O = 6
So the empirical formula = $C_7H_5N_3O_6$ *[1 mark]*
The molecular mass = 227
The empirical mass = (7 × C) + (5 × H) + (3 × N) + (6 × O)
= (7 × 12) + (5 × 1) + (3 × 14) + (6 × 16)
= 227
The empirical formula is the same as the molecular formula as they have the same mass *[1 mark]*.

b)

*[1 mark, allow different placing of groups around ring]*

## Page 115 — Practical Techniques

1 a) The purer sample will have the higher melting point *[1 mark]*, so the sample that melts at 69 °C is purer *[1 mark]*.

b) To purify the sample you could dissolve it in hot propanone *[1 mark]* and allow it to partially recrystallise *[1 mark]*. You'd then filter the crystals
*[1 mark]*, wash them with very cold propanone *[1 mark]* and dry them
*[1 mark]*.

c) The purity could be checked by measuring the boiling point or melting point OR by spectroscopic means *[1 mark]*.

## Page 117 — Organic Functional Groups

1 a) A — hydroxyl *[1 mark]*
B — hydroxyl and alkenyl *[1 mark]*
C — hydroxyl and phenyl *[1 mark]*

b) C *[1 mark]*

c) A *[1 mark]*

d) C *[1 mark]*

2 a) carbonyl / ketone OR amide (–$CONH_2$) *[1 mark]* and (primary) amine / amino *[1 mark]*

b) i) C=O *[1 mark]*
ii) It is a double-ended molecule *[1 mark]* with 2 amine/amino groups *[1 mark]*.

3 a) phenyl *[1 mark]*, hydroxyl *[1 mark]* and ester *[1 mark]*

b) ester *[1 mark]*

c) Expanded structure (with C and H atoms showing):

So molecular formula of methyl salicylate is $C_8H_8O_3$. *[1 mark]*

d)

*[1 mark]*

Look back at esters on p57 if you had trouble with this one.

## Page 120 — Organic Synthesis

1 Step 1: The methanol is refluxed *[1 mark]* with $K_2Cr_2O_7$ *[1 mark]* and sulfuric acid *[1 mark]* to form methanoic acid *[1 mark]*.
Step 2: The methanoic acid is reacted under reflux *[1 mark]* with ethanol *[1 mark]* using an acid catalyst *[1 mark]*.

2 Step 1: React propane with bromine *[1 mark]* in the presence of UV light *[1 mark]*. Bromine is toxic and corrosive *[1 mark]* so great care should be taken. Bromopropane is formed *[1 mark]*.
Step 2: Bromopropane is then refluxed *[1 mark]* with sodium hydroxide solution *[1 mark]*, again a corrosive substance so take care *[1 mark]*, to form propanol *[1 mark]*.

# Index

## A

absorbance-time graph 5
acid chlorides 59, 103, 104
acid dissociation constant 40
acid hydrolysis of esters 57
acids 38-46
activation energy 16-18, 23, 77
acyl chlorides 59, 103, 104
acylation 103, 104
addition polymerisation 108
addition reactions 100
adsorption 94
alcohol as a fuel 82
alcohols 53, 54, 56-59
aldehydes 50-54
alkalis 43, 45
alternative reaction pathway 17
amide links 110
amides 59, 103, 104
amines 59, 102-104
amino acids 106, 107, 111
ammonia 59
        - manufacture of 26, 36
amphoteric substances 93
anticlockwise rule 76, 77, 91
arenes 96-101
aromatic compounds 96-101
Arrhenius equation/plot 16, 17
asymmetric carbons 48
atom economy 36, 37, 94
azo dyes 105

## B

bar graphs 122
base hydrolysis of esters 57
bases 38-41, 44
Benedict's solution 52
benzene 96, 97, 98, 100, 101
bidentate ligands 87, 89
biodiesel 58
blood 46
Brady's reagent 52
breathalysing drink drivers 69, 83
Brønsted-Lowry acids 38
buffers 45, 46
burette 43

## C

carbonyl compounds 50, 52, 53
carboxylates 55
carboxylic acids 52, 54-57, 59
catalysts 8, 12, 16-18, 34, 94
catalytic converters 17
cell potential 74-77, 91
CFCs 60
charge density 25
chemical shift 64, 65
chiral molecules 48, 107
chlorine radicals 60
chromatography 70, 71, 106, 107
chromium ions 91, 92
chromium(II) ethanoate 92
cis-trans isomerism 47
cisplatin 95
citric acid (measuring the amount of in fruit juice) 55
classifying compounds 116
clock reactions 4, 16
closed system 26
collision theory 35
colorimeter 4, 5
colour 87, 88, 89
combinatorial chemistry 120
complex ions 86-90, 102
concentration 5, 6, 8, 9, 11, 78, 80
concentrations in equilibrium mixtures 28, 29
concentration-time graph 4, 6, 7, 10
conclusions 123
condensation polymerisation 108, 110, 111

condensation reactions 56
conjugate pairs 38
Contact process 17, 26, 94
coordination number 86, 88, 89
copper, calculating the percentage of in an alloy 81
copper compounds 91
correlation 122

## D

d-block 84
data
        anomalous 121
        categoric 121
        continuous 121
        discrete 121
        ordinal 121
dancing Santa 82
dative covalent bonds 86, 87
delocalisation of electrons 96, 97, 101
delocalised model of benzene 96
dependent variable 121
diamines 110
diazonium salts 105
dicarboxylic acids 110
dichromate(VI) ions 78
diffusion 19
diluting acids 42
dimers 54
diols 110
dipeptide 111
disorder 19
disproportionation 72, 91
dissolving 24, 25
drawing optical isomers 48
drug development 120
dynamic equilibria 26

## E

E/Z isomerism 47
$E_{cell}$ 74
$EDTA^{4-}$ 87
electronic configurations 85
electrical conductivity 4
electrochemical cells 74
electrochemical series 76
electrode potential 74-77
electrode potential chart 76
electromagnetic radiation 60, 61
electron configurations 84
electronegativity 61
electrophilic addition 100
electrophilic substitution 98-101
emf 74
empirical formulas 112, 113
enantiomers 48, 49
end point 43
endothermic reactions 20-22,
                24, 33, 34
energy gap 87
enthalpy cycles 24
enthalpy of hydration 24
enthalpy of solution 24
enthalpy profile 18
entropy 19-23, 32, 33, 36, 37, 77, 89
enzymes 17
equilibria 26-29, 31, 34-36, 38, 39, 77
equilibrium concentrations 27-29
equilibrium constant 27-30, 32, 37,
                39, 77
equimolar solutions 41
ester links 110
esterification 56
esters 56, 57, 58, 59
ethanoic acid manufacture 94
ethyl ethanoate 56, 57
evidence 2-3
exothermic reactions 21, 33, 34
exponential relationship 16

## F

fair test 121
fats 58
fatty acids 58
feasibility of reactions 77
Fehling's solution 52
first order reactions 7-9
fission 60
fractional distillation 115
fragmentation pattern 62, 63
free radicals 60
Friedel-Crafts acylation 99
Friedel-Crafts alkylation 99
fuel cells 82, 83
functional groups 116, 117

## G

gas chromatography 70, 71
gas syringe 4
gas volume-time graph 5
geometric isomerism 47
glycerol 57
gradients 4, 6, 10, 16-17
graphs (types of) 122
green chemistry 94

## H

Haber process 17, 26, 36
haemoglobin 87
half-cell 74
half-equations 73, 75, 76
half-equivalence 44
half-life 6, 7, 9
halogen carriers 98-100
halogenoalkane 14, 15
Hess's Law 24
heterogeneous catalysis 16, 17, 94
heterogeneous equilibrium 28, 31
high-pressure/performance liquid chromatography
                (HPLC) 70, 71
homogeneous catalysis 17, 94
homogeneous equilibria 28, 31
homolytic fission 60
how science works 2-3
hydration enthalpy 25
hydrogen bonds 50, 54
hydrogen cyanide 51
hydrogen environments 64, 65
hydrogen fuel cells 82
hydrolysis 57
        of esters 57
        of halogenoalkanes 14, 15
        of nitriles 54
hydroxynitriles 51

## I

ibuprofen 36
industrial processes 18, 26, 36, 37
infrared (IR) spectroscopy 68, 69
initial rate of reaction 4, 10
initiation step 60
independent variable 121
instant cold pack 22
integration trace 66
iodine-clock reaction 16
iodine-sodium thiosulfate titrations 80
ionic charge 25
ionic half-equations 73
ionic lattice 25
ionic product of water 39
ionic radii 25
ionisation energies 85
iron tablets 79
isoelectric point 106
isomerism 47-49

# Index

**K**

K 30
$K_a$ 40, 41, 46
$K_c$ 28, 29, 34, 39
Kekulé structure of benzene 96
ketones 50, 51, 52, 53
Kevlar® 110
$K_p$ 31, 34
$K_w$ 39, 40

**L**

lattice enthalpy 24, 25
Le Chatelier's principle 34, 38, 45
ligand exchange/substitution 86, 89
ligands 86, 87, 88, 89
line graphs 122
logarithmic form of Arrhenius equation 16
logarithmic scale 40

**M**

M peak 62, 63
magnetic resonance imagery (MRI) 67
manganate(VII) ions 78
mass spectrometry 62, 63
Maxwell-Boltzmann distribution 18
mechanisms 12, 13, 49, 51, 60, 98, 100
metal-aqua complex ions 86
methyl carbonyl groups 53
methyl orange 43
microwaves 61
minimising costs 36
mole fractions 30
molecular formulas 112, 113
monodentate ligands 87
monoprotic acids 40
Mr Clippy 62
multiplets 66
multi-step reactions 12

**N**

n+1 rule 66
naming compounds 116
neutral solutions 39
nitration of arenes 98, 101
nitriles 54
nuclear magnetic resonance (NMR) spectroscopy 64-66
nucleophilic addition 51, 53
nucleophilic substitution 14, 49
nylon 6,6 110

**O**

optical activity 49
optical isomerism 47-49, 51, 107
order of reaction 6-10, 12, 13, 15
organic functional groups 116, 117
organic synthesis 118-120
oxidation 72-74, 76, 92
oxidation numbers/states 72, 86, 88
oxidation of alcohols 54
oxidation of aldehydes 54
oxidising agent 72
ozone 60

**P**

paper chromatography 106, 107
partial pressures 30, 31
peer reviews 2
peptide links 111
percentage composition of compounds 112
pH 40-46
pH curves 43, 44
phenolphthalein 43

phenols 100, 101
pipette 43
$pK_a$ 41, 44
$pK_w$ 39
poisoning of catalysts 17
polar bonds 14, 50, 61
polar molecules 54, 61
polyamides 110, 111
polychromic sunglasses 95
polydentate ligands 87, 89
polyesters 58, 110
polymer electrolyte membrane (PEM) 82
polymers 58, 108-111
position of equilibrium 34
practical techniques 114, 115
precipitation reactions 89, 90
predicting the feasibility of reactions 77
pressure
    of a gas in a mixture 30
    effect on equilibrium position 34
    effect on reaction rate 35
primary halogenoalkanes 14
propagation step 60
proteins 111
proton NMR 64-66
purifying products 114
purity, checking with chromatography 71

**Q**

quanta 19

**R**

racemate 48
racemic mixture 48, 49, 51
rate constant 8, 9, 16
rate equation 8-15
rate of reaction 4-13, 17, 35, 36
rate-concentration graph 6
rate-determining step 12, 13, 14, 15
reaction rates 4-13
redox reactions 72-74
redox titrations 78-81
reducing a carboxylic acid 55
reducing agent 72
reduction 72, 73, 74, 76, 78, 92
reference cell 74
refluxing 114
reformer 82
results of investigations 123
relative molecular mass (finding with mass spectrometry) 62
retention time 70
reversible reactions 26, 34, 77

**S**

salt bridge 74
saturated fats 58
scatter graphs 122
scientific process 2-3
second order reactions 7, 9
secondary halogenoalkanes 14
shapes of molecules/ions 86, 89
shape of rate-concentration graph 6
$S_N1$ mechanism 14, 49
$S_N2$ mechanism 14, 49
soap 57
solution, enthalpy change of 24
spectrometry 62, 63
spectroscopy 68, 69
spin-spin coupling 66
split peaks 66
spontaneous reaction 20, 23, 32
stability 19
standard conditions 20
standard electrode potentials 74, 75, 76

standard entropy 20, 22
standard hydrogen electrode 74
standard lattice enthalpy 24
states of matter 19, 20
stereoisomerism 47, 48, 49
stoichiometry 73
structural isomerism 47
subshell notation 84
sulfonation of arenes 98
sulfuric acid, manufacture of 26
sustainability 82
synthesis 118-120

**T**

table of results 121
tangent of a graph 4-6
temperature
    and the rate constant 8
    effect on equilibrium position 34
    effect on reaction rate 35
termination step 60
tertiary halogenoalkanes 14
terylene (PET) 58, 110
tetramethylsilane (TMS) 64
theories 2-3
thermodynamics 23
titration curves 45
titrations 10, 43, 44, 55, 78, 79, 80, 81
Tollens' reagent 52
total enthalpy change 24
total entropy change 21-23, 32, 77, 89
transesterification 58
transition elements 84-88, 94, 95
triesters (triglycerides) 57

**U**

unidentate ligands 87
units of rate constant 8
unsaturated fats 58
UV radiation 60

**V**

vanadium pentoxide 17, 94
variables 121-123
voltage 74, 75
voltmeter 74

**W**

weak acids/bases 38, 40-44

**Y**

yield 36

**Z**

zero order reactions 7-9
zwitterion 106